Acclaim for 1

Destination Unstoppable

The Journey of **No Teammate Left Behind**

"If you are looking to gain an edge on your competition, read Destination Unstoppable. The book shows you how to maximize individual and team performance by identifying and leveraging team members' strengths. In my experience, this is how professional sports teams and businesses become champions."

– Christopher Ilitch
President & CEO
Ilitch Holdings, Inc

"The best book on strengths. Ever. It will touch your head and your heart and inspire you to find your Destination Unstoppable!"

– Stephen Shapiro
Hall of Fame Speaker
Author of *Best Practices are Stupid*

"As a member of the one of the most successful teams in NFL history, my experience as a professional athlete and entrepreneur has taught me that building a winning team requires more than recruiting talented people. You can't stop there - history is littered with gifted individuals and teams that failed to reach their full potential. You must invest in a player's strengths to bring out their best on the field and off. You must invest in the strengths of the collective to build a championship team. This book will teach you to discover the untapped talent on your team, and harness it to reach your Destination Unstoppable."

– Ryan Diem
Super Bowl XLI Champion, Indianapolis Colts '01-'1'
Director/Investor, CloudO

“Like many tech startups, our team members are spread all over the globe. Maureen Monte and her No Teammate Left Behind system helped us to know each other, despite our distance. She provided us with a currency of communication that improves our ability to collaborate on behalf of our clients. Her program provides the human glue that gives us the strength to persevere, stand tall and succeed. My employees always ask for more time with her. I want to buy the movie rights to this story, and I'm not kidding!”

– John McDonald
CEO, CloudOne

“Calling all business leaders - it's time to practice what we preach! *Destination Unstoppable* is a true success story about harnessing the strengths of individuals to deliver extraordinary team results. The best news is that you can do it, too - roadmap included! A must read!”

– Steve Schultz
President and COO
GOJO Industries

"Maureen's ability to bring the initial conflict the team felt and their migration to understanding each other by learning their respective strengths in an exciting and taut read is truly remarkable. I have used her program with my own management team and it was very revealing regarding the strengths of each team member. I found personal biases colored team member's real strengths."

– David P. Wood, Jr., MD.
Executive Vice-President
Chief Medical Officer
Beaumont Health

“When we made the Destination Unstoppable journey with Maureen and empowered players to use their strengths in a defined role, the players were able to help each other and help the team achieve success. There was more continuity and cohesiveness, both on and off the ice. The players were way more relaxed and the tension was gone. Team chemistry dramatically improved and everyone added value to the team.”

– Head Coach Andrew Weidenbach
Cranbrook-Kingswood Boys Varsity Hockey

"If you want to create a high-functioning team, whether in sports or in business, read *Destination Unstoppable* and put its principles to work. The book tells the story, in a very readable manner, of how to create strengths-based success. Team members benefit individually from a strengths-based focus, and the results are magnified exponentially when all members commit to reaching their full potential. This book helps you plot your team's Destination Unstoppable - the road less traveled."

– Barbara Korte
Former North American Director of Sales

After (we worked with Maureen) the team was more focused toward a common goal. In the beginning of the season they seemed like a herd of young colts running around, sometimes in circles with no direction or focus. Later they were like a herd of stallions, running in a pack toward the same goals, not asking questions, just doing & achieving. Following the words of Yoda: "Think not, do!"

– Assistant Coach Patrick Ronayne
Cranbrook-Kingswood Boys Varsity Hockey

Don't just be inspired by this story of how a high-school hockey team harnessed their strengths and pulled together to achieve lofty goals. Embrace the principals that sparked their success: agree on clear and compelling team goals, build shared awareness of the unique strengths that each team member brings to the team's work, commit to using those strengths for the success and well-being of the team, behave in ways that generates trust among team members, and promise to not let any team member fail. Maureen Monte brings these principles to life in a compelling narrative that not only taps into her deep expertise with strength-based approaches but her pure joy in applying that expertise to help teams achieve their best. At the same time, her work with teams dispels the myth that focusing on strengths means that failings are ignored. She gets teams to see the habits that inhibit as well as those that boost team trust and illustrates how strengths overdone can undo a team. The bottom line: When a team uses a keen awareness of its human system to accomplish the contradictory task of accentuating differences to bind themselves together, they create an unstoppable force for realizing their aspirations.

– Cindy McCauley
Senior Fellow
Center for Creative Leadership

"A season on the brink, a scuffling team not realizing their potential. More Practice? Work Harder? How about a radical approach of optimizing performance by unleashing the inherent strengths of each personality on the team. This insightful and provocative book tells how a high school hockey team went from mediocre to champions by changing the culture through a strengths-based approach. 'Unstoppable' shares individual accounts of team leaders who were a part of the transformation of a hockey season, and the transformation of self-awareness that will last a lifetime. You will undoubtedly be inspired to find ways to do the same with your team to produce equally dramatic results."

– Shawn Patterson
Vice President
Organizational Effectiveness
DTE Energy

DESTINATION

Destination Unstoppable

The Journey of **No Teammate Left Behind**

Maureen Electa Monte

Maureen Monte Consulting
2016

First Printing: 2016

ISBN 978-0-9974648-5-6

eBook ISBN 978-0-9974648-0-1

Maureen Monte Consulting, LLC
2886 12 Mile Road
PO Box 725343
Berkley, MI 48072-5343

MaureenMonte.com

Special discounts are available on quantity purchases by corporations, associations, educators, and others. For details, contact the publisher at the above listed address or at Maureen@MaureenMonte.com.

U.S. trade bookstores and wholesalers: Please contact Maureen Electa Monte at Maureen@MaureenMonte.com.

Acknowledgements

I pause to celebrate the hundreds of people, colleagues, friends, clients, and members of my family who have supported me on my strengths-based journey. You know who you are. Thank you!

I specifically thank Stephen Shapiro, Jane Miller, Dean Jones, Jim Collison, Benjamin Erickson-Farr, Blanca Estella Garcia, Brian Brim, Todd Johnson, Paul Allen, Jon Clifton, Scott Wright, Heather Wright, Shawn Patterson, Vicky Flaherty, Lisa Cobbs, Jennifer Pelham, Hazel Woodcock, Khalid Raza, Celia Bobrowski, Susan Brueckman, Karen Sallee, Barbara Korte, Ed Brunner, Donna Satterfield, Jeff VanDeusen, Paula Kube, Amy Peterson, Dr. David Wood, Jody Rogow, Kirstin Dumas, Ellen Rogers, John McDonald, Robert Baillargeon, and Duncan Seidler, all of whom have provided guidance and encouragement.

Three important people in my life are no longer here, but their lessons remain in my heart and I strive to reflect them in my actions.

Michael Fezzey, Huntington Bank regional president and former president and general manager of WJR-AM (760). Mike gave me my first big break. He led from his heart and was a human connector like no other. He passed away in March of 2015. It was Michigan's loss and Heaven's gain. I miss him.

Curt Liesveld, for leading me and believing in me. A reluctant guru, Curt was the wellspring of Clifton StrengthsFinder experiential knowledge and wisdom. His soul was definitely connected to his role, and he was magnificent in his generosity. Curt passed away in May of 2015. I miss him.

Kenneth Monte, my father, for teaching me to love hockey and baseball. He passed away just after my 11th birthday. I miss him, too.

I offer special gratitude to my editor, Conny Coon, who helped me polish this pearl, and to my brother, Matthew Monte, and his team at Monte Consulting for designing the cover of this book and my website.

Contents

Introduction

I build winning teams. I help identify the untapped talent on the team and align it with a common view of success. This process offers my clients a greater appreciation of the strengths they bring as individuals and teammates, and a plan to harness that collective horsepower to achieve goals and objectives. Together we drive momentum, trust, chemistry, and a belief in one another. It is a smart investment in the human system of success. It is not touchy-feely; it's effective. It is how we reach Destination Unstoppable – the place where teams realize their full potential. It is how we build championship teams in the conference room, the boardroom, or the locker room.

In early 2015, I had the opportunity to bring my approach to the Cranbrook-Kingswood Boy's Varsity Hockey Team. They were talented but struggling and did not play like a cohesive unit. We ignited and harvested their competitive spirit, while at the same time, built a trust bank to deepen their commitment and connection to one another. The Clifton StrengthsFinder enabled us to reveal and utilize their strengths so that they felt understood and valued. We harnessed the intangibles that often make or break success but rarely show up in statistics or a win column. It provided a game-changing competitive advantage. The daring and eager young men defined, owned, and achieved their destiny. They became unstoppable because they felt unstoppable. No teammate was left behind on our journey.

Some books offer leadership lessons and use stories to support them. This book is different. It tells a true story with personal and team lessons revealed along the way. After all, isn't that how we learn and experience them in real life?

This narrative serves as a model for leading, accelerating, and fully harnessing the talent on a team. Any team. It was the most rewarding experience I have ever had. I hope you enjoy the ride as much as I did.

Learning with Head Coach Andrew Weidenbach was an honor and a privilege. Working with the young men brought me great joy.

This is our story.

The Roster

Maureen Electa Monte (The Leadership & Team Consultant)

Martin Monte (The Junior Success Architect)

My Boss (The Messenger)

Coach Andrew Weidenbach (The Maestro)

The Company (The Antagonist)

The Cranbrook Varsity Hockey Team (The Protagonist)

Karla (The Connector)

Red Fox, Silver Fox, and the Fox family (The Anonymous Funders)

Ed Brunner (The Human Calculator)

Mason Schultz (The Energy Guy)

Cooper Stahl (The Co-captain and The Calminator)

Jack Blumberg (The Learner)

Jake Nestell (The Thinking Man)

Austin Alger (The Co-captain and The Constructor)

Nolan Rogow (The Harmonizer)

Blake Rogow (The Team Competitor)

Shawn Patterson (The Strengths Executive)

Coaches Lock, Ronayne, and Slavick (The Greek Chorus)

The Clifton StrengthsFinder (The Game Changer)

About the Clifton StrengthsFinder Tool

Much of the discussion in this book is about how I partnered with Head Coach Weidenbach to transform his team by identifying and harnessing untapped talent and aligning it with success. My approach is founded in ten years of building winning teams in the corporate world. The starting point for all of my clients is a game-changing assessment tool called the Clifton StrengthsFinder. It measures 34 remarkable forces of excellence that are present in each one of us. The process of discovering and leveraging your strengths is a nourishing experience and a performance strategy that is described in detail in this book.

What About Your Strengths?

I invite you and your work teams or sports teams or book clubs to take the StrengthsFinder. You can follow along with your results as we make the success journey with the Cranbrook hockey team. It is a little bit like reading about climbing the Eiffel Tower in Paris; it is more rewarding and interesting if you have been there. If you have children of high school age, I recommend you make this a family adventure! Please feel invited, not obligated.

If you would like to assess your strengths, please visit gallupstrengthscenter.com. Today, it costs $15 to unlock your top five strengths. One point of clarity: I do not receive a dime if you take the StrengthsFinder assessment. I do not want you to do it for me; I want you to do it for you.

Prologue

Even though I was cruising along at 500 mph and 35,000 feet on my way to Sin City, I was watching the clock and wishing I was on my way home. I would land just before the puck dropped, and it was killing me that I couldn't be there. The rivalry between Cranbrook and Brother Rice went back years, maybe even back to before I was born. The tension was heightened by Brother Rice's current ranking as the #1 team in the league. Of course, Red Fox was watching the game for me, and she would email or text me with the results. Still, I would rather be there in person, huddled under a puny overhead heater that was perpetually outgunned by the frosty air. I wanted to gauge the team myself. Would the work we had put in over the past few weeks pay off? Would this immensely talented group of high school boys finally band together and achieve their potential? Would they align their individual strengths behind their definition of success? Would they refuse to let each other fail? Would the insertion of the Clifton StrengthsFinder be the game changer they needed to become a high-performing team? Just how far would they go in their quest to win the state championship?

I turned to the window and gazed upon the frozen tundra below. There were no answers to my questions because only time would provide them.

PART 1: WHAT I SAW

Chapter 1: Valued for Being Valuable

**"Try not to become a man of success.
Rather become a man of value."**

Albert Einstein

* * *

It was not the result I had hoped for.

I tugged my headset off, tousled my hair, and sighed. My eyes ran down the scribbles on the page. They mirrored the awkwardness of my conversation, for I had just completed my annual performance review with My Boss. For the third year in a row I was left crumpled and bruised on the side of the corporate highway, a sad case of emotional road kill.

I glanced at my notes again, equally irritated by my rating and the performance review process itself.

Creative…

Star performer…

Your partners love you…

Visibility has gone up…

Sales have gone up…

Your strategic partners have won awards…

Scope of your role isn't big enough to justify a higher grade…

If you want an A, you'd have to get a new job…

Brimming with disappointment, I leaned back in my chair and stared blankly across the galley of my colorful kitchen. Comprised of hues one might find in a Tuscan garden, it was warm and vibrant, a place where I had enjoyed many "What does success look like for you?" strengths conversations with family and friends.

It was where Moira, gifted with strengths that made her one of the most amazing relationship builders I have ever known, had shared that she had discovered the perfect volunteer role. My mind instantly imagined all sorts of things that Moira would be great at – helping kids learn to read or helping high school teens avoid the perils of drugs, alcohol, and smoking. But those activities were for mere mortals. What did Moira do? Moira chose to go to the hospital one night a week and sit with people who were dying but had no family to visit them. When she told me, I felt a tightening of my gut and a rising sense of terror.

"I really like it," said Moira.

"Why?" I asked, still wrestling with the idea.

"It makes me feel like I'm helping someone who really needs it."

"What do you do there?" I asked, not sure I really wanted to know.

"I hold their hand if they'd like that," said Moira, with a gentle smile. "If they want to talk, we talk. I read to them. I get them water. Many times they are asleep, and I just sit next to them and read my own book. I want to be there in case they wake up and are frightened."

"Oh my God," I involuntarily muttered under my breath. I studied Moira's face across the span of my kitchen table to see if I could find a selfish chink in that mantle she was carrying, but there was nothing but pure joy. I glanced at her StrengthsFinder profile. Her number one strength was Empathy, and it was followed by six other relating talents that made her a leader in the Kindness Special Forces unit. Moira was wired to feel and give. She had found a place in the universe that valued her special gift and allowed her to do what she does best.

I could not imagine myself in her shoes. However, I had infinite admiration and respect for Moira's ability to flourish in that role. I will treasure that precious conversation forever, and she remains one of the people I love to spend time with.

I had experienced dozens of similar strengths coaching sessions with immensely talented people over the years. Those remarkable discussions were human, joyful, and a celebration of all that was right about us. My kitchen was made for those kinds of moments. It was incongruent with the one I had just completed with my Boss.

My Boss lived near London, so this was not the first time I had received my annual performance review via some intergalactic satellite bouncing bits and bytes of voice data across the Atlantic. A conference call was not exactly ideal for important conversations. Morse code would have been less painful. An old-fashioned ham radio system would have been more fun. My mind, at its creative best when it is unhappy, dropped me right into the middle of that imaginary conversation.

"What's that, Boss? Over!"

"You got a B!" My Boss would shout into the microphone. "Over!"

Crackle, crackle, crackle… Squawk.

"Boss, is the weather in London foggy or just your mind? Over!"

"All clear here, Maureen! A 'B' is a GREAT grade! Congratulations! Over!"

"Boss, I thought we agreed that…"

"The Company isn't issuing many As this year. Keep up the good work! Over!"

"But Boss…"

Static, static, static…ffffft.

"Over and out."

The Company I worked for had proudly transitioned to a mostly virtual workforce which saved a gazillion dollars in real estate costs. Many employees worked from home, with a computer and a phone being the only contact with colleagues and customers. After four years in this role, it felt like death by isolation. Social connections to colleagues were lost because in-person interactions of any sort were few and far between. It was hard, even for me, a certified thinker and introvert. Our days were long because our work was global. A noon meeting in Germany was held at 6 am my time.

"Ugh," I said aloud. "I hate this frickin' company!"

I rose wearily from my chair, thinking for the millionth time that sitting in front of a computer all day long was going to kill me, and walked to my front window.

It was frigid. It was a cold winter, even by Michigan standards.

"Forget it," I said. "I'm going for a walk."

Then, I hesitated. My sense of responsibility kicked in, and I knew I could not miss a meeting, no matter how unhappy I was. I walked back to my computer, opened my calendar, and checked the date. Thursday.

What? I was even more annoyed with myself. I did not work on Thursdays! Why had I agreed to conduct a performance review on my day off? I shook my head in disgust. This was a pattern I needed to break this year. I was free to go for a walk. I would run out of warmth before I would run out of time.

I pulled on my heavy winter gear and thought about my situation.

Six months prior, when I hit 55 years old, I received an innocuous corporate email from The Company, which basically said: "Hey Maureen, we want you to retire, and here's how you can do that! You can work part-time for 18 months and then leave!" The program was a "transition to retirement." One could work three days a week and have the other two days to work elsewhere, start a company, or do nothing. I read the email twice, thinking it was too good to be true. Once I had confirmed its validity and double checked my qualification to participate, I was all in.

The program, in theory, was perfect for me. I had wanted to focus on my very-part-time strengths-based success business for a while. However, launching a new business while working 60 hours a week in a demanding role for The Company is not exactly the best strategy for successful entrepreneurship.

I immediately sent My Boss an instant message (IM) asking if I could retire. He replied with a simple, "No." It became an entertaining exchange as I explained the program via IM. The Company was not offering this program in London, where My Boss works, so he was naturally a bit skeptical. I promised that if he let me do it, I would not let him down. In the end, he said yes. I will forever be grateful.

Here's the rub: I moved to three days a week and took a considerable pay cut, but there was no corresponding reduction in my responsibilities. Once I was on the program, I typically worked three 12 hour days (6 am to 6 pm), and then had Thursday, Friday, and the weekend, to launch my business.

This, I soon realized, was a great deal for The Company. They got at least 36 hours out of me, I did not drop a single ball, and they paid me a lot less money! But, because I was time-poor in terms of creating my future, those extra two days of the week were like precious gold.

The payoff associated with my decision slowly emerged. My strengths-based success clients included a few high-tech startups, and I had just landed a wonderful opportunity to help increase the success of an executive leadership team that was part of a regional bank. I had another large and challenging engagement on the horizon. It was not easy because I worked most days of the month, but it felt like progress. Projecting my vision like a movie on a big screen, I wondered if I could truly make a decent living by pursuing my dreams and doing what I do best. I believed it, but I could not see it. Like that mythical island that cannot be seen unless you believe it exists, the future eluded me.

I snapped up my winter boots, stomped down the stairs, and shoved the side door open, overcoming the resistance posed by six inches of new snow. The cold wind slapped my cheeks. I emitted an involuntary groan, lowered my head, and kept going. It felt good to be out of the house and away from the office.

My mind frolics on these thought walks. That's why I need them. I even measure my thinking time on my personal well-being tracker. Freed from the tortuous confines of a computer screen and a telephone headset, my mind replayed the conversation with My Boss.

"Let me start by saying how great it is to have you on my team," he began in his delightful British accent.

I truly loved My Boss because he was one of the few people at The Company who appreciated my ability to build strong strategic partnerships with the small software companies we worked with.

My role had an element of David and Goliath about it. I worked for Goliath, and it was my job to identify and build partnerships with the Davids of the software world. This approach benefited our customers because our partners' products helped increase the value of our own software solutions. Despite the advantages achieved by building a strong ecosystem of partners (think Apple and app developers), The Company did not always behave as if it valued them. That really bugged me.

Imagine a marriage where the wife believes that she is very pretty, extremely smart, very accomplished, a perfect cook, and hasn't made a mistake since the last century. Outside the home, she is perceived as being super amazing. She professes to be completely committed to the success of the marriage, and even makes it part of her conversations at parties. But deep down, she believes that her husband got a waaaay better deal than she did and that he is most fortunate to be married to her. She behaves towards him in a dismissive manner when others are not around. Not exactly a recipe for success, is it?

Similarly, Goliath had never fully embraced the value of the Davids I worked with. The Company spoke passionately about the importance of a partner ecosystem and it was part of our public strategic plan, but our words were not evident in The Company's deeds, systems, or sales support. I worked hard to make up for it, took my strategic relationships to heart, and our results reflected that commitment.

I had doubled the expected revenue generated by my partners and had a large pipeline of opportunities going into January. Last fall, both of my strategic partners had received corporate awards – no one else on my team had ever accomplished that level of success. My strategic partners loved me and were very grateful for my commitment to the partnership. I had achieved these results while working just three days a week for months. Didn't that make my results even more exceptional? What else could My Boss give me but an A grade? Not so fast.

What else could My Boss give me but an A grade? Not so fast.

"You know it's been crazy with the reorganization," My Boss said.

Yes. Crazy was one word for it. The Company had conducted yet another massive reorganization. On my lowly rung of the ladder, it felt like there was little planning and even less communication. We were flung about like the tip of a flag, flapping wildly in the face of a strong corporate wind.

"There are some sales people who don't even know what group they are in yet," he added. "There are lots of rumors."

I began to wonder what that had to do with me. I am not in sales. I craft strong partnerships. I build winning teams. Then I realized that My Boss was just making small talk to avoid the meat of our conversation. Uh oh.

He cleared his throat. "So let's get right to it. Your rating for last year is a B."

I felt like I had just been pushed into an ice bath after leaving a Finnish sauna.

My Boss forged ahead. "It's an excellent score. I don't know anyone who received an A. I didn't have one to issue. Plus, you are retiring at the end of this year."

I was struck mute as my poor, tired brain tried to process the grade.

"Receiving an A is mostly ego," added My Boss, eager to diffuse the tension. "It impacts raises in middle of the coming year. If I had an A to give, it would have been hard not to give it to someone else on the team, someone who will be here next year."

As if I were in a dream, my mind dropped me into the middle of a conversation I'd had a few years back with a manager named Janet. I had conducted strengths-based success training with her group. She managed a team of high performers who had worked together for years.

When it came time for the annual performance review, they begged Janet to simply draw names out of a hat in front of them. "Charlotte, this year, you get the A!" Pull another name from the hat. "Joanie! You got the B!" and so on. It would have made more sense and been less personally painful. However, The Company was not in the business of making sense or reducing pain. And as with any form of gambling, The Company always wins.

"You are a star performer!" injected My Boss and jolting me back to reality. "Your partners love you. Duncan considers you a member of his family, like a sister. Their visibility in The Company has gone up. Sales have gone up. They are winning awards!"

"And?" I said, my voice dripping with sarcasm.

"And..." replied My Boss, hesitating for a moment in the face of my anger, "the scope of your job is part of it. With The Company's team-based decision-making process for evaluating individual performance, there are people at your same level in Singapore who generated $10 million dollars in sales."

The Company had gone to a global team-based approach to performance. Employees were now compared to people they did not know, and would never know, in disparate roles. Imagine comparing the work of the head designer of the Chevy Corvette in Detroit with the results of the best accountant in Singapore.

Then, with one more statement, everything became clear. "If you want an A," said My Boss, "you would have to get a different job with a greater scope of impact."

No wonder My Boss sounded uncomfortable. There would be no A grade for me in my role, no matter how well I performed. I was beginning my fourth year in this position, and this was the first time I had heard that bit of significant news. It was different from what I had been told in last year's review.

Last year, I had been told that if my partners generated $X million in sales, I would get an A grade. My partners had generated $2X million in sales – hence my high expectations. I had received a B grade in this position year after year. Now, in some dysfunctional parallel universe, the grade made more sense.

Didn't I feel like a fool? Blind as a bat. From the moment I had joined this team, an A grade was never, ever in my future because the scope of the role was too small. What a dummy I was. And what an awful, ludicrous performance management system that generated fruitless, unattainable goals and false hope. It was an exercise in futility that was executed hundreds of thousands of times a year, all over the globe, with poor souls like me.

What an awful, ludicrous performance management system that generated fruitless, unattainable goals and false hope.

My Boss and I have a good relationship. Sensing my disappointment, and perhaps remembering the conversation from last year's review, he began to offer additional information that was likely confidential in nature, but important to share. He cared, after all, even though he couldn't show it by giving me a more fitting grade. Plus, he needed to keep me motivated during this coming year, my last year with the team. Twelve months is a long time to be unhappy, unmotivated, and disengaged. Unfortunately, even though I knew My Boss truly valued me, I was feeling unhappy, unmotivated, and disengaged. I wanted to yell at the Management Gods: "Hey! If we agree that the purpose of a performance review is to improve performance, why do they crush us and suck the life out of our souls?" Poorly conducted performance reviews lower performance in individuals and teams. I had seen it over and over again at The Company.

In an attempt to put a bandage over the wound and reduce the pain of the message, My Boss kindly stated that he hoped that there was a way to keep me past my retirement date. I felt a pang of sympathy for him, because I knew that this conversation was not easy and that he did genuinely appreciate me. However, I also knew that it was not legally possible to stay beyond my exit date of December 31. And then there was the reality of the situation – I did not want to remain. In fact, I suddenly couldn't wait to leave. Between his desire to minimize conflict and get back to business as usual and my distaste for a pill that was impossible to swallow, our conversation ended quickly.

My Boss added one last bit of advice. "I want you to enjoy your last year. Have fun, hold yourself to your very high standards," instructed My Boss. "But," he cautioned, "don't do it for the grade."

Between the lines, My Boss was telling me that no matter how well I performed in the coming year, there would likely be no reward beyond my salary. Therefore, it was on me to manage my time and energy in proportion to my reduced income. I am wired to work hard, especially when people outside The Company – such as my strategic partners – depended upon me.

Lost in my thoughts, I turned down Cumberland Street, plodding through the snow. The wind was at my back. It pushed me forward, and my thoughts followed.

Disillusionment grows like mold in the gap that lies between expectations and reality. Stung by the disappointment of my performance review, I felt a sneaky, mean sense of doubt crawl into my heart, and it stabbed at my entrepreneurial dreams. Most startups fail. Could I make a living? Were my services valuable? What was reality for me? When would I know?

Move forward through the fog, and trust that the road will appear.

A gust of wind threw snow into my face, momentarily disrupting my vision. I wiped it away. Then, I was reminded of the advice I give my clients when they feel frustrated by the dense fog of uncertainty: *Just because it is difficult to see does not mean there is no road. Move forward through the fog, and trust that the road will appear.*

Following my own counsel, I believed that all would become clear. I simply had to trust in the universe and be ready. My deep expertise in building strengths-based teams would bear fruit. I could take my disappointment and use it to fuel my energy toward my next client. This was not the end of the world. The obstacle in the path is the path. This was all practice for something bigger, something yet to come. As Einstein advised, I would be ready to demonstrate my value, and be valued for it.

I took a deep breath and trudged toward home.

Chapter 2: Divine Intervention

"Be bold, and mighty forces will come to your aid."

Basil King and/or Goethe

* * *

Two days after my performance review drama, I was becoming more philosophical about it. It was yet another road sign indicating that I needed to exit The Company.

During a telephone conversation with my brother Marty, who always supports me, I self-talked my way to a new spot on the map.

"My long-term future does not include The Company, so why am I killing myself for rewards that haven't come for years?" The telephone receiver was working just fine, but my voice was raised, reflecting the intensity of my feelings.

Marty remained silent. He knew when to let me rant.

"Yes, I need to keep my strategic partners successful. Beyond that, not a single ounce of my precious energy should be directed, for any reason, at The Company. No more battles to fix broken processes. No more begging for better demonstrations of our products. No more wrestling with sales teams trying to prove that my strategic partners can help them win more business. In the future, I'm going to let it go – Every. Single. Bit. Of. It!"

"I see," said Marty, with just the right touch of skepticism. He had heard this song before.

"I mean it this time!" I said, even louder. Before long, he would not need a phone to hear me, for we only lived about a mile apart. To prove my commitment to a new way of working for The Company, I gave him an example.

"Imagine a cup full of water," I began. "Now, imagine that the water in the cup contains all the energy that you have for one day. Going forward, only one-third of the water will go to The Company. The rest will go to my strengths-based success business. If nothing else, it is an investment in my mental health."

"Gotcha."

His response barely registered. I was too worked up to hear him. "I told you what my colleague said, right? She said my expectations of excellence are too high for other employees at The Company!"

"No, I hadn't heard that before."

He was teasing me. I had shared that story at least a dozen times. My colleague's indictment of my commitment to excellence – think polishing a pearl – happened ages ago. Clearly, it had set its hook in me. I reiterated my idea that I should go to my CEO, whom I used to work for back in the day, and ask her if she preferred high expectations or low expectations of excellence. I hoped it was a rhetorical question. Shoddy work discourages me, and it violates my strengths.

Marty, sensing that the steam was out of the pot, offered an observation. "You're in a great position," he began. "You've worked with all those teams in The Company, so you've had the chance to perfect your use of the StrengthsFinder. How many teams did you work with? 80? 100? You've got the results to prove it."

I reminded him that I had never been paid a dime for those workshops. Improving the effectiveness and awesomeness of my colleagues at The Company was never part of my day job, and I had worked hundreds of extra hours to deliver the programs.

"True," he conceded, "but there are very few consultants out there who can walk into a large or small firm and say, 'Hey, look what I did for The Company. Now, I can do that for you.' Like a great sports team, you're peaking at just the right time."

Marty had a point. Over the past eight years, I had established and leveraged a really great training ground. It was volunteer work. My paid roles never included the responsibility of helping teams at The Company discover and engage their strengths. It was annoying to have a Master's degree in Leadership, and continually be passed over for roles in Leadership Development. My volunteer investments created a higher performing company by leveraging the strengths of our employees, yet my efforts failed to yield a full-time role.

My perseverance paid off in other ways. The experience was invaluable. I had honed my craft. I had a methodology that had been tested and refined through my work with individuals and teams. My vast experience with the Clifton StrengthsFinder resulted in a personal ocean of knowledge that was wide and deep. As a result, I could help people and teams identify, leverage, and communicate their value proposition with confidence and clarity. I helped organizations define success and harness their collective strengths to achieve it.

My methods had driven improvements in The Company's North American sales force. As word spread about my strengths-based success programs, I was invited to work with teams far beyond the shores of the U.S., including India, Singapore, Brazil, Central Europe, and Australia.

I was discovered by an internal group in Europe after a renowned StrengthsFinder expert had quoted a speaking fee that ran in the tens of thousands of dollars. I went in his stead and spoke to hundreds of managers at a large company event in Ireland, where I achieved the highest speaker rating. The woman who had recruited me, a lovely executive from Spain, was thrilled. She was competitive in nature, and when I received the highest rating, she, of course, considered it a reflection upon her. I was fine with that and thrilled that my workshop had been received so well. I called her "my favorite executive sponsor," and she called me, "her precious gem," which, when uttered in a Spanish accent, sounds delightful. I was proud to be her precious gem.

That led to more work with the European vice president and his senior leadership team. My extensive global experience gave me immense confidence. I was entirely comfortable working with leaders at any level, in any industry, to leverage a strengths-based approach to success. It is hard to place a dollar figure on all those opportunities, but it certainly wasn't zero – for me or for The Company.

It was hard to place a dollar figure on all those opportunities, but it certainly wasn't zero.

At the same time, it was frustrating. I wanted to be valued for being valuable. In baseball terms, I was hitting home run after home run, waiting for a talent scout to come by and say, "Hey, I want you to play on my team!" There was no cohesive program linking my workshops to a particular organization within The Company, so while every group was grateful and higher performing, they were disparate and disconnected. I had broached the topic with a few vice presidents, but times were tight, and no one had room on their roster for me.

Weary of one-off workshops that were not landing me the role I wanted, I partnered with my colleague in India, Khalid Raza, to offer a global *Succeed With Your Strengths* webinar series. Over 6,000 employees signed up. Employees of The Company were hungry for the kind of nourishment provided by my strengths-based approach to success. I knew my colleagues were talented and awesome. I wanted them to know it, too, and to understand why. The Clifton StrengthsFinder assessment was both accessible and budget friendly and would help them identify how they solved problems, built relationships, influenced others, and executed tasks. All I did was introduce it to them, walk them through their results, and provide next steps. They loved it. The feedback from the webinar series was outstanding. It led to even greater possibilities.

If employees knew their strengths, they'd be more productive, happier, and more likely to be engaged.

One forward thinking leader in Malaysia was building a new center, and he was interested in using my strengths-based success approach to develop the 3,500 employees he planned to hire. He understood that if new employees knew their strengths, they'd be more productive, happier, and more likely to be engaged. Engaged employees are less likely to leave. Turnover was a problem in that region of the world. It was a volunteer opportunity that was too wonderful to pass up, and I jumped in with both feet, without missing a beat in my day job responsibilities. I was working crazy long hours, but it was worth it.

As my success with the webinars and the Malaysia team gained steam, it landed on the radar of two vice presidents at The Company headquarters. They interrupted their important work in the Department of Internal Navel-Gazing long enough to make inquiries. The result of said inquiries led to an excruciatingly painful outcome. I was whacked unmercifully with a blunt corporate 2x4 as they demanded to know who I was working with, why, and for how long. Just who did I think I was, anyway? Fear is a driving factor in the culture at The Company. Previously strong allies fled like vermin from a sinking ship. The Malaysian leader decided it was not in his best interest to move forward, and I did not blame him. Unfortunately, that was not the worst of it.

A witch hunt was underway. I actually welcomed the fight for myself. If folks in HQ wanted to burn me at the stake for building a better, happier, and more engaged workforce on my own time, go for it. There was no other global initiative that was as successful in improving morale, and I knew it. My position was honorable and defendable. However, I was concerned for the well-being of my 20 *Succeed With Your Strengths* volunteers around the globe.

My fears were realized when one of them was informed that being associated with our movement would be detrimental to their career. This colleague immediately called me and asked me to remove any reference to their name from our materials and collaboration site. The panic in my dear friend's voice was palpable and upsetting. In that single moment, I knew it was over. I was willing to risk my job, but would never, ever want others to do the same. In one fell swoop, I shut the program down. We were done.

The public outcry from the global community was loud and intense. People naturally wanted to know why I was closing the doors. I would only say that it was not possible to continue. I did not want to give any energy to the fear-based culture, so I kept the details to myself. In the end, there was no middle road, no demilitarized zone that could make it work without inadvertently damaging people's careers.

Despite the crash landing, I was proud of the results. Four years after I introduced my strengths-based success program to The Company, we estimated that 15,000 employees had assessed their strengths and were happier and higher performing as a result. My webinar materials had been downloaded over 24,000 times in one year. I had feedback from leaders, teams, and individuals that proved the value of my work. Believe it or not, even the drubbing from HQ was a blessing in disguise because it shifted my mindset. I stopped hoping for a role in The Company, and instead, believed there was a place, beyond the rigid walls of The Company, where my value proposition would be valued. When the retirement offer arrived, I grabbed it with both hands.

"Hey," said Marty, interrupting my thoughts, "I'm off to run some errands."

"We will continue this later." I said, "Thanks for listening, and by the way, you're in the same boat I am."

He laughed in agreement, and hung up.

Our journeys were aligned. We became certified in the use of the StrengthsFinder at the same time, which was a lot of fun for me. Marty also worked for a large company, and his experiences were not dissimilar from mine. He cared too much, worked too hard without receiving the financial or emotional benefits, and fomenting change in the workplace was a never ending exercise in frustration. However, there is something so compelling about engaging in a StrengthsFinder movement, that it is nearly impossible to walk away from. He felt it, too. I also believed that he would be more successful than I was – he had a StrengthsFinder profile comprised of higher influencing talent that I have. And if he was learning and honing his craft, I supported his efforts 100%.

I opened my laptop and fiddled around on the internet. I was stalling. I needed to work on a manuscript I was writing about personal success. My book would capture and make accessible the techniques I had developed over the past ten years of my experience with the Clifton StrengthsFinder. Knowing your strengths is the starting point, not the landing point. Success – as defined by each person or team – was the destination. I was helping people discover and accomplish what they had been put on this earth to achieve. One can only reach that summit when they know themselves really well, define what success looks like for them, and fully leverage their natural, God-given strengths. This was the purpose of my manuscript.

I was helping people discover and accomplish what they had been put on this earth to achieve.

I opened the file for chapter three, which began with my own Clifton StrengthsFinder results. I smiled, thinking about what a wonderful journey it had been to discover my personal rocket fuel. My top six StrengthsFinder results included lots of thinking, a little doing, a little relating, and a little influencing. See the table on the next page.

Maureen's Top StrengthsFinder Results

Executing Strengths (Get it done!)	Relating Strengths (Human Glue)	Thinking Strengths (Navigators)	Influencing Strengths (Energy to Move People to Action)
Achiever (to-do list, personally productive)	Individualization (everyone is unique in their own way)	Strategic (connect dots to best outcome or spot on map)	Maximizer (polish the pearl, good to great, reaching excellence)
		Ideation (idea machine, creative)	
		Learner (curious, happy in new environments)	

In a nutshell, my strengths profile revealed that I was an idea machine (Ideation) focused on maximizing (Maximizer) the excellence of individuals (Individualization), teams, and projects (Strategic). I loved to learn for the sake of learning (Learner). I would gladly work myself to death (Achiever). When I took the StrengthsFinder, it simply explained so much. The more I learned about the tool, the more I valued it. It soon became the centerpiece of my leadership activities, and I was determined to make a career out of it. The StrengthsFinder measures 34 patterns of excellence, and I knew my whole profile. Key to my happiness and well being was having time to think, for I had six thinking strengths in my top 14 talents. When I used my strengths in my work, I was in hog heaven. I was in seventh heaven when I was *valued* for using my strengths in my work.

When I used my strengths in my work, I was in hog heaven. I was in seventh heaven when I was valued for using my strengths in my work.

How did my strengths compare to Marty's? It's always interesting to compare siblings. Here are Marty's top strengths.

Marty's Top StrengthsFinder Results

Executing Strengths (Get it done!)	Relating Strengths (Human Glue)	Thinking Strengths (Navigators)	Influencing Strengths (Move people to action)
	Individualization (everyone is unique in their own way)	Context (historian, looks backwards to solve problems)	Activator (impatient, urgent need for action)
	Adaptability (go with the flow)		Communication (gift of gab, verbal influence)
			Self-Assurance (supremely confident)

Comparing my results to those of my brother, one can see that Marty was more easy going (Adaptability), looked backwards to solve today's problem (Context – he loves history), and was able to rouse the troops to action (Communication, Activator). His poise in tackling tough challenges (Self-Assurance) made him a leader that people liked to follow. He had helped multiple colleagues improve their interviewing skills by focusing on and communicating their strengths (Individualization). His three influencing strengths delivered energy, conversation, and confidence. Frankly, he really was better suited than me to inspire a strengths movement inside his company. Plus, he was well aware of the mistakes I had made.

I encouraged myself to refocus on my writing, but my mind had other plans. I indulged in a series of important distractions such as gazing out the window, quenching my thirst with a large glass of water, checking the weather forecast, starting a load of laundry, and adding items to my to do list. I realized it had been at least ten minutes since I had checked my email, and off I went to see if anything exciting had happened during that time.

There was an email from my friend, Karla! Karla was a bundle of energy, and it was always good to hear from her. We were working together to find her a new role, with better pay, that leveraged her amazing strengths and provided more opportunity for growth. I clicked on her email.

Hi Maureen,

A friend of mine has a team building opportunity for the Cranbrook hockey team. I thought of you. Is that something you could do? If not, any ideas?

Karla

My jaw dropped. I scanned the email again, unable to believe my eyes. Work with a sports team? Using the StrengthsFinder and my methodology? It was a dream come true. I love sports! Sports teams are the ultimate system of strengths-based success. I often pored over articles about sports figures, guessing at their StrengthsFinder profile and seeking insight into what success looked like to them. I leveraged these gems in the business world to help professional talent do the same thing.

Sports teams do it right. They select people for talent in the role and then develop that talent. If there is a talented pitcher, they work on pitching. They do not take the best baseball pitcher and move that fellow behind the plate in order to improve his pitching nor do they throw him in at shortstop to help him improve his footwork. We make that mistake in the corporate world all the time. "Fix your weaknesses and you'll be a rock star!" No. It is not true. Hone your strengths and you'll be a rock star.

Sports teams do it right. If there is a talented pitcher, they work on pitching. "Fix your weaknesses and you'll be a rock star!" No. Hone your strengths and you'll be a rock star.

The opportunity to work with a sports team of any caliber had been a dream. Thanks to Karla's email, it could become a reality.

My fingers flew over the keyboard. (I was typing champion at Romeo Junior High.) I replied with multiple "Yes!" statements because one simply wasn't enough and explained that the project was everything I love all rolled into one delicious bundle. I hit send and then leapt to my feet in the V pose that all humans strike when they feel victorious. I could not believe my good fortune! I paced around my kitchen, processing the good news. How cool would it be to work with Cranbrook? It was one of the most exclusive high schools in the area. I often visited and wandered the beautiful grounds, enjoying the elegant splendor of its architecture and gardens.

I tried to shift my focus back to my writing but was unsuccessful. I was wound up and antsy. The dark clouds from my performance review were swept away by the winds of excitement generated by this new opportunity. Plus, it was hockey! I had played hockey and worked at Romeo Ice Arena many, many years ago. I would be perfect for this job.

A few hours later, I saw that Karla had forwarded my email to her friend, Red Fox. Red Fox was the code name used for this project because it was veiled in a shroud of secrecy. Red Fox was working privately with the hockey coach and did not want other parents to think she was interfering in some way.

I had met Red Fox some years before. I wondered if she would remember me. Her email, which arrived the next day, was filled with enthusiasm. She suggested that the very best next step would be to speak by phone. After agreeing upon a time, I phoned Red Fox.

We began with the normal pleasantries and the customary historical exchange required between folks who haven't talked in years. I listened to her son's plans for college and how much he had enjoyed playing hockey for Cranbrook. That led us to the business at hand.

"Maureen, the team has a problem, and we don't really know what it is," she began. "They just had their fifth tie against teams they should have beaten. Cranbrook won the Michigan state championship two years ago, and with all the talent on this team, they should have won last year as well. This year, there are at least a dozen seniors. It's an awesome team, and we should be doing better. Coach Weidenbach wants to do some teambuilding."

My mind was churning away on the information, and my first question was one I often ask leaders in the corporate world, because you can't help someone who doesn't think they have a problem. "Does Coach think there is anything wrong?"

"He does. He says he's never seen anything like it before, which is shocking and proves there is something amiss because Coach has this down to a science." Red Fox paused for a moment before adding, "I could tell there was something wrong in the beginning of the year. They don't have good chemistry, and they don't play like a team. I told Coach I was going to talk to you and see what you thought."

I was silent, letting my mind race through multiple scenarios. There could be a lot of things going on. Like a doctor trying to guess what's wrong with a patient simply by listening to their symptom (and we don't always recognize our own symptoms, do we?) I could guess. Or, I could assess the group with the StrengthsFinder and see what the results indicated. I decided to continue to mine for information.

"Has Coach identified specific issues?"

"Yes," she said. He had witnessed disrespectful behavior that goes unpunished. The two captains did not have the authority or respect needed to guide the team. Players were perpetually jockeying for position. There was a lack of team-regulated discipline for mindless behavior such as forgetting one's hockey sticks.

I processed the information. It was not unfamiliar territory.

I had seen executive teams behave this way. They are driven and high-powered by nature. Then, when you add the pressures of sales quotas, business growth, or fighting for every square inch on the corporate ladder, jealousy and lashing out make a regular appearance. If unchecked, these unproductive behaviors spread like weeds, and undermine the success of the organization. The funny thing is that the executives are generally well intentioned. They want to be successful. They want to be effective. They want to achieve the team goals. But because they do not know their own strengths or the strengths of their colleagues, and they receive little guidance from above, they sometimes behave poorly.

"The talented kids are sassy. They all operate as individuals," continued Red Fox. "The five ties are a symptom, but we don't know what's causing it or why they won't play as a team."

Aha! Now we were getting somewhere. A slow smile moved across my face. Determining what's wrong with a talented team is my idea of a good time.

This team was suffering, and it was not from lack of talent. How often does that happen in the corporate world? I have seen many a business work group who had the formal skills to perform well and were working like mad to get the work done. However, with zero emphasis on the human system, they failed to reach their goals. They felt miserable and drained. They were malnourished in the human sense. This is where my strengths-based success program is most effective because it nourishes talent. We invest in the human system.

Red Fox described the sense of urgency surrounding the project. "We've got to do something quickly," she exclaimed. "The playoffs are practically upon us. Coach would need to do something in the next couple of days, in the evening, or even on a Sunday. He'll even give up an ice slot for it."

I did not really need to know anything else. My experience had shown me that every single individual and organization derives a boost of energy and a sense of appreciation for those around them when they embark upon the strengths-based success journey. We do not change the people; we change their point of view. It improves team chemistry, particularly if that chemistry is weak.

We do not change the people; we change their point of view. It improves team chemistry, particularly if that chemistry is weak.

I jumped in with both feet. "I think I can help. Let me just quickly share my approach, and we'll go from there," I said. I shared that it was entirely likely that each player had a different view of what success looked like. I described my process of building the definition of success with the team in order to get buy-in from the players. Then, we would identify and analyze the strengths of the team and target ways to bring all of the talent to bear against the success statement. This method results in an instant shift of energy that would drive improvements in collaboration with less conflict.

"It sounds great!" exclaimed Red Fox. Then, she hesitated. "I didn't talk to Coach about fees. Would there be a charge?"

This was a pivotal moment for me. I wanted this opportunity. At the same time, I had taken a pay cut at The Company so that I could pursue this path as a career. I needed to generate some income. I was leaning towards doing it for free when a little voice inside my head said, "No!" It was time to be bold so that great forces could come to my aid.

"I'd have to charge something," I said, clearing my throat and buying time. I mentally ran through the costs. There was the fee to take the strengths assessment, and my time associated with preparing and delivering two workshops. I quoted a fee that was one-third of my corporate rate, plus the cost for 25 players and coaches to take the Clifton StrengthsFinder assessment.

"I think that is very reasonable," said Red Fox. "Let me speak to my husband about funding it. I think it would be a great experience for the boys! Would you be willing to work on a Sunday?"

"You bet," I replied.

I regularly worked Sundays as part of growing my business. Plus, we have already established that I do not have great work/life balance during normal circumstances, let alone something as wonderful as this. I like the idea of a Sabbath, I just do not know how to do it. Achiever is my third StrengthsFinder talent, and that basically means that every day I must do something productive. Making my dreams come true trumps my wistful longing for a Sabbath every time.

She offered to talk to Coach and get back to me. I promised to send her a paper I had written about strengths-based teams. It had a corporate flavor, but I encouraged her to share it with Coach. We agreed to reconnect after she had spoken to Coach Weidenbach.

I hung up the phone, giddy with excitement. I did not have all the facts, and I had yet to engage with Coach Weidenbach, but from what I knew so far, it looked like a clear-cut case of a train that was barreling full speed ahead on the wrong set of tracks. Maybe it was time to pause, redefine the destination, and fire up the team strengths engine.

My mind was deeply embroiled in the art of the possible when another thought entered the mix. If The Company didn't think I was all that valuable, maybe a boy's hockey team would.

Chapter 3: Meeting the Maestro

**"No one can whistle a symphony.
It takes a whole orchestra to play it."**

Halford E. Luccock

* * *

I emailed a summary of our conversation to Red Fox so that she would have the information to review with Coach Weidenbach.

1. It is most effective to implement change from a position of abundance – what is RIGHT about you versus what is WRONG with you.
2. StrengthsFinder is a holistic tool that measures talent in how we relate, influence, think, and execute tasks.
3. Teams that are strengths-based are more productive, collaborative and have reduced conflict.
4. Understanding and valuing our strengths, and then aiming them at a common purpose, is a high-energy endeavor that yields great benefits and provides a competitive advantage.

For good measure, I sent her a blog post I had written about Brad Ausmus, Detroit Tigers manager, along with the white paper I had created on strengths-based teams.

Red Fox shared my plethora of strengths-based success content with Coach Weidenbach. He read it all and was interested in a conversation with me. Meanwhile, back at the ranch, Red Fox spoke to her husband Silver Fox, and they agreed that the Fox family would cover the fees. I thought it was extraordinarily generous of the Fox family to invest in the young men's future. I knew from experience that it was an investment that would last a lifetime. Now, it was up to me to convince Coach Weidenbach that this was a strategically sound path to pursue.

Coach and I dove right into a frank discussion about the status of his Cranbrook varsity hockey team. He confirmed much of the information shared with me by Red Fox – they were talented but struggling. The team had started well, but the group slowly began to change to the point that they were far less effective than they should be. The multiple tied games were symptoms. There were other clues of a more human nature.

"We still have a winning record," said Coach, "but I don't like the selfish behavior I see on and off the ice."

I needed specifics. "How does that behavior manifest itself?"

"They play as individuals, not as a team. They snipe at one another when things don't go as planned. There's not a lot of respect for the leadership on the team," said Coach. "We've preached a mindset of achieving success with a positive attitude, and I've told them that they've got to believe, but they still seem disengaged. That message doesn't sink in."

My first thought was that the team dynamics described by Coach sounded an awful lot like the corporate leadership groups that I had worked with. I wondered if this team had a purpose that they were universally and deeply connected to. Talent does not automatically translate to achieving the desired outcome. Talent demands focus and structure, and a net to harness all that energy. Winning teams require massive amounts of human glue – connection points to one another and to the purpose – to boost cohesion as they journey along the arduous path to success. Creating a culture of character is also an important part of the equation. Without these critical success factors, a team with a lot of horsepower can rip itself apart.

I also suspected that there were a lot of "you" statements flying around the locker room. They sound like this:

"You didn't do x!"

"You did y!"

"You need to stop doing z!"

"What's wrong with *you*?"

There's no 'I' in team. But there is no 'U' in it either. The bottom line? Pronoun usage is an indicator of team health.

There is a popular saying in sports and business. "There is no 'I' in Team." That is true. But there is no "U" in Team, either. I believe the "U" problem is bigger than the "I" problem on most teams. In fact, I have seen the "You" problem result in an "I" response. "If YOU won't do what needs to done, then I will!" This behavior almost always results in the opposite of the desired outcome.

In the corporate world, there is an additional pronoun that raises a red flag: "They." The word, "they" is often used to refer to the little people, the lower level worker bees, or anyone that is sublevel to a leader in the organization. "They don't understand our strategy," is vastly different from, "We have a communication problem because our strategy is not well understood up and down our team." The same word is often used to indicate an opponent within a different organization inside the same company. "They don't get it," is different from, "We have conflicting objectives across our lines of business." In both examples, the first statements imply blame; the second statements imply ownership.

The bottom line is this: pronoun usage is an indicator of organizational health.

This led me to an important question for Coach. Was he participating in the blame game, or was he willing to own the solution? It is not the kind of question I would typically ask in my first conversation with a client. However, time was not on our side. I decided to broach the topic from an oblique perspective and gauge his response.

"Coach, what do you see as your role on the team?"

"I'm the Maestro," he said. "I tell them all the time that we have to make music, not noise. The Maestro makes the music happen. If they don't make music, it's the Maestro's fault."

Coach Weidenbach did not have pronoun trouble! "It's on me," was the wise general's response. It had been a long time since I had heard a leader take full responsibility for the outcomes achieved by a team. I felt a sense of relief. I could help him.

I also appreciated Coach's word choice. "Maestro" is a term that had been used for centuries to represent mastery of a subject or form. It was used in fencing and in painting. It was a term of reverence and respect. It implied a sense of responsibility for the outcome. If things do not go well, one should look to the Maestro for answers. The Maestro provides clarity and structure around an art that is difficult to comprehend. A Maestro provides a sense of control and timing across a team.

Have you ever heard an orchestra warm up before a performance? It sounds awful. It's chaotic. Great musicians are playing their own notes, their own way, whenever they feel like it. Some are tuning, some are warming up their hands or fingers. Each musician has his or her own routine. Collectively, there is nothing lovely about the sounds they are making. Then, the Maestro steps to the podium, lifts his baton, and the chaos is transformed into magic. All that talent is aligned behind the Maestro as he leads them through the score.

Continuing the music metaphor, the Maestro does not play the instruments; the musicians do. They play the notes and play them well. The Maestro conducts the talent in the room to play as a team, and if they do not, the music begins to disintegrate. Musicians step over one another's parts and play at the wrong time. It sounds like a spinning carnival ride that has gone off the tracks and eventually comes to a screeching halt. It is nearly impossible to recover from that problem. The orchestra must stop, regroup, and start again.

My plan was to do just that. I would work with Coach Weidenbach to hit the pause button so that we stop the spinning and crashing. We would meet and regroup to help the team reconnect with one another. Then, we would revisit the purpose of the team and agree that everyone would recommit to remaining true to their role and to the musical score, as conducted by the Maestro. Plus, we would make them feel like it was their idea. By the way, this issue is not unique to a sports team. In the corporate world, I would tackle this same problem, in the same way, within the confines of an executive retreat.

"Coach, I have worked with troubled teams before," I said, speaking so quickly that my words were practically stumbling over one another. "I know how to fix this problem."

I shared my experience of redirecting struggling teams by starting from a position of abundance. I explained that I focus on what is right about the team, not what is wrong with them. I talked about the strengths philosophy of achieving excellence by focusing on our strengths rather than fixing our weaknesses. "The purpose of using the Clifton StrengthsFinder tool is to focus on what's right about them by evaluating their strengths. We'll use that information to build a solid foundation of collective understanding for the group. Then, we'll align and leverage their strengths to help the team play like a team."

My energy was on the rise, as it always was when I spoke about my favorite topic. I suddenly realized that my right leg was jiggling like I had consumed 15 cups of coffee. I paused for a millisecond, giving Coach a chance to insert a comment. He was silent, likely overcome by my intensity. I decided to push forward with the next important step: building consensus around success.

I spoke about launching with StrengthsFinder and then navigating toward a new destination because the team could only move forward when they knew which direction forward was. I told him we would build a success statement that defines our landing point as well as how and why we were going there. Finally, we would align the strengths of the team with the success statement. "Coach," I explained, "the ultimate goal of our work together is to connect each player's strengths to their role on the team and to the team's definition of success."

"The ultimate goal of our work together is to connect each player's strengths to their role on the team and to the team's definition of success."

I paused, figuring I had talked long enough.

"Okay," said Coach. He did not sound negative. He sounded like he was processing the concept. Well, he was about to get another big dose of information.

I began to describe the StrengthsFinder, explaining how it measures and adds a language around talent. I said it was holistic in nature, identifying 34 patterns of excellence. I acknowledged that 34 strengths is a lot, but people are messy and success is complex. I became increasingly animated as I shared the four StrengthsFinder categories focused on how we relate, execute tasks, influence others, and think to solve problems. We cannot look inside anyone's head and see how they solve problems! Some people like to think about the future. Others like to think about the past. Some people love data. Thinking is such an important part of what we do, and the StrengthsFinder helps us understand that aspect of success. "Coach, wouldn't you like to know how the guys on your team think to solve problems?"

"I would," said Coach. "I'd like to know everything about what makes them tick."

"This tool will help you do that," I said, like an eager lawyer bargaining with a judge. "I don't know what we're going to find when they take the StrengthsFinder, but I guarantee you we will discover new ways to motivate them and leverage the team's strengths. When we connect what's right about them to their definition of success, everything changes. Good things happen."

"I like that idea."

"One more thing. I hear your concerns around the team chemistry. The outcome that I have observed over and over again is this: when the players understand their strengths and the strengths of those around them, the chemistry is much improved. Conflict declines, appreciation rises, and performance takes off. I have worked with a lot of teams, and I have never seen it fail."

I paused to take a breath. I am passionate about this topic, and I have learned that this dialogue is best made in small steps, each one building upon the other to drive impact and understanding.

Coach was on board. He said he liked the ideas I had shared and was eager to give it a try.

We built a plan that rotated around two team meetings over the next nine days. In between meetings, the team would take the Clifton StrengthsFinder assessment. I would compile their results and create a team analysis. We established three milestones:

1. Meet to define what success looks like and gain buy-in from the team. Build our success statement.
2. Have the team complete the StrengthsFinder before midnight the next day (giving me time to process the team results).
3. Meet to explore their strengths and gain their commitment to align their strengths behind the success statement.

I told him that I would work on draft agendas for both meetings, email them, and together we would build a final one. At the end of our call, I made sure to share how much this opportunity meant to me. Working with him and the Cranbrook hockey team was making my dreams come true.

After my call with Coach Weidenbach, I sat right down at the computer and accomplished two tasks. I purchased StrengthsFinder codes for 25 people, and I crafted an email to Coach, summarizing our call and next steps.

He replied with additional information about what he saw as desired outcomes. His list spoke volumes about what a high-performing team looks like. It transcended hockey and was just as valid in the boardroom as in the locker room.

Coach Weidenbach's definition of success:

1. To build a team with great chemistry.
2. To have players respect each other at all times.
3. To have players who care about each other and the success of the team more than just caring about themselves.
4. To win a state championship (optional)

Coach added that winning the title was not the most important thing to him, but said it would be nice for the players to have that experience, and that it was a byproduct of his first three statements. Coach said that he had good kids, but no William Wallace (Braveheart) or General George Patton in the locker room. He wanted the players to take ownership in the team. He ended with a final observation: For the team to be successful, the coaches could not care more about the goals and achievement of the team than the players did.

I considered each item one by one.

Team Chemistry

The team entering my workshop would not be the same team leaving my workshop.

When people speak about great team chemistry, they are really describing a workgroup that has figured out how to embrace and leverage all the talent on the team. It also implies an effective strengths energy management system. I was pretty certain that a group of talented hockey players possessed an abundance of energy. Chemistry is the result of harnessing and aligning that talent-based energy and blending it with the right touch of human glue to help the team coalesce and remain connected when the going gets rough. This aspect of high performing teams is undervalued in the corporate world, largely because many leaders and managers do not know how to foster it.

After a big win, Michigan State University football Coach Mark Dantonio spoke about the importance of team chemistry. "…I just credit our team's belief system. I keep saying over and over we win because of chemistry on our football team. And chemistry is something that is almost magical at times… It's intangible…It's a feeling of belief in each other …We don't give up on each other."[1]

Do you hear the power in those words? Notice he doesn't mention talent. Talent is your ticket to the game, your ante. Great team chemistry delivers a competitive advantage.

Team chemistry is rarely mentioned in the board room or conference room. This was something I was trying to change through my work with executive teams. I was completely comfortable that we would fix the Cranbrook team chemistry problem relatively quickly. The team entering my workshop would not be the same team leaving my workshop.

Respect

Respect among peers is one of the outcomes many people seek when they decide to embark upon my strengths-based success journey. It definitely improves respect, and I touched upon this process in my paper about strengths-based teams. I used the analogy of an eagle and a dolphin as talented fisherman. They are unlikely to respect or even like one another because they go about catching fish in such completely different ways and are on the opposite ends of the personality spectrum. However, if we assess and communicate their strengths, the odds of them valuing the talents of one another greatly increase. That drives respect, which compounds over time.

Success

I wondered if everyone was on the same page. What did success look like to the captains? To the stars? How about to the younger players who might spend more time on the bench than on the ice? What did success look like for them? The answers to these questions were critical to building a winning team. I had worked with many organizations that

---

[1] Hondo S. Carpenter, Sr., "Mark Dantonio & Multiple Players Discuss the Cotton Bowl Victory over Baylor," www.spartannation.com, (January 1, 2015)

had a chasm between their definition of organizational success and their employees' ability to connect their role to that definition. It is a productivity killer because it is demoralizing when one's role seems insignificant. Conversely, when a leader is able to connect organizational success with every single role and person on the team, productivity and engagement skyrocket.

In my corporate work, I often share a powerful example. It is the true story of a hospital orderly. When teased by a colleague about mopping floors day after day, the orderly replied that he was not mopping a floor. He was preventing diseases from spreading. The orderly had formed a real connection between his work and the importance of caring for the sick in a hospital. Now, don't you want your loved ones to be in a hospital where employees have a strong bond between their role and the corporate definition of success?

Winning

The fourth criteria really grabbed my attention. Winning was not everything for Coach Weidenbach. Respect was important. Pronoun choices were important. Caring was important. Team chemistry was important. The state championship was important *only as a byproduct of everything else working well.* I was beginning to understand just how unique Coach Weidenbach was.

Leadership

I chuckled when I saw Coach reference General Patton. On my 40th birthday, I held a *Come as Your Favorite Dead Person* party. I chose to dress as General Patton. He had many flaws, but his greatness was undeniable. Regulating my inner General Patton had been an important part of my strengths journey. I had the talent to take command, and it was triggered most frequently when there was a leadership void. But just because one can do something does not mean they should. Effectiveness matters. One of the outcomes of our work together would be to help Coach and his captains understand how to lead with the strengths they had on the team. General Patton and William Wallace stand out because there are not many people like that out there. Authenticity is essential. There is nothing worse than reporting to a copycat who is flailing around like a fifth-rate General Patton. Understanding how to help the players lead with their strengths and leverage the strengths of their followers would take time and focus, but we would take an important first step by leveraging the Clifton StrengthsFinder. My individual and team analysis would help them climb the learning curve. Would it be enough? Our runway was short with only six weeks left in the season, and the playoffs were just around the corner.

I fired off an immediate response, thanking Coach for sharing his goals with me, and assuring him that we would work together to get everyone to land on the same spot on the roadmap of success.

Before long, I had one last reply from Coach Weidenbach.

I tell my players all the time that there are 3 kinds of people in the world:

1. *Those who make things happen*
2. *Those who watch things happen*
3. *Those who wonder what happened*

#1 is the person you should aspire to be. Not just regular Navy – be a Navy SEAL!
aw

With each interaction, my appreciation of Coach and his point of view deepened. As I shared earlier, I have a strength called Individualization. This strength helps me see each person as a human snowflake, and for me, knowing a person's StrengthsFinder profile is like knowing their DNA. Everyone is unique. There is no person on earth like me or Coach or you. Individualization allows me to understand and honor the talents of each person. The more I interacted with Coach, the more I understood and valued him. That process is delightful for me.

I noticed he signed his emails "aw," short for Andrew Weidenbach. I wondered what he would prefer to be called. Coach? Andy? AW? I thought about it for a moment. I could not call him Andy. I could not call him AW. It felt disrespectful. He was Coach Weidenbach. Period. Without even knowing his history, I could tell that he was an accomplished leader and deserved the respect of the title. In my mind, Coach was his first name and Weidenbach was his last. The day I called him Andy was the day I would eat nails for lunch.

Tomorrow, I would meet the team for the first time. What would I say? I jotted down a few notes about sharing the strengths philosophy with the boys and building a success statement.

- I like to work with talented people who desire success. You are motivated or you wouldn't be here.
- I am not here to fix you. I don't believe you're broken.
- Make a journey together to achieve our success goal. You can't whistle a symphony.
- Individual success is complicated. Team success is complicated. If we align your natural strengths against a goal or a purpose, we are more likely to succeed.
- Introduce the StrengthsFinder Assessment. (Thank sponsor.)
- Define what success looks like for this team. Why does the Cranbrook hockey team exist, and what is your impact on the universe? What does progress look like?
- Next steps

I sat back, and stared at my rough outline. I was well prepared and did not need to do more. I wouldn't follow it anyhow – I never do. I would say what needed to be said in the moment. All I had to do was show up, share my enthusiasm and knowledge, speak from my heart, and help the Maestro and his team define and commit to success. This was my secret sauce.

Suddenly, I felt the full impact of the gift I had been given. The excitement and energy of working with Coach Weidenbach and the Cranbrook hockey team was my reward for the dozens and dozens of volunteer team engagements with The Company. Marty was right. I was peaking at the right time. I had prepared for this opportunity for years. I was ready for this.

I leaned back in my chair and stretched. The future felt pretty cool. Tomorrow, at 4 pm in the boy's locker room at the Wallace ice arena, I would take the first step toward making the talented Cranbrook hockey players a functional, high-performing team. Would my approach to building successful teams in the business world translate well to the sports world? Could I help high school hockey players look, behave, and play differently than they did today?

There was only one way to find out.

Chapter 4: Meeting the Team

"If everyone is moving forward together, then success takes care of itself."

Henry Ford

* * *

The next afternoon, I left my tiny brick bungalow and drove toward Woodward Avenue. To head north on Woodward, I made a Michigan left (Michiganians love to avoid left turns at intersections, and instead design lengthy detours comprised of a right turn, left turn, and another left turn. This marvelous system consumes valuable time and gasoline to achieve the same outcome.) I had allowed myself plenty of leeway, for I am never late. I did not have far to travel; the geographical distance between Chez Monte and Cranbrook is a mere six or seven miles. However, the distance in personal income and power was considerably more significant.

When I told one client that I was excited about working with the Cranbrook hockey team, he sniffed and replied, "Trust fund babies." I was surprised, for he was at the top of the financial heap. I have never understood the resentment toward kids raised in wealth. Spoiled brats are not the exclusive fruit of the rich. Plus, none of us chose our parents, rich or poor. By the way, does a hefty bank account prevent cancer? Does a piece of paper with an image of Ben Franklin on it soothe your heart after your boyfriend cheats on you? It did not do much for me. If you've had an easy life, please raise your hand.

That aside, my client raised a good point. What kind of character would these young men have? Would they feel entitled based on where they go to school? Would they have poor manners? Would they have a strong work ethic? I am at my best when I am working with people who want success bad enough to look within to find it. The internal work is more challenging than the external. Roger Staubach said, "There is no traffic jam along the extra mile." That quote applies equally well to the internal world. Few are willing to make that journey.

I turned left off of Woodward Avenue onto Lone Pine Road. Elegant mansions lined both sides of the street and gazed benevolently upon me as I passed. Some of the homes on Lone Pine are like beautiful movie stars from long ago – they do not make them like that anymore. I admired them without experiencing house envy. I had lived in a one room apartment in Paris and in a two room carriage house in Savannah. I was blissfully happy in both. I had long ago concluded that my "big rooms" are in my head, and that is where I spend most of my time. I look at a large dwelling and see a 6,000 square foot burden. It is not what success looks like for me, but I don't mind that it is what success looks like for others.

I passed below Christ Church Cranbrook, perched upon a pretty bluff. Its gothic structure and long steeple reached toward the heavens and towered over the Cranbrook campus like a staunch sentry. Enter if you dare.

I had always wanted to embark upon a church tour of my area to see where I was most welcomed, and find a spiritual home. I never executed my plan, and instead, slid in and out of a few congregations, vaguely dissatisfied. I did not have the social moxie to enter a place like Christ Church Cranbrook. Pity, for they may have embraced me. We find what we seek, yes? Seek injury, and ye shall find it. Confirmation bias, I believe it is called.

I drove past the Cranbrook Gardens' front entrance, and my mind leaped back to an adventure I had experienced in the summer.

Occasionally, I will get up at 6 am, grab my camera, and head to Cranbrook to walk the gardens and campus. One never knows what gifts Mother Nature will present on any given day, between the weather, the fowl, and the fauna. This visit was no exception.

I entered the tiny Japanese garden, tucked between Kingswood Lake and Cranbrook Road. The garden was nearly silent and beautifully illuminated; it was one of those soft Sunday mornings that keep our souls alive. I worked the vista, shooting from various distances and angles, to capture the serenity of the garden, while keeping the tiny, bright red walking bridge in the frame as a focal point.

I moved west and walked along the edge of the lake, keeping an eye out for Mr. Snapping Turtle, whom I had seen on a log, basking in the sun, just a few weeks prior. My attention was drawn to a ruckus off to my right, an apparent territorial battle between a flock of Canadian geese. There was screeching and hissing and honking. I was glad my bedroom was not located next to the natural selection process at work. It was loud.

Out of the corner of my eye, I noticed a goose waddling toward the water with some urgency. Then, I realized why – there were tiny, furry balls of feathers following her. Babies! Really little babies. Brand new, practically. This was going to be fun.

I cautiously approached, watching for signs of resentment. Mother Goose glared. I paused. She nudged her babies into the water. I advanced. She glared. This happened multiple times until I was almost upon them. I lowered myself to water level and began to shoot.

The results were amazing. The babies were fluffy, and because the water was calm, I could capture not just the babies, but also their reflections in the water. Sometimes Mother Goose would go bottoms up, reaching her long neck toward the food along the lake floor, so I had images of her tail feathers raised towards the heavens, surrounded by her goslings. I kept a watchful eye out for Father Goose. He was mostly engaged with keeping the competition at bay, but I did not care to be on the wrong end of a sneak attack. Things proceeded along nicely for about five minutes, when suddenly, everything changed. Mother Goose and Father Goose began to honk nervously and rounded up their babies in a tight circle. I lowered my camera and looked to my right.

I saw him. It was a white swan barreling down upon the Goose family in full royal puffed up mode. His feathers were raised and the tips of them formed a circle above his back. His neck was arched, which resulted in an intense and intimidating eye contact with anyone in his way. He was paddling effortlessly but swiftly, and I'm not kidding when I say that Mr. Swan had bow waves, like those you see on a freighter. I began to shoot furiously as he made his way from one Goose family to the next, delivering a clear message: Don't forget who is king around here.

I had seen photos of swans in this mode and had found them beautiful. I hadn't realized it was a power posture. It was still beautiful, but now I knew what it stood for. It had a dual message, a combination of

"Look at me" and "Don't mess with me." It was a hierarchical statement of authority, beauty, and riches.

The Goose families got the message and almost all gave him room. The few that did not were instantly warned to kneel and state their purpose. If they did not, they were chased out of the water.

There is a connection between these encounters in nature and the interactions between people in the workplace. In fact, American humorist Evan Esar quipped, "Zoo: an excellent place to study the habits of human beings."

It was true. Think about the interactions between Mr. Swan and the Goose Family. They rarely get along, they posture for authority and control, they protect their children, they resentfully cower to a social pecking order, and they fight over water and land. It was a social dynamic we see in humanity all the time. It was interesting how we allow, and even expect it, from animals, yet we resist and attempt to curb the same behavior from people. I suppose that part of developing our level of consciousness included the process of rising above our animal instincts. How are we doing with that, as a global population?

Bullying is not limited to children or animals. I had worked with more than a few Mr. or Ms. Swans in the corporate zoo, especially at the executive level. The Swans were not easy to coach, but when I was able to reach them, the results were amazing.

Imagine coaching a Ms. Swan after watching her bully a workplace team like the Goose family. I had been in this position. Sometimes Ms. Swan had the StrengthsFinder talent of Significance, the need to be seen as important and significant. Poorly regulated Significance can manifest itself in a "Look at me!" and "I'm the best!" behavior. I would encourage Ms. Swan to seek the spotlight, but then turn it on her fellow teammates. Make it "Look at what WE did", not "Look at what I did." What would Ms. Swan's world look like if she made that shift? How would her colleagues and team feel?

I had also run into a Mr. Swan who had the strength of Command, which, when poorly managed, can sound like, "Don't forget who is boss around here!" or "Because I said so!" I helped this particular Mr. Swan soften his approach after telling him that he was scaring the babies (the new hires). I wasn't sure if sharing the information would help regulate his behavior or add fuel to his self-importance. It did both. First, Mr. Swan was pleased with himself. Then, when we focused on effectiveness, he realized that employees who feared their leaders do not perform well over the long haul. It took some time, but small improvements were achieved. These baby steps had a measurably positive impact on team morale. Regulating our talents is required for all of the strengths, not just those named in these two examples.

This brings us to an important point. We cannot presuppose that the Mr. or Ms. Swans in our life are coachable. There are people with that kind of talent, beauty, and power who are not coachable. They require a few more lessons from the universe to help them become ready for feedback. Frankly, some never do reach that point.

A large part of my work with teams focused on helping them understand that each person is different and has a specific value proposition. I achieve success when I help a group of diverse people understand how to value themselves and value those around them, and then lead them toward collective greatness.

It is a shift in mindset from, "You are different. I will fix you." to "You are different. I will leverage you."

There is a line in the book, *Now, Discover Your Strengths*, which captured this concept perfectly.[2] It describes how truly successful organizations not only make room for the uniqueness of each employee, but they capitalize upon those differences. I love that it removes judgment from the equation. It is a shift in mindset from, *You are different. I will fix you.* to *You are different. I will leverage you.* The first statement is reformatory in tone. The second statement implies a competitive advantage, like a power play is in hockey, and is part of a winning business strategy.

The discovery path from fixing people to leveraging people was at the core of the work I've done with teams in the corporate world. I fully expected that this concept would be front and center on the journey I was about to forge with the Cranbrook hockey team.

I returned to the present as I made the turn off of Lone Pine Road, eventually landing at the mouth of the ice arena. I found an empty parking space, gathered up my handouts, and cautiously tiptoed my way

---

[2] Marcus Buckingham and Donald Clifton. *Now, Discover Your Strengths.* (New York, The Free Press, 2001), 5.

across the slippery frozen pavement. My boots had a bit of a heel on them, so it was a challenge.

I hoped that I was dressed okay. What does one wear to a locker room to speak with high school kids? I had on jeans, black boots, a white t-shirt, and a black jacket. I wasn't corporate, and I wasn't casual. I was going for smartly cool.

I passed through the front doors with no idea where to proceed next. The ice arena appeared deserted. I stood there for a moment and then saw signs of life at the far end of the rink. I headed there.

"I'm looking for Coach Weidenbach," I announced. One of the men stepped forward, and we shook hands.

Meeting Coach Weidenbach is like meeting an intense cup of coffee. His dark eyes have the energy of an electric storm. He stands ramrod straight and grabs your attention like the snap of a rubber band. I liked him immediately.

Coach invited me into his office, offered a chair, and said, "The boys are almost ready."

I could feel my adrenaline kick in. We made pleasantries, but I could not tell you what was said. It was show time. I always enter some sort of high energy force field when I am about to share my commitment to a strengths-based approach to success.

Another man poked his head into Coach's office, and said, "We're good to go."

Coach tilted his head to the left, and I followed him into the locker room. I had a weird moment of "what am I doing here?" I was in a boy's locker room, for heaven's sake. I took a breath and glanced around the facility. I realized that the locker room was pristine – not a skate, jersey, or person out of place. It was u-shaped. The young men sat in front of their lockers on perfectly aligned Cranbrook-logoed chairs. They were motionless, a seated version of standing at full attention. All eyes were on me. I walked to the front so that everyone could see me. I think Coach introduced me, but I can't be sure.

I hesitated and then smiled. I was about to do what I do best: invest in the greatness of these young men and their coaches.

I launched into my history with emotional guns blazing. I talked about my first job. I was a Zamboni driver and a poor sharpener of skates at Romeo Ice Arena because I had three brothers who played hockey. I shared that I donned my Bauer hockey skates and played on my brother's team when they were short a man. I could skate with the best of them. This information was important for me to communicate so that they'd know that I had grown up in their environment.

"I am so excited to work with a sports team," I said. "It's been on my wish list for a while. It's not because I don't like working with business teams, because I do. But, there is a difference between teams that show up because they are paid to do so and teams that are motivated to excel. I have a strength called Maximizer. Maximizer likes excellence. Sports teams thrive on excellence."

I paused for a moment. What I said next would set the tone for the rest of the meeting.

"I want to make one thing perfectly clear before we begin," I said. "I'm not here to fix you because I don't believe you're broken. I'm here to work with you from a position of abundance. I don't care about your weaknesses. I care about your strengths. I'm here to help you identify your strengths and then leverage those talents against the common purpose of this team."

At that point, I knew I had done enough talking. It was time to engage the guys. I posed a question to get the dialogue rolling.

"What is one characteristic of a great defenseman?"

Silence. I waited patiently. I'm good with silence.

Finally, a young man to my left raised his hand. He had large blue eyes, curly dark hair, and a friendly demeanor. I glanced at the name on his locker: Stahl. I nodded at him.

"Responsibility!" he said.

I was secretly thrilled with his response. I had expected the players to respond with skills, such as having a wicked slap shot. I glanced around the room and nodded my approval. "I like that," I said with a smile. "Responsibility is a strength."

Bolstered by my encouragement, more characteristics emerged.

"Disciplined."

"Full effort."

"Anticipate the opponent's next move."

"Focused."

I noted that these descriptions were internally sourced. They have external consequences, but they are rooted within. Many a victory is won by

Many a victory is won by players who have mastered the inside world – that fertile ground between the ears, the chambers of the heart, and the core of one's soul.

players who have mastered the inside world – that fertile ground between the ears, the chambers of the heart, and the core of one's soul. We were going to explore that internal world in a new way – from a position of strength.

The dialogue continued as the boys added skills to the strengths, including the ability to skate backwards, check hard, and shoot from the line. This is the natural progression of success: start with strengths and then add skills and experience to make those strengths stronger.

I moved onto the universal truth surrounding the pursuit of a worthy endeavor: Success is complicated. People are messy. Describing our strengths is difficult, yet our best performance lies in the bedrock of those strengths. Teams are even more complex! Our collective talents must be aligned with a common goal or purpose. It was my job to lead them on this journey. To support my point, I shared a story.

I pulled out a newspaper article about one of the Detroit Lions' coaches. In his first year as a defensive coach, the Lions' defense ranked second overall, first against the run, and third in points allowed. Pretty good results for a first-year coach.

"These results are part of the formal system of managing and measuring success," I said. "In hockey, we look at goals scored, shots blocked, penalty kill success – we need those metrics. They support the formal system of success. However, there is another system that matters, too. In the business world, I call it the human system. Investing in the human system drives improvements in the formal system, like those success metrics we were just talking about, but the human system is more difficult to appreciate."

I paused, and pointed at the article again. "Listen to what these pros say about their coach. They love playing for him because the coach puts them in a position to utilize their strengths and hide their weaknesses. They don't talk about the metrics. They talk about the human system. The human system is founded in knowing, nourishing and leveraging our strengths. Then, as a secondary project, we focus on mitigating our weaknesses."

The room was utterly quiet. When I can hear a pin drop, it means that the team is engaged. I had one more point to make. I wanted to plant the seed that what we learned would be useful beyond the hockey season. I explained that investing in the individual and team strengths applies in business as well as sports. Our learning journey would extend far beyond the walls of the ice arena.

I talked the team through the process of taking the StrengthsFinder, shared our deadlines for completion, and talked about timing for our second workshop on the following Sunday. I told them that our work together was possible because of the anonymous donation, and we offered a round of applause for the Fox family.

The Strengths Philosophy

Then, I introduced the Strengths philosophy with my story about a manager hiring two fishermen – a dolphin and an eagle. While each could catch fish, they would achieve success differently. We talked about each animal's lens to the world and how each lens could be useful in different situations. The eagle will fly solo, high above the earth, examine the horizon, swoop in, and catch a fish. A dolphin will work in a group, leveraging a playful and social strategy to success. This is a real example of exploiting the differences between individuals. A great manager would support the approach that works best for the individual, knowing that each will make their fish quota in their own way.

A great manager would support the approach that works best for the individual, knowing that each will make their fish quota in their own way.

However, many managers make the mistake of trying to reform their star players. The manager might attempt to make the eagle charming like a dolphin, or teach the dolphin to see over the horizon like an eagle. This is frustrating for the eagle, the dolphin, and the manager. Ten semesters of charm school will not result in the eagle being as warm, friendly, and approachable as the dolphin. The poor dolphin will never leap high enough to see over the horizon like an eagle. The well-meaning manager is confusing weakness management with performance management. They are not the same. Reform school is hardly an engaging experience and rarely achieves the desired outcome. This mistake is costly because it demoralizes people and results in a lower-performing team. Most of our systems in society are reform- and deficit-based. There is another choice.

The well-meaning manager is confusing weakness management with performance management. They are not the same.

A strengths-based performance management strategy focuses on the natural talents of each individual and allows them to leverage their strengths to achieve success in their own way. The eagle has an abundance of flying talent. The dolphin has an abundance of charm talent. Great managers would recognize it and send them to perform school! The eagle would be enrolled in flight school, and receive a course in strategic planning. The dolphin would attend charm school and participate in Toastmasters. This would allow each one to hone their natural gifts. They would return from perform school energized, high performing (imagine that!), and ready to deliver world-class performance in their roles.

How do we mitigate their weaknesses? Pairing the dolphin and the eagle together offered a weakness strategy. The dolphin could introduce the eagle to clients as the best strategic planner in the world: a little quiet, a little fierce, but brilliant at looking over the horizon. The eagle could rely on the dolphin when a particular message required communicating. The manager could put the dolphin in a client-facing role to leverage her friendly energy and put the eagle in a consulting role to leverage his navigation talents. They would all work together to craft their partnership strategy, each honoring and leveraging the strengths of the other.

I explained how the Clifton StrengthsFinder would help each player in the room understand their lens to the world and how knowing that information would benefit them as individuals and as a team. We would be in perform school, not reform school. The goal was to leverage every single ounce of talent in the room.

Then, I took them to the next level. Knowing our strengths is not enough. Purpose matters.

What Success Looks Like

It was time to embark upon a discussion around success. Not success in general, but specific success – the point of being in the locker room at all.

"Why are we here?" I asked.

One boy spoke up. "To win the state championship." Heads nodded. This was the ultimate goal.

"Okay," I agreed. "That's the WHAT portion of our accomplishment. But, does the HOW we win matter?"

Oh yes, it mattered, claimed many of the boys. Unwilling to put words in their mouths, I probed for specifics. "Tell me more. Tell me more about the HOW."

"Respect."

"Brotherhood."

"Full effort."

"Caring."

I made careful notes because ideas generated by the team would operate as fuel and guard rails for the journey to come. Ownership of the content was critically important. It would help achieve one of Coach Weidenbach's goals – having the team care about the outcome as much or more than the coaches.

I asked if their success statement was limited to the on-ice part of their life. After some consideration and dialogue, they said, "No. On and off the ice."

I continued to take notes and then repeated what I had heard from them. I used sound bites, not whole sentences – that would come later.

"You guys are all in?" I asked. They nodded. The coaches nodded. I paused, and let my gaze roam the room. I noticed that one young man had been watching me with a particular intensity. I couldn't really read what was behind it. Was I reaching him? Was he confused? Was he interested? I glanced at the name on his locker: Blumberg. I would want to examine his strengths, as well as the young man who spoke first, Stahl.

Were we done? Not quite. Based on what Coach Weidenbach had told me about the unproductive behaviors of the team, I pulled one more arrow from my quiver.

"Let's talk about failure."

Ears perked up, and everyone was studying me with interest.

"I've got an exercise that I've used only once before. I save it for the teams who truly desire success and are willing to do what it takes." I paused for a moment, wondering how transparent I should be. I decided to go for it.

"Frankly, I don't find many individuals or teams in a business environment that really want success badly enough to make the tough journey, the internal journey – the very journey I am going ask you to commit to. But, I think you guys are different. I think you do want it. What I am about to ask is unusual. It is about being more than personally 'all in.' Real success runs deeper than that. It's about being 'all in' for the guy next to you and across from you. Are you willing to make a real commitment to one another?"

They nodded, either from conviction or capitulation.

Turn to the person next to you and say, "I refuse to let you fail."

"Okay," I continued, "turn to the person next to you and say, 'I refuse to let you fail.'"

There was a slight hesitation as the boys processed this instruction. Then, they did it, first on one side, and then the other. The voices got louder as they upped their energy, committing to the success of the teammates on either side of them, and then a few seats down the line. I let this run its course until the waves of power and excitement began to diminish.

"Now, point to the player across the room from you, and say, 'I refuse to let you fail!'"

They complied, and it got even louder as they shouted across the locker room. It was u-shaped, and the folks at the back were left out when we pointed to people across the room because I failed to participate. When I realized my mistake, I pointed at them and said, "I refuse to let you fail!" They reciprocated. I have to admit, it felt good to have a small army of hockey players shouting that they refused to let me fail!

Considerable buzz permeated the air; a good sign. It was on me to harness it and maintain it. That was my next step.

As things quieted down, I introduced one more concept. I spoke about what the Gallup organization calls HumanSigma. In a nutshell, HumanSigma means this: every single time there is an encounter between an employee and a customer, the outcome either adds to the relationship or subtracts from it. The encounter is never, ever neutral.

To illustrate my point, I provided an example.

"If we compiled the series of encounters between a waitress at a local restaurant and a regular client, there would either be a negative balance, indicating low trust, or a positive one, indicating high trust. The goal is to have a positive balance in the trust account, because this drives engagement, and engaged customers recommend the business, spend more money when they visit, and don't depart for the diner down the road. They can become your best brand ambassadors."

I explained that the trust account premise exists between managers and employees, and between hockey players and coaches. It was time to draw an important line. "From this moment on, there is a Cranbrook team trust bank in play. Therefore, every single interaction you have with one another will either invest in the team trust bank or subtract from it."

From this moment on, there is a Cranbrook team trust bank in play.

I glanced around the room, making sure that each person realized they were included in the conversation, and I began to tick off a list of behaviors and their impact.

1. If you support a teammate, it adds to the trust bank.
2. If you blame a teammate, it subtracts from it.
3. If you throw your stick, you deplete energy, set a bad example, and subtract from the team trust bank.
4. Bickering and gossip deplete the trust bank.
5. Encouragement increases it.
6. Mistakes and bad plays are going to happen – how the team responds when they happen will determine if there is a deposit in the trust bank or a withdrawal.

"Each of you must choose how to react to setbacks. Whatever decision you make will impact the balance in the trust bank."

The group rustled as they absorbed the information. I sensed that this concept added an element of responsibility to our dialogue that wasn't there before.

"Now, let me ask you a question. Do you think the exercise we did, the one where we committed that we wouldn't let anyone fail, was an investment in the trust bank?"

A chorus of agreement rang out.

This was good news. My "I refuse to let you fail" exercise was designed to build a hefty starting balance in the trust bank. If "I refuse to let you fail" remained part of their conversations going forward, it would keep surplus flowing to it for the rest of the season. This emotional currency would help sustain them in hard times, for they would surely be challenged along the way.

"How about this," I continued. "Is there a link between the trust bank and our strengths?"

This connection was more difficult to make, and I knew it. They hesitated. I let it linger for a moment as they glanced at one another. A few heads nodded, but not many. That was okay. I had thrown a great deal of new information at them. We would get there, as a team, in the next workshop.

I explained that knowing our strengths was a starting point, like the "start here" location on Google maps. Building the trust bank happens over time as we remain committed to valuing the strengths of one another, and to refusing to let anyone fail. Achieving goals comes from aligning all the strengths in the room behind a success statement. "What I described is simple and fun, but not easy. Very, very few teams make this journey. I think you guys are one of those very, very few."

I had nothing more to add. I asked if they had any questions, and there were none. I told them I would craft a success statement from their input and would share it with Coach Weidenbach for distribution and feedback.

Coach Weidenbach rose, and addressed the boys. "Hey, remember the deadline to take the assessment – tomorrow night by 11 pm." The young men nodded.

I packed up my notes and smiled to myself, wondering what the odds were of 22 high school boys and three busy coaches completing the assessment by the deadline. Many of the corporate teams I have worked with could not (or would not) meet a deadline. I certainly expected less from kids in their teens.

A tall, blond-haired young man approached. "Hi," he said, extending his hand. "My name is Mason Schultz, and that was great!"

I was pleased and impressed by his social courage. "Mason, it's nice to meet you! I can't thank you enough for your kind words."

"I think this will help us," he added.

"Good!" I said, "We all do better when we know our strengths. We are going to have so much fun exploring the talent of your amazing team, I promise!"

"I look forward to it," he replied, with a friendly wave of his hand as he headed to the locker room door.

A few others also thanked me in a swift, shy manner. I understood, for I would have been more like them than Mason when I was their age.

Coach Weidenbach approached. It was hard to gauge his reaction. I spoke first. "What did you think?"

"I thought it went well," he replied.

"Yes, it was a big step today. A lot of information. I think it will become more relevant to them once we know their strengths."

Coach nodded. He was making the same journey the boys were.

I told Coach I would craft a draft success statement and share it with him for review. Once he felt that it captured the essence of what the boys meant, we would distribute it for review and buy-in. He agreed with the plan. We shook hands, and parted.

Building the Success Statement

I could not wait to dig in. The process of helping people and teams define success is a joyful one for me. My Ideation, Strategic, Individualization, and Maximizer strengths are all having a party. After fiddling with their words for a half hour or so, I came up with:

The 2014/2015 Cranbrook Hockey Team is determined to win the state championship by recommitting to unselfish play, discipline, focus, trust, respect, team chemistry, brotherhood, and by caring for one another, on and off the ice. We refuse to let anyone fail.

I placed the team's success statement on a photograph I had taken in the Upper Peninsula. It showed a silver trail across a meadow, surrounded by trees adorned in stunning fall colors. Some were nearly pink, others orange and yellow, with evergreens mixed in for contrast.

In my mind, the image was a metaphor for our journey, offering a pathway to success while allowing for, and embracing, everyone's cacophony of colors. In the photo, each tree was different. Some had long limbs, some had stubby limbs. Height, width, and weight varied. Each tree was beautiful in its own right, and together, they formed a perfect portrait. I created a PDF file that could be printed, almost like a poster.

I emailed it off to Coach Weidenbach for his review and said that once he felt good about it, we'd share it with the boys – I wanted them to own it, drive progress toward it, and align their strengths behind it.

He gave it the thumbs up and distributed it to the players for their review. I had suggested we start our workshop with their success statement, ensure that it accurately reflected the collective view of the team, and use it to remind us of why we were, as Henry Ford said, "moving forward together."

I re-read the team's success statement, letting it sink in. I thought about corporate groups that could benefit by executing against success metrics with an attitude of unselfish play, focus, trust, respect, team chemistry, and brotherhood. Imagine a workplace where everyone cares for one another, in and outside the office, while refusing to let anyone fail. That would be a pretty remarkable place of employment.

After reading it one more time, I said to myself, "Not bad for high school boys."

They had the talent. They had the skills. Once they knew their strengths, the energy in the room would skyrocket. If they harnessed that energy, tweaked their behavior, and pursued success in the manner they described above, that would feel amazing. Saying it is one thing. Doing it is another. Would they have the will to walk the talk?

Chapter 5: Being Different

"If you are going to do something truly innovative, you have to be someone who does not value social approval. You can't need social approval to go forward. Otherwise, how would you ever do the thing that you are doing?"

Malcolm Gladwell

* * *

Before we look at how amazing the Cranbrook hockey team is, I want to share some basic StrengthsFinder information. If you have taken the Clifton StrengthsFinder, then you are making this journey with your own strengths in hand and may be curious about all 34 patterns of excellence. This table can help. We are going to talk about the hockey players' strengths, and it will be helpful to have this chart handy. Each column is a different StrengthsFinder category type.

Clifton StrengthsFinder: 34 Patterns of Excellence

Executing	Relationship-Building	Thinking	Influencing
Achiever: high stamina, to-do list	**Adaptability**: go with the flow	**Analytical:** values data, practical	**Activator:** impatient, foot on gas
Arranger: organizer, conductor	**Developer:** takes pride in small steps/progress	**Context:** historian, looking backward	**Command:** willing to take charge
Belief: strong value system	**Connectedness:** we are all one (connected)	**Futuristic:** looks over the horizon	**Communication: verbal,** loves an audience
Consistency: do things the same way, process	**Empathy:** senses people's feelings	**Ideation:** generates ideas, creative	**Competition:** hates to lose, always comparing
Deliberative: risk sensitive, foot on brake	**Harmony:** common ground, diplomat	**Input:** human data base, collects info	**Maximizer:** polish the pearl, good to great
Discipline: structured, sticks to schedule, etc	**Includer:** no one left out, social inclusion	**Intellection:** needs time to think	**Self-Assurance:** leads with confidence
Focus: not easily distracted, prioritizes	**Individualization:** every person is unique	**Learner:** loves to learn new things, curious	**Significance:** loves to make a difference
Responsibility: done right or not at all	**Positivity:** inserts optimistic outlook	**Strategic:** connects the dots, builds pathways	**Woo:** never met a stranger, social courage
Restorative: fixes things, removes roadblocks	**Relator:** small group of close friends		

What I love about the StrengthsFinder is that it his holistic in nature. To achieve success in life, we must think, execute, build relationships, and influence others. Yes, 34 patterns are a lot. However, it helps us answer the question, "What are you great at?" The StrengthsFinder helps us add confidence and clarity to your specific answer to that difficult question!

If you've taken the StrengthsFinder, let's look at how amazing you are! Add your own top five strengths in the table below.

Your top five strengths are:

	Strength	Category
1		
2		
3		
4		
5		

* * *

Less than 24 hours after our first team meeting, I could see that a few of the players had taken the assessment. Oh, and remember that deadline? Good thing I did not bet my 401K on the odds of the team meeting it. Every single boy and coach finished the StrengthsFinder assessment by the midnight deadline. This fact also made the team unlike the corporate work groups I had engaged with. Busy professionals often missed the deadline established for them, whether it was established by me or by their leaders. The timeliness of this team spoke volumes about their respect for discipline.

As the players' results began to roll in, I initially assumed that what I was seeing was just a coincidence. After the first ten or twelve arrived, I realized that we were on to something great. The amount of Competition talent on this team was astounding.

To help clarify my point, let's say that we were studying hair color. The global distribution of hair color ranges from black to white, and the least common hair color is red, at only 1% to 2% of the world's population (it is 13% in Scotland – isn't that amazing?) The strengths patterns I was seeing would be akin to having 75% of the hockey team walking into the locker room with red hair. It could happen, but it was very statistically unlikely.

I began to notice the emergence of other astonishing patterns including unusually high amounts of the Futuristic, Learner, Restorative, and Command strengths. I had never seen anything like it, even with leadership teams at the highest level of The Company, or any of my other executive clients, for that matter. The disparity increased when I compared the hockey team's StrengthsFinder results with the statistical distribution from the global data base. Some of the hockey team's StrengthsFinder results were off the charts. My excitement began to rise. I felt like I had discovered a new chemical element in the universe.

Some of the hockey team's StrengthsFinder results were off the charts. I felt like I had discovered a new chemical element in the universe.

I leapt to my feet, dashed to my phone, and speed-dialed Marty.

"Hello?"

I did not bother with pleasantries. "Okay, guess how many guys on the hockey team have Competition?" My brother paused, and I wondered if my words had been smashed into one long incoherent syllable. I talk fast when I am excited.

"Come on," I urged him. "How many?"

I heard a deep inhale. He was clearly giving the question the proper consideration it deserved.

"I think… eight," he replied.

"Ha! Try again."

"Ten?"

"Nope."

"13?"

"Try 18!" I said, practically shouting. "18 out of 25 people! Can you believe it? Do you know how much horsepower that is? It's insane."

"How many should they have?" asked Marty, referring to the statistical norm provided by the Clifton StrengthsFinder top five strengths database of 11 million people.

"Three," I said. "Actually, 2.75 people, but I'm going to round up to three."

"Wow."

"Exactly! So, here's the $64 million question: With all that Competition in the room, who is it directed toward? Who is the opponent? Is it the guy sitting next to them on the bench, or is it the guy on the opposite team?"

"Right," agreed Marty. "And how do you harness all that energy to a positive outcome? That's not easy. Maybe that's part of the reason they haven't played like a team. Are you seeing anything else that might provide insight into why the group hasn't gelled?"

"I need to dig further into it," I replied, "but they look low on relationship building strengths."

Relationship building strengths are critical to a team's success, because they provide human glue. That glue is what keeps the team together during a tough loss, a bad bounce, or a disappointment of any sort. In the pursuit of a strategic win or an important business objective, investments in the relationships on the team tend to diminish. Did this team have enough human glue to hold them together? Would we need to place more emphasis on building connections on the team? Was this lower amount of relating talent hurting team chemistry? We would have to explore it in the workshop.

Marty and I delved into why the team might be higher than average on the strength of Futuristic. Perhaps it helped them with the critical success factor of mentally turning the page when they have a bad game. Then, I went in the opposite direction.

"Guess how many Learners there are on the team?" I asked.

"Five Learners?" Most teams do have a fair amount of Learners because nearly a quarter of the people who have taken the StrengthsFinder have Learner in their top five strengths.

"Nope. One guy has Learner."

To underscore this surprising result, I reminded my brother that I had recently worked with an executive leadership team of medical doctors. Seven out of nine had Learner in their top five StrengthsFinder profile. Granted, they were scientists, and scientists are in the knowledge business. Their product is making use of that knowledge to help us heal. Having high Learner makes sense, but it provided an even more interesting contrast with the hockey team. On the medical team, 78% had Learner in their top five strengths profile. On the hockey team, only 4%.

I shared that the Cranbrook hockey team had more influencing strengths by percentage than any other team I had worked with. The message was clear: *This team was different!*

Different is good, right? It is very good – as long as being different is recognized as being valuable. Being different also increases the odds of being misunderstood and undervalued. Being different often results in receiving less social approval. This team's StrengthsFinder makeup was so unusual that normal means of managing and leading them were unlikely to succeed. A unique approach was required, one designed to leverage all the energy that comes part and parcel with influencing strengths.

Being different also increases the odds of being misunderstood and undervalued. Being different often results in receiving less social approval.

I could not wait for the actual workshop to dive into the awesomeness of these boys and align all their horsepower behind their team success statement.

Being Different

When I had all twenty-five StrengthsFinder results, it was time to perform a deeper team analysis. I popped open my StrengthsFinder Team Analysis tool. This tool was created for me by my former boss, Ed Brunner. He is an Excel power user. Ed built a tool for me that automatically inputs StrengthsFinder data, and performs all kinds of whiz bang analysis, automatic categorization, color coding, strengths frequency analysis, everything. It is very handy when seeking a team-at-a-glance profile of large groups. When I worked for Ed at The Company, he valued me for being valuable (and graded me accordingly!) and I shall always be grateful for that.

The hockey team had 25 people, each with five strengths. Therefore, the sum of all the strengths on the team was 25 x 5 = 125 total strengths. Below, you'll see those 125 strengths categorized by type. Instantly, I had insight into both why this team was different, and why they were struggling with the human system.

Cranbrook Hockey Team's Strengths Summary

Executing Strengths	Relating Strengths	Thinking Strengths	Influencing Strengths
32%	18%	18%	31%

Nearly a third of the team's strengths fell in the executing category. That was a bit higher than a normal team. The players were inclined to get it done with a lot of horsepower and energy. They were likely very productive as a result, but in the corporate world, I have observed that a task-oriented team may achieve goals at the expense of thinking or relating.

They were lighter on the human glue strengths, the relationship-building strengths, than a statistically normal team.

They were also light on thinking strengths. How was this impacting the team? Were those who possessed thinking strengths valued by other players and by the coaches? Thinking strengths are less visible, and, therefore, easier to overlook. Any time there is talent that is overlooked, the team is, by definition, sub-optimized. Sub-optimized teams cannot achieve maximum performance.

Sub-optimized teams cannot achieve maximum performance.

The Cranbrook hockey team was loaded with influencing strengths, with more than double the amount we would expect to find on a normal team. Influencing strengths always have a lot of energy associated with them. Harnessing that energy, while building stronger team collaboration and chemistry, would be a challenge because it requires changing how the players view one another. This is a problem I have confronted repeatedly in the executive ranks of the corporate world. It would take a very special leader to manage this transformation effectively.

For a point of comparison, I pulled up the top five strengths distribution data base of 11 million people.

My eyes raced down the list of the most common StrengthsFinder strengths on the Cranbrook hockey team. Only two strengths fell into the statistically normal distribution. Those were Strategic (finds and connects dots) and Relator (small but deep circle of friends).

My findings are documented in the next table.

Comparing Cranbrook Hockey Team's Most Common Top Five Strengths vs The Norm

Hockey Team's Most Common Top Five Strengths	# of Players With This Strength	# of Players if the Team were Statistically Normal *
Competition	18	3
Restorative	12	4
Futuristic	11	3
Achiever	10	8
Relator	7	7
Significance	7	2
Strategic	6	6
Command	5	1
Learner	1	7

* The statistically normal team results were calculated from the data provided by Gallup and is based upon the top five StrengthsFinder results from 11 million people as of May, 2015. I rounded to the nearest whole number.

The data was fascinating! My mind was full of thoughts and questions, all battling for proper attention. Let's go one by one and explore these strengths – you might even have some of them in your top five strengths profile.

1. **Competition** was their most frequent strength. Eighteen players or coaches had Competition. A statistically normal team would have three. This influencing strength manifests in people who hate to lose (more than they love to win.) Who did these boys view as their competition, both individually and as a team? By nature, there is competition for being on the first line (usually the best combination of talent on the team.) It would be difficult to manage your emotions if you viewed the guy next to you on the bench as your competition and also try to compete against other teams. Where was the energy channeled?
2. **Restorative** was their second most common strength. Twelve people had this strength in their top five strengths profile. Normal

would be four. Restorative is in the executing category and is the consummate problem-solver strength. It is not the same as *thinking* to solve a problem; it is *acting* to solve a problem. It can look like persistence with a bulldozer: that roadblock will be removed. I once read an article about an emergency medical technician who said that when he was trying to save the life of someone, he did not see the person, he saw the problem. He tackled the problem, and once the problem was solved, the result was a life saved. That is an example of Restorative at work. What roadblocks needed removing on the Cranbrook hockey team? Did anyone view their teammates as a roadblock? Or, was that talent directed toward the opposition or stopping a goal? Also, people with Restorative rarely give up. Perseverance is part of their makeup. Imagine a bunch of bulldozers going at it like some sort of demolition derby. That could be a source of team friction.

3. **Futuristic** was third. This thinking strength looks over the horizon. Did the players have the same future in mind? Or a different one? If everyone is running to a different spot on the map, that is not effective. We'd have to explore it. Perhaps the high presence of the Futuristic strength in the athletes had to do with the critical need to turn the page when mistakes, losses, or bad calls happen. Athletes must move past setbacks lest they get caught in the emotional quagmire of "That's not fair!" or blaming themselves or someone else. Futuristic might help them leapfrog over those deadly mental potholes so that they focus their energy on the next play. Having a high frequency of Futuristic on the hockey team might also indicate that they could envision that winning moment in their mind. That would provide rocket fuel to the individual, and when communicated, to the team.
4. **Achiever** was fourth. It is the most common strength in the global data base. This executing strength reflects the power of personal productivity, and the reward of accomplishing a great deal in one day. Was this team in alignment on what a productive practice looked like? Did the Achievers expect others to be as productive as they were? Pace-setting may not be well appreciated unless all agreed to that approach ahead of time. The team was slightly higher than the norm on this strength.

5. **Relator** was fifth. This relating strength manifests itself by building deep friendships within a small circle of friends. They were statistically normal in this strength. That was good, because as a group, they were lower than normal on strengths from the relationship-building category, which begged the question: Was there enough human glue on this team?
6. **Significance** was sixth. This influencing strength drives people to want to make an impact on the universe and feel a sense of importance. Players with Significance would want to make a difference and be rewarded for success. This team had an unusually large amount of this strength on their team. That could account for some of the pronoun trouble. If a player is not getting enough atta-boys or believe they should receive more, the "me" focus can drown out the "we" focus. On the other hand, pushing hard to win a state championship would feel significant and rewarding.
7. **Strategic** was seventh. Players with the thinking strength of Strategic would plot the best path to the desired outcome. Of course, this path is seen through the lens of our strengths and experiences, so there might be some incongruence between how one player would plot the path versus another.
8. **Command** was eighth. As you can imagine, it is an influencing strength. People with command have a sense of presence and are comfortable taking charge. In fact, they prefer it. Command is the least common top five strength on the planet. There were five people on this team with Command. How challenging would this be? It would be akin to having five generals from five separate countries sitting around the table discussing a battle plan. Each wants to take charge and do things their own way. They may not be inclined to listen to or support, another general's plan. Friction city.
9. **Learner**: I added Learner not because it was high on the team, but because it was so unbelievably low. I had never seen a 25-member team with only a single Learner thinking strength in the team's top five StrengthsFinder profiles. Never. Normal would have been seven players with Learner.
10. **Hockey Team vs. Data Base of 11 Million People**: Only Relator and Strategic were statistically normal.

The message was clear: On the Cranbrook hockey team, normal was different. As such, motivating and leading them would be more challenging. This team had unique needs.

I was so excited about the StrengthsFinder results from the Cranbrook hockey team that I decided to compare their most common strengths against the frequency of those same strengths on other teams that I have recently worked with. It resulted in a great deal of interesting information. However, unless you are very familiar with StrengthsFinder usage in organizations and teams, it might not be interesting to you. Therefore, I placed that information in Appendix C. There you will find a comparison of the Cranbrook hockey team's StrengthsFinder analysis with a technology start up, bank leadership, medical leadership, and sales leadership teams.

I have one additional data point. In my reservoir of team-based strengths data, I located one client with more total Competition strengths (19 people) than the Cranbrook team. For this engagement, I was invited to New York City to work with the highest performing employees from a large, global inside sales organization. Yes, they had 19 people with competition, but the size of the team was exactly 100 people. Therefore, only 19% of the sales team had Competition in their top five strengths. Cranbrook had 72%. Not even close to the relative amount of Competition talent on the Cranbrook hockey team.

Social Approval

It would take a special academic environment to make space for this unusual group of young men.

It is easy to get caught up in the amazing statistics of this group. Let us spend a moment on the human side of the equation. Pause and consider how these high-horsepower teens might be perceived in a classroom environment. They likely compete for grades, attention, and approval. They may be mentally living in the future and appear unfocused in class. They might tackle bullying face-to-face with little fear, even if it was from someone in a position of authority. With all the influencing talent on the team, they would have more energy than many students. It would take a special academic environment to make space for this unusual group of young men.

Influencing strengths have a lot of energy associated with them because they are used to move mountains of people at one time. Consider what happens when we introduce a competition into a school event, or even a corporate environment. Some companies are holding their own weight loss contests to increase employee well-being and influence them to permanently change their eating and exercising habits. The competition motivates people to do what they might not do otherwise. This is why Competition is an influencing strength – and it can influence volumes of people to take action.

Influencing strengths like Competition, Command, and Significance occur with low frequency in a top five strengths profile; therefore, these boys might be less appreciated in the classroom or the office than when they were on the ice. Competition, Command, and Significance are not only less common in the global population, they are also less common in the teaching population. Therefore, the odds of being misunderstood increase dramatically. This likely made the players feel more out of place in the school room than in the locker room. They may receive less social approval than they would on a hockey team.

Were you ever misunderstood in high school? How about in the workplace? At home? In a volunteer role? It is a miserable experience. This problem is not limited to young people, nor is it limited to the world of education. It is a universal problem, which is exactly why 6,000 were signed up for my webinar series. We all struggle with being misunderstood or undervalued. We may not even understand or value ourselves. The StrengthsFinder experience helps individuals identify their talent, which is positive and energizing in nature. When that experience is wrapped in encouragement and structure from me, it moves people into the possibility of breakthrough performance. No longer do they feel like misunderstood outliers. They feel powerful and engaged, which naturally generates better results.

Imagine introducing the StrengthsFinder into the high school environment so that all talents are valued and understood, not just those strengths we see most often in the global population or in the teacher population. This is particularly important with young people because they do place such high emphasis on being liked by others. If a young man or a young woman has low frequency strengths in their StrengthsFinder profile, they may receive less social approval. How unfortunate, for that can lead to bullying and low self-esteem. In reality, such people are undervalued and underutilized human beings. They are left behind, which hurts everyone involved.

Valuing and Aligning Strengths

I began the process of summarizing the information for Coach Weidenbach so that he would have time to think about it before our next workshop. I also started to think about alignment within the team and how we would accomplish it in our next meeting. It was critical that we make forward progress on using their strengths in their role, or the StrengthsFinder data and experience would lose its impact. This would hurt their ability to reach their goals.

My experience with corporate teams has shown me that teams that do not capitalize upon all strengths in the workgroup tend to underperform. They are more prone to conflict, and less likely to collaborate. The team chemistry may suffer. Recent research supports this point of view.

In an article published in the Harvard Business Review[3], researchers observed that teams comprised of mostly high-powered leaders underperformed when compared to those teams who had a mix of levels. The team of executives demonstrated unproductive conflict and poor collaboration. They were unable to reach an agreement nearly 60% of the time! Contributing factors included battles for status, control, point of view, information, position, and preventing loss of face. These behaviors can be symptoms of poorly managed strengths like Competition, Belief, Significance, Restorative, Maximizer and Command. The team of executives wrestled with issues similar to those experienced by the hockey team. It is difficult to build team chemistry and achieve goals when the loudest engines are roaring against one another rather than with one another.

My program is designed to mitigate that problem. Naturally, on a sports team, Competition would clearly be a strength that was welcomed and brought to bear. However, could we say the same thing about those strengths beyond Competition? What about Adaptability or Ideation or Belief? Were all the strengths of the hockey team leveraged to help the

---

[3] Hildreth, A. & Anderson, C. (2016). Powerful People Underperform When They Work Together. *Harvard Business Review*. 24 Feb 2016. (https://hbr.org/).

team win? Our upcoming workshop would be the first step in addressing that question.

The purpose of building the success statement was to identify the team's definition of success. Then, each player could align their different strengths behind it. As a reminder, the Cranbrook hockey team's success statement was:

The 2014/2015 Cranbrook Hockey Team is determined to win the state championship by recommitting to unselfish play, discipline, focus, trust, respect, team chemistry, brotherhood, and by caring for one another, on and off the ice. We refuse to let anyone fail.

None of us can value our strengths or the strengths of others unless we understand them and appreciate their power. The StrengthsFinder tool helps us do that from a holistic perspective. Thinking is as important as executing, which is as important as relating, which is as important as influencing. No strengths are better than others. What is better is to know our strengths and use them to attack the objectives at hand. This approach gives teams a competitive edge.

A Closer Look

Still marveling over the team's unique StrengthsFinder profile, I emailed Coach Weidenbach with the team analysis and the individual profiles of each person. I explained how and why the team was different and asked him to identify the captains for me.

Coach Weidenbach swiftly replied that he found the analysis interesting. He shared that the co-captains were Cooper Stahl and Austin Alger.

Stahl was the boy who spoke first when we met in the locker room. He was a captain. Was he showing leadership or was he naturally that kind of kid? I glanced at his strengths profile. He was an outlier, with three relationship-building strengths. I reviewed the strengths of the other captain, Austin Alger. Jack Blumberg had studied me when I spoke. Mason Schultz had approached me after the workshop. Then, one more person caught my eye. Jake Nestell had three thinking strengths, placing him outside the norm on this team. Cooper Stahl and Jake Nestell carried a good share of the team's relationship building and thinking horsepower, respectively. Let's look at their strengths in more detail.

Cooper Stahl	Austin Alger	Jack Blumberg	Mason Schultz	Jake Nestell
Futuristic	Competition	Achiever	Restorative	Strategic
Adaptability	Consistency	Command	Communica-tion	Restorative
Developer	Significance	Learner	Includer	Adaptability
Relator	Arranger	Competition	Strategic	Futuristic
Significance	Harmony	Activator	Woo	Analytical

Cooper Stahl: Why did he speak first in the locker room? Perhaps his Significance (make an impact) kicked in. He also may have felt the need to share some of that human glue (Adaptability, Developer, Relator). As co-captain, Cooper could help build a vision (Futuristic) and use that human glue to connect the team to his vision, thereby maximizing his contributions to the team.

Austin Alger: Austin was the other co-captain. As a leader, his hate-to-lose mentality was likely contagious. He also had the Significance (make an impact), liked people to follow the system (Consistency), was able to drive team productivity (Arranger), and may dislike dissention (Harmony). Coach had talked about tension on the team. I wondered if Austin found that distracting.

Jack Blumberg: Jack had listened with particular intensity when I spoke earlier in the week. As I looked at his strengths, he had the ability to take charge (Command), was personally productive (Achiever), was curious (Learner), hated to lose (Competition), and was action oriented (Activator). I suspected his Learner was engaged when he studied me as I spoke. He had three influencing strengths – a lot of horsepower.

Mason Schultz: Mason was the first person to approach and speak to me. That takes social courage, which is the definition of the Woo strength. Woo is an acronym for "winning others over." In addition, seeing me standing up in front of the room alone may have triggered his Includer strength. Conversation would come naturally to him (Communication). Restorative (problem solver) may have said, "No one is talking to Maureen. I'm going to fix that problem." During and after games, I noticed that Mason was always chatting it up with the referees. He was engaging his strengths.

Jake Nestell: Jake is a thinking machine who connects the dots to a better future after analyzing the situation (Strategic, Analytical, Futuristic). He was also a problem solver (Restorative) that would go with the flow (Adaptability). I suspected that he would have a quiet demeanor, for people with multiple thinking strengths in their profile often observe before speaking or acting. In a room full of race cars, his quietness might be misunderstood or seen as different. Did he fit in on this hockey team?

I hoped we would have more answers to those kinds of questions as we made our way through the workshop.

Later in the week, Coach Weidenbach and I chatted by phone. We confirmed the high-level agenda and agreed that we should leave room for some detours along the way. Then, we dove right into his StrengthsFinder profile:

Coach Weidenbach
Individualization
Responsibility
Activator
Command
Relator

1. Individualization is a relationship-building strength that sees each person as unique. Do you remember when Coach said that he would love to know everything about what makes his players tick? That was Individualization showing up for him.
2. Responsibility is an execution strength that likes things done right. Remember when Coach said don't be regular Navy, be a Navy SEAL? That was his Responsibility showing up.
3. Activator is an influencing strength that is impatient for action. One minute can feel like an hour. It did not take Coach long to decide to work with me, did it?
4. Command is an influencing strength that is comfortable with being in charge. Coach did not seek permission to work with me. He made the decision that it was right for the team, and we moved on.
5. Relator is a relationship-building strength that likes a small, tight circle of close friends. Think deep rather than wide. Getting to know Coach well would take time.

I explained that his top five strengths are his greatest assets for achieving world class performance in his role, and when used daily, result in maximum effectiveness, happiness, productivity, and a sense of well-being. We do use our strengths like we breathe – without effort or thought. It's satisfying.

Coach and I both have Individualization in our top five strengths profile, so we talked through the content in our respective StrengthsFinder Insight Reports. They were quite different. This is a value proposition offered by the Clifton StrengthsFinder. Each Insight Report is unique, even if people have the same strength. I explained that we would make this same journey with the boys. By sharing their Insight Report content, they would more deeply understand their specific flavor of a given strength. The 18 teammates with Competition in their top five strengths would have different descriptions in their Insight report.

As we dug deeper into his Individualization strength, Coach had a few questions.

"Is Individualization a good strength to have as a coach?"

I had been pacing around my house as I shared the team analysis. I love to talk about the nourishing process of understanding people's strengths, and it always winds me up like a toy. When Coach asked that question, I paused. I did not want to be overzealous simply because I have it in my profile as well. "I believe it is, and I'm not just saying it because I also have Individualization as a top five strength," I replied. "Individualization is the human snowflake strength. It gives us the ability to notice even tiny details about what makes each person different from the next. I think that many managers of sports teams may have Individualization, which helps them fully exploit the unique talent of each player and place them in a role where they can be most successful. They know, and value, what makes a person tick."

Many managers of sports teams may have Individualization, which helps them fully exploit the unique talent of each player and place them in a role where they can be most successful.

To make my point, I shared how helpful I had found my Individualization to be in the corporate world, citing my experience with a particularly difficult vice president. One of my colleagues called me "the handler" because I was able to predict and prevent disasters by guiding and crafting messages to this VP. I knew what the hot buttons were, and

I knew how they would respond in almost any given situation. My ability was often tested.

One of my colleagues was determined to tell the vice president that the VP's leadership team was not responsive enough for his liking. I knew the VP would not like it because the executive would take that remark as a reflection upon their ability to lead. I advised my colleague to find another way to say it and even gave him an example, something like, "We love hearing from your leadership team. Can you help us increase the amount of time they spend with us on this topic?"

He was determined to speak his mind and told the VP in no uncertain terms that the leadership team was falling short. The VP promptly crushed and dismissed him, and moved to the next person on the agenda. This was exactly what I was trying to prevent. Not only did my colleague feel hurt, the mission failed. He did not accomplish the desired outcome of engaging more deeply with the leadership team. He blew it, not because he would not listen to me, but because he would not focus on the effectiveness of his approach. Effectiveness is the gold standard in a corporate environment. Sometimes, it is more important to be effective than to be right.

I told Coach that when I know someone well, which doesn't take long with my Individualization strength, it enables me to manage information flow to them in a manner that is most productive. This is not manipulation; this is effectiveness. We want to bring out the best in people, don't we? Why else are we here?

"Individualization helps us honor and leverage the differences between people. You and I will love the StrengthsFinder because it helps us do that. Does that make sense, Coach?"

"It does," he replied. "It helps a lot. I like this approach already."

Later on, I would learn how very powerful Coach's Individualization strength was and the role it would play in guiding the team on their difficult journey.

We worked through a few more logistics and then deemed ourselves ready for the team workshop on Sunday. I couldn't wait!

Chapter 6: The Success Workshop

"The best teamwork comes from men who are working independently toward one goal in unison."

James Cash Penney

* * *

The big day arrived! I was there about 15 minutes early to be sure I could get from the parking lot to the building. It was all of 50 yards, but then again, I did not know the Cranbrook school buildings that well because I spent all my time on the nature trails and in the gardens. Coach met me as I was headed up to the building, and we arrived at the room two minutes later.

Guess what?

Every single player and coach had arrived before I did. I was astonished. Clearly, this was not the normal high school student environment. Coach did things differently. He treated them like professionals and he expected them to behave like professionals. Professionals are not late; it is unprofessional! I got it intellectually, but was still blown away by it.

The players settled in. I had butterflies because this workshop would be different from the dozens and dozens I had conducted in the business world. I smiled at the row of eager faces before me, aware that they were in for an amazing treat and confident that the team who walked in the door would not be the same team that walked out.

I thanked them for being prompt and for making time to invest in themselves and one another. Then I set the stage for the remaining two and a half hours.

First, we offered a round of applause, giving public appreciation for the anonymous Fox family who paid for everyone to take the StrengthsFinder assessment and for my services.

Second, I established our rules of engagement for the workshop.

1. When we learn our strengths and speak about them publicly, it can make us feel vulnerable. We would need to lower our walls just a little bit so that we could all learn and grow with one another.
2. The Cranbrook hockey team trust bank was still in effect, and we would need to be mindful of our choices. Every single thing we say or do in that room would either increase the balance in the team trust bank or diminish it.
3. The room was a safe place to explore our strengths, our roles, our hopes, and our dreams. All questions were welcome.

Could the young men and coaches commit to that? They nodded.

Then, I began by speaking openly about the unique nature of the team. "I have never seen a team with this much influencing horsepower," I said. "This is good news. However, the hard part about all of your influencing horsepower is that it can be difficult to manage."

To help drive the point home, I posed a scenario. "Imagine a baseball pitcher who can throw the ball 100 miles per hour."

They murmured – 100 mph is the Holy Grail of pitching speeds.

"If this talented pitcher who can throw a fast ball at 100 MPH can't hit a target, is he an asset or a liability?"

Long pause.

"Liability!" said Coach Weidenbach.

I dug a dollar bill out of my pocket, and gave it to Coach. He looked at the players with a Cheshire cat grin. The boys were instantly mad that they did not answer the question, and all assured me that they knew the correct response. Coach's expression indicated, "If you know, speak up!" I chuckled, for I knew that rewarding Coach would tap into the team's competitive profile and drive the desired outcome, which was involvement in the discussion.

We must understand how to harness all the horsepower you have on this team, making it an asset, not a liability.

"A strength that is poorly managed is a liability," I confirmed. "One of our goals today will be to understand how to harness all the horsepower you have on this team, making it an asset, not a liability. Being a team asset is an internal challenge focused on regulating your strengths. Once you harness your power and combine it with your skills and experience to make it into your own secret sauce of success, you will be more effective as individuals and as a team. Then, we will align your talent and energy behind your success statement. It is an amazing journey with real results. Results that are reliable and repeatable."

With the preamble complete, we reviewed the success statement. I asked if it was still valid after they had had a week to think about it. It was. I reaffirmed its importance, describing it as our compass for the afternoon. Everything we did would support our success statement. From that launching point, we dove into the topic of their strengths.

A poll of the group revealed that they had found their individual results interesting and largely right on. This was the typical reaction of most teams when we use my methodology to drive success. Taking the StrengthsFinder is a rewarding and affirming experience. It is nourishing, and it helps us start from a place of abundance. The hard part is to move beyond that to connect their strengths to their role, understand their teammates, and then execute with alignment to the success statement. It takes time, and there are no shortcuts. I was going to cut a few corners today, simply because we had such a limited runway.

"I'm going to ask you some questions that might seem odd, but bear with me." I glanced at my notes, lifted my head, and said, "If you have Achiever in your top five strengths, please stand."

Ten boys stood, and this was met with some mumbling from the group as they tried to figure out if this was good or bad. I nodded, and then motioned for them to sit.

"If you have Responsibility, please stand." Five boys stood, and then sat.

"If you have Learner, please stand." One player stood, looking a bit embarrassed.

I suddenly recalled his face – he was the young man who studied me intently in the locker room. Jack Blumberg. No wonder he was zeroed in on me when I was speaking. He was using his Learner strength and was absorbing information like a sponge.

"It is good to have Learner, Jack," I said, "I bet you are unafraid of new experiences and can visit places that others might not have the courage for." He smiled and nodded. I gave him permission to sit.

"Guess how many players with Learner your team should have, if you were like the rest of the world?"

The players began to throw out numbers.

"Two?"

I shook my head

"Four?"

I shook my head again. "Your team should have seven young men with Learner. Your team is *different*," I exclaimed.

I couldn't stand it any longer. It was time to deliver the most interesting news of all.

"If you have Competition, please stand."

The air in the room was filled with the sound of chairs scraping against the floor. A whole herd of people stood – 18 in total. 18 out of 25 people standing makes for nice visual exclamation point. They responded with, "Wow!" and "Cool!" Even they could not believe it.

I asked them to remain standing, and then added the additional influencing strengths of Command, Significance, Communication, Woo, Maximizer, Self-Assurance and Activator. The number of folks standing continued to grow. When it was all said and done, only three people on the team were without any influencing strengths in their top five strengths profile. You will see that we found a way to make them feel special in their own right – they had talents that the others did not. I shared with the team that influencing strengths were the least common category in the general population's top five strengths. This group was really, REALLY unique.

I told the players that managing all these people with influencing strengths in their top five profile had to be a challenge for Coach Weidenbach because influencing strengths generate energy. It is why I used the color red to represent them. The boys glanced at the Coach as if to see how he felt about this responsibility. He smiled. Coach was totally up for the challenge.

To help the group understand what I meant, I shared an analogy. "Imagine that each one of you is a race car. You are a Tesla," I said, pointing at one player. "And you're a Ferrari," I said, pointing at another. I added Corvettes, Mustangs, Challengers, and Maseratis. "That's a lot of energy and power," I said. "Coach Weidenbach has to harness your race car potential to maximize both individual performance *and* team performance. Sometimes the 'me' win can conflict with the 'we' win. The team that could align all those race cars and have them pull with all their energy, in the direction of the success statement, would be practically unstoppable. This is the objective of being here today."

The boys gazed about, perhaps seeing one another, and the team, through a different lens.

Once we were done visually demonstrating all the influencing capability of the team, for comparison, I asked those who had Empathy to stand. There wasn't a soul in the room (including me) who had Empathy in their top five profile. We agreed that Mother Theresa did not make the hockey team.

In addition, remember that Coach Weidenbach had talked to his team about winning with belief and a positive attitude? Not a single member of the team had the Belief or Positivity strengths in their top five. Therefore, that message did not connect with this group like it would have if there were multiple players on the team with Belief and Positivity. I acknowledged Coach's attempt to reach them through Positivity and Belief. "It's like speaking Chinese to Germans," I said, exaggerating slightly.

The room was abuzz, energized by the information about the unusual makeup of the team.

I walked them through the statistical profile of the team at a high level, simply helping them understand what they had an abundance of, and what was missing.

I wasn't finished. I wanted to address the concept of social approval. "Because your team is so unusual, you might fit in well in the locker room, but you might be misunderstood, or even undervalued, in the classroom or out in the real world."

I could see this last statement resonating with the group – they were different. They saw the world through lenses that would not commonly be recognized. They felt, thought, and behaved with a lot more energy and fervor than a normal person or team. As a result, they were likely treated differently by teachers, parents, other students, and eventually, by the corporate world. It probably felt good to be on a team where they were birds of a feather because we recognize what we know, and we know what we have.

Before we shared their individual and team strengths, it was important that they have an understanding of the value associated with each of the StrengthsFinder categories. I walked them through each one, focusing on how they provide a competitive advantage.

Executing	Relating	Thinking	Influencing
Get it done! Task oriented	Human glue and caring	Navigators and observers	Move mountains of people to action

Executing Strengths: I pointed at the executing strengths category, color coded in purple, and I explained that these strengths are associated with productivity and completing tasks. They describe how we will be productive in school, hockey, or cleaning the garage.

Relating Strengths: I moved to the relating strengths category, color coded in green, and spoke about the benefit of human glue associated with them. This conversation was critical because this team was below average on this strengths category. That meant that the guys with these talents might be overlooked by people focused on goals and achievements. Relating strengths are like oil for a hard working engine. They help remove friction from the system. "Human glue talents hold the team together during tough times," I said. "As you strive to achieve your success statement, the guys with human glue can help the team move forward in unison."

Relating strengths are like oil for a hard working engine. They help remove friction from the system.

Thinking Strengths: I moved to a category that is a personal favorite of mine, the thinking strengths. I color code those in blue. I explained that one reason I love the StrengthsFinder tool is that it is holistic in nature and measures eight ways we think to solve problems. This particular category happens inside people's head, and we cannot look at someone and see these strengths in action. Thinkers are master observers and navigators, collecting, analyzing, and using information to get us to the right place on the map. "Over 50% of you have a thinking strength called Futuristic. Wouldn't it be great if we can find a way to leverage all that thinking power? And we would not even have known you had it if you hadn't taken the StrengthsFinder."

The boys glanced at one another, wondering who had Futuristic on the team. I shared a story about the value of navigators. Remember reading about the herds of buffalo that would run like heck toward a cliff? Blindly following the leader, they would race full speed toward the precipice. When it was too late to change direction, over the cliff they would go. I compared the buffalo with people who are so task-focused that they do not realize when they must change direction. "If the head buffalo had listened to the thinkers on the team, who were quietly saying, 'We should make a 90 degree turn,' the disaster would have been avoided. I believe that thinkers are underserved and undervalued. Don't leave your thinkers out of your success equation. It's easy to do, but it is a mistake."

A murmur arose. This category sparked some interest.

Influencing Strengths: I color code this category red, because of the energy associated with these strengths. This category is difficult to discern from the relating strengths. On the surface, they seem similar, because both have a connection as to how we relate with people. However, there is an element of scale and outcome associated with influencing strengths. I provided two examples to drive home the difference.

I asked them to imagine a disappointment in life, like not getting into the college you want or being discriminated against in some way. You seek solace in friendship. If one of those friends should be high in the strength of Empathy, that person would know how you felt, and would simply listen or talk about the situation. It is a one-on-one connection that builds human glue between you and your friend.

Then, I invited them to consider the same scenario. This time, before talking to a friend about it, you happen to hear Martin Luther King Junior's *I Have a Dream* speech. At the end of it, your outlook has changed. You feel full of energy, ready to take on the world again. You go back out and fight for what you want. You have been influenced by Martin Luther King, Jr. I pointed at the influencing strength of Communication. "Perhaps he had Communication," I said. "That's the power of giving an amazing speech that influences hundreds of thousands of people. We were changed and influenced by him. Yet none of us sat down to dinner with him. We did not have a chat with him. He's no longer alive, yet he influences more people every year."

That is the inherent energy of an influencing strength. It can move mountains of people at one time, even when we do not know them personally, and drive us to take action.

Their faces were eager as they studied the two categories, relating and influencing.

"Think about the power of Competition," I continued, pointing at the red colored influencing strength. "Think about all the kids in the stands who are motivated to play hockey when they watch you play. Or think about all the little girls who take up gymnastics after watching the Olympics. We are influenced by athletes, even if we never meet them. Influencing strengths also have the highest horsepower and energy associated with them." I paused for a moment, for there was a good news/bad news aspect to influencing strengths. It was not something I would typically bring up this early in a strengths-based success journey, but we did not have the luxury of time. All the influencing strengths on this team might tear the team apart.

I broached the point using the analogy of a double-edged sword. The good news was that influencing strengths bring immense energy. The bad news was that they often give people the most trouble if they are not well managed. To help them relate, I referred back to the sports car idea and asked a simple question. "Would you spend $100,000 on a car that did not have a brake?"

"Would you spend $100,000 on a car that didn't have a brake?"

They chuckled, appreciating how the example related to this team.

Talent is Talent

Now was the perfect time to dive into our exercises. I knew they would enjoy it, and it is where the real learning takes place. But first, I had a point to make.

"Boys," I said, "whether we like it or not, society places expectations on men and women, and those expectations vary depending on where you live in America or Europe or India or China. But let's talk about two scenarios. Imagine a leader who has Command. Command is an influencing strength and has no problem taking charge. In fact, they expect to be in charge. That's a good talent to have, right?"

They nodded.

"Now, imagine the leader who has the Command strength and happens to be a woman who looks like a beauty queen. Imagine the surprise on the team when she speaks and General Patton jumps out."

They laughed.

"Our expectations of men and women vary, yet a talent is a talent. We expect men to have Command, and we embrace it. We are less accepting of a woman having the same ability. An essential element of this journey is embracing the strengths of people no matter what planet they are from, what god they believe in, or the color of the skin. Talent is talent. It's not easy, but it is important."

I let them noodle on that for a few moments. Then I provided an opposite example showcasing a man who has the power of Empathy. In a sales role, this fellow would have the awesome ability to sense how clients are feeling. That is a huge advantage because he can tell how they are responding to the product or service. Yet, how might he be perceived in a dog-eat-dog corporate culture? He might be perceived as soft, not tough enough for business. A woman with Empathy in the same sales role may be viewed more positively. The bias goes both ways. "In this room, we will value all the talents on the team equally. The goal is to identify, understand, and leverage them so that you achieve your mission."

I added the percentages of each category, reflecting the cumulative strengths of the Cranbrook hockey team.

Executing Strengths (Get it done!)	Relating Strengths (Human Glue)	Thinking Strengths (Observers and Navigators)	Influencing Strengths (Moving people to take action)
32%	**18%**	**18%**	**31%**

A young man sitting in the back of the room, who had been largely silent up to this point, raised his hand.

"Yes?" I asked.

"Your numbers don't add up."

I glanced at my chart, did a quick summary in my head. He was right. The numbers did not add up. They totaled 99%. They should have totaled 100%. I looked back at him and headed in his direction so I could engage with him more directly.

"What's your name?"

"Jake."

"Jake," I repeated, swiftly searching the team chart for his strengths. Aha! Remember Jake? He was one of the boys with an outlier top five StrengthsFinder profile. Jake had three thinking strengths, more than anyone else on the team. Jake was also one of the three people in the room that did not have any influencing strengths, possibly making him even more of an outsider. I recalled wondering if he was accepted by the players who were more likely to value action.

Jake had a particular thinking strength that had motivated him to raise his hand: Analytical. People high in Analytical like numbers and data. Jake would likely need to think first and analyze first, then execute or relate with others.

"Jake," I said, pointing at him with energy, "Good for you! You were using your strengths! Thank you for calling me out. That took a lot of courage. You found a rounding error in my Excel spreadsheet!"

I was delighted that Jake raised his hand, not just because he was right to catch the rounding error in my Excel spreadsheet and had the courage to bring it up, but because it gave me an opportunity to speak about an important aspect of our strengths journey: the dreaded strengths violation.

I probed a bit. "How did it feel to see that the numbers did not add up?"

The young men listened intently; it is always exciting when a student catches the instructor in a mistake.

"I noticed it," said Jake, with a shrug. Then, going further out on a limb, he added, "I didn't like it."

"That's right, and you shouldn't like it. It violates your Analytical strength. You pay attention to data. Anytime our strengths are violated, we feel really frustrated."

This led us on a lively discussion of what it was like when this team's strengths were violated. I handed out a few more dollar bills because the boys were really participating. They shared how annoying it felt to be told not to try so hard to win or to be upset when you lose, (18 players had Competition in their top five strengths, remember!) to not focus on the future, to be nicer. In short, to be told that who you are is not who you should be. Having your strengths violated is not a lot of fun, and it is a significant source of conflict in the workplace.

They shared how annoying it felt to be told that who you are is not who you should be. Having your strengths violated is not a lot of fun.

I made a mental note to fix my StrengthsFinder Team Analysis tool to carry numbers out to a single decimal point to fix the rounding error that Jake had identified.

We spent a little bit more time on the team StrengthsFinder profile to help the young men understand that we had a huge opportunity before us. We had the ability to capitalize on their differences by understanding and harnessing their horsepower in Competition, Restorative, Futuristic and other unusual strengths. At the same time, we needed to pay special attention to the strengths that were not common on the team, like Learner, Ideation, Analytical, Harmony, and Adaptability. Having Competition did not trump having Harmony, for example. All talents are valuable, and we would need every single one of them to achieve our desired destiny.

All talents are valuable, and we would need every single one of them to achieve our desired destiny.

When we were finished exploring the most common strengths on the hockey team, it was time to shift our focus to the individual perspective.

Individual Strengths

The goal of this part of the journey is to understand, leverage, and communicate our strengths in our given role in life, in school, on a corporate team, or on a hockey team. It is also very important to note that we are more than our top five strengths. For the purpose of cost, and for the sake of managing a team of 25 people, we focused on only the top five strengths. However, the reality is that our performance toolkit lies in our top 10 – 12 strengths. In corporate teams, it is not uncommon for me to focus on the top 10 – 12 strengths of each person, and the collective team, as we seek to drive performance, collaboration, and alignment to success. It results in a deeper understanding of success.

I presented the group with a handout that showed the StrengthsFinder profile for each person, categorized by type/color. This naturally creates a lot of chatter because everyone is looking at everyone else's strengths. It is fun to understand what makes you and your colleagues tick.

Throughout the room, I heard players say, "Look at all that red!" Influencing strengths were shown in red on the handout, and it was fun to watch them visually process the amount of horse power on this team.

As part of this process, we explored a few important points.

- We are more than our top five strengths. Our real performance toolkit is our top 10 – 15 strengths.
- Self understanding comes first, followed by understanding the strengths of the other individuals on the team.
- People with the same strength manifest that talent differently. There were 18 unique versions of Competition on that team. I compared it to coffee beans from 18 different parts of the world. While all coffee beans are beans, Kona coffee beans do not have the same taste as Sumatra coffee beans. It was important that each player embrace and dig into their unique flavor of Competition, or any other strength they shared with others on the team.
- Strengths envy is a waste of time. It is not better to have Woo or worse. Embrace and leverage your highest talents, and allow others to do the same.
- Strengths-based success is not a pill. It is a practice. Our workshop was a first step toward a success practice, founded in the powerful potential of our strengths. This concept is applicable to all aspects of life, in and outside the hockey rink.
- The information would help Coach Weidenbach and his coaching team maximize the contributions of each player.
- Aligning all the talent in the room behind their success statement was the critical next step.

I asked if there were any questions. Mason raised his hand.

"I am the only person with the Woo strength," said Mason. "What does that mean?"

"It means you have social courage. Here's my test for Woo. Do you speak to people in the grocery store line?"

"Of course," he said. Everyone chuckled.

"Woo is a low strength for me, Mason. I don't talk to people in the checkout line. You are unafraid of meeting new people. When you walk into a room filled with people you don't know, you likely have a boost of energy. Many of us would find that experience draining and maybe even intimidating."

Mason nodded, absorbing the information, and indicating that the description sounded like him.

"Does it matter that I have one of every color?" Mason had one strength from each of the thinking, relating, and executing categories, and two strengths in the influencing category. His corresponding profile had the spectrum of colors: blue, green, purple, and red.

"It doesn't matter," I replied, "but it is unusual." Looking at the team strengths, there was only one other player who also had the rainbow of one strength from each category. I went on to describe that it is not better or worse to have a rainbow. It is not better or worse to have a profile that has strengths from a single category, like relating. It is just different. The goal becomes one of leveraging those strengths, regardless of category, to achieve success in life. Your strengths don't tell us *what* you will do. They tell us *how* you will do it.

Your strengths don't tell us what you will do. They tell us how you will do it.

"For example, Mason, your Woo strength can be useful for a doctor, an accountant, or a hockey player. The key takeaway for you is to leverage your strengths to drive success in your role."

There were a few more questions. One young man asked about Ideation. He was the only player on the team with that strength. I encouraged the group to look to him for ideas on how to creatively solve problems, or how to think differently about a challenge.

A player sitting near the front of the room raised his hand. I nodded at him.

"What if you don't have any relationship building strengths in your top five strengths?" he asked.

"That is a great question!" I said. "It's normal. Remember, the tool measures 34 patterns of excellence, and we are only seeing your top five strengths. If we were able to see your top 10 or 12 strengths, which comprise our true performance toolkit, we would likely find some relationship strengths in there. We began with the top five because it's less costly, and because we have a limited time. You build relationships, don't you?"

He nodded.

"Of course you do. We may not know which strengths you're using, but they are there. We are all more than just our top five strengths, but it's a good place to begin."

He nodded, appearing cautiously satisfied. I was in the same boat. "In my top five," I said, "I don't have any influencing strengths. One could conclude I can't influence, which would be incorrect, because I have four influencing strengths in my top 14 strengths. I just don't influence first. I tend to influence others after I've had time to think and build relationships."

With no more questions, it was time to dig into the exercises.

I broke the team into small groups of three people. Well, to be more accurate, Coach Weidenbach helped me do it. Something went wrong as I had the boys count out and be a group of 1, 2, or 3. And then I told them to join a particular group. People were milling around rather aimlessly, which was not my intent.

Coach walked over and said, "You can't do that. You have to tell them exactly what you want them to do."

I laughed helplessly because total chaos had ensued. He asked me what I wanted. I said I wanted groups of three. Coach fixed it, and we were swiftly back on track. It was a good example of teamwork. His ability to organize and deliver instructions with clarity was infinitely better than mine.

Once they were re-assembled into small groups of three players, we proceeded to run through a series of exercises designed to:

1. Help each person better understand their individual strengths
2. Help understand the strengths of the others in the small group
3. Help them build their Secret sauce statement to reflect their strengths in action

What Makes You Unique?

One reason I break teams into small groups is to support peer-to-peer learning. The energy in the room rises when people talk about their talents with those they know well. There's a lot of joy and laughter. This is good. It is human glue in action and it invests in the team trust bank. Hearing about the strengths of others on the team helps them understand and value each other more deeply. It also expands their strengths vocabulary beyond their own results, to include understanding about strengths they do not possess in their own StrengthsFinder profile.

We began this journey by exploring each person's Strengths Insight Report. As I mentioned early on, that report is customized. I demonstrated this fact by having two people with Competition read aloud the first four or five lines from their Insight Report. To the astonishment of everyone on the team, the description of Competition for the first boy varied greatly from the description of the second boy, even though they were reading about the same strength. Understanding our customized report is an important milestone in our success journey.

To prepare for this part of the workshop, the team had been asked to print and read their Insight Report, highlighting those phrases that resonated with them. In their small groups, I had them share their favorite lines from their StrengthsFinder Insight Report, and provide an example of when they had used that strength on the ice. This process of selecting and expanding upon content that describes their talent is a way of internalizing it. They must know their strengths and connect them to success in the past in order for them to become part of a repeatable future.

They must know their strengths and connect them to success in the past in order for them to become part of a repeatable future.

As each player shared a personal example of the strength in action, it quickly became clear that they were making the connection between their strengths and how to use them on and off the ice. It was a big leap along the learning curve. It was time to ask the boys to be a bit more advanced. Our final exercise was one of crafting our own Secret sauce.

Our Secret sauce is the blend of all of our strengths combed with particular knowledge, skills, and experience that result in you doing one or two things really, really well. To help them understand how to begin this process, I shared the story of T.J. Oshie.

Never heard of T.J. Oshie? I had not either until he helped the U.S. beat the Russians in the 2014 Winter Olympics. He is a living example of the Secret sauce approach to success. In a nutshell, T.J. Oshie is a young hockey player who does one thing exceptionally well: He is the best penalty shot expert in the National Hockey League. When he goes one-on-one against a goalie, it's as close to an automatic goal as it can get. He is a good hockey player, but he is superb in one-on-one situations, like penalty shots or shoot-outs to resolve a tied game. Here is what his Secret sauce looks like. T.J. Oshie first stares down at the goalie from behind the middle line for about 10 to 20 seconds, which probably feels like two hours to the goalie. Then he meanders (you cannot call it skating as it is very slow) towards the goal. At some point, his skates flutter, his head twitches, the goalie goes left, and T.J. Oshie goes right.

Goal. There is a wonderful four-minute YouTube video compilation of his best penalty shots, culminating with the winning goal against the Russians in the Olympics.

I shared the same story with the boys. Then, I distributed a form designed to help each player build their own Secret sauce, focusing on what they most enjoy on the ice, what they do that has the most impact upon the team, and what strengths they use when they are at their best. This approach is called reflective learning, and it helps make education personal. Each player and coach traveled their own path, and it was important to capture the lessons learned along the way.

As each boy completed their Secret sauce form, it was very quiet. They were focused, absorbed in thinking and writing about what they do best and why. I asked each boy to sign and date their form, adding formality to the commitment they were making to honor the success statement, to refuse to let anyone fail, and to play as a team.

I then began to call on each young man to read their Secret sauce statement aloud. Some were short and simple. Some were longer, and offered more detail. Neither is right or wrong. It just has to be something that resonates with each individual and connects their strengths to their role and to the success of the team. We applauded after each one, reinforcing and supporting their public commitment to the team and celebrating investments in the team trust bank.

We were already beyond the two-hour mark for our workshop. I wanted to be sensitive of their time. After all, they were in high school, playing hockey, and it was a Sunday. The young men were wonderful, always displaying a friendly, polite, and respectful demeanor. They had given me their undivided attention throughout the day. I could not have asked for more.

To end on an inspirational note, I shared one of my favorite quotes about effort and adversity, Theodore Roosevelt's *Man in the Arena* speech. I read it aloud, with extra emphasis on daring greatly and pursuing a worthy cause. When I was finished, I paused, eyed them evenly, and added, "You guys are not timid souls. You are daring greatly. You are pursuing a worthy cause. Now, go win the state championship."

They clapped, as they would have regardless, but it felt sincere. I noticed that Mason snapped his fingers instead, and I laughed out loud. That mode of expressing appreciation was around back in the 60s and 70s. What goes around, comes around, and on the second coming, people think they are seeing it for the first time. I took it to be a sign of approval.

I distributed a feedback form to measure their value of the experience and thanked them for their time, attention, and awesomeness.

The boys were excited and energized by their newfound knowledge about self and teammates. Many players approached me to personally express their gratitude, which was deeply rewarding. I watched them file out, observing body language and conversation. They looked energized and sounded happy.

Coach and I spoke afterwards. He gave me my dollar bill back, saying that he had only taken it to inspire the boys. He had tears in his eyes as he spoke about how much he wanted the team to behave as a real team and that he believed this was a giant step forward. Over and over, he said, "I love this stuff!" It was clear he meant it. I also knew why. People high in individualization connect well to the StrengthsFinder experience. It fed his need to know what makes each person tick. Understanding the strengths of each boy would be like manna from heaven for Coach.

"You know," Coach said, "I made a choice a long time ago. I chose high school coaching over professional coaching because the measurement of success is different."

I was instantly curious. "How so?"

"Well, if you are a pro coach in the NHL or in its farm programs, there really is only one goal. The goal is to win. That's what is deemed most important. Player development has its place, and building great men is a contributing factor, but in the end, it's the win/loss record that matters. If you're a high school coach, the goal becomes teaching life skills. Success is judged by building great men, not by the win/loss column or the number of trophies you win."

Success is judged by building great men, not by the win/loss column or the number of trophies you win.

It was no wonder Coach valued our workshop and the content in our success statement. We were investing in the greatness of his boys. Hockey was the vehicle and winning the Michigan state championship was a desired outcome, but helping each person understand how they could maximize their performance and character, on and off the ice, well, that was what success looked like to Coach Weidenbach.

I compared Coach's clarity about what success looks like with the leaders I have worked with in the business world. I often ask, "What does success look like for you in this role? What does success look like for this team?" Many executives have not given it a great deal thought. Often, they reply with metrics. "We need to make our numbers." This is normal because the world has become so fast paced that execution has been placed at the top of the corporate shrine. However, remember the story about the buffalo galloping over the cliff. It is important to engage the thinkers. Human glue is required to prevent fragmentation. If we do not leverage every single talent on the team and honor thinking and relating as much as executing and influencing, the odds of the organization achieving victory decline considerably.

If we do not leverage every single talent on the team and honor thinking and relating as much as executing and influencing, the odds of the organization achieving victory decline considerably.

Coach and I walked out of the classroom. He expressed his gratitude, and I thanked him for trusting me with his team. Austin Alger, a tall, lanky young man of few words, joined us. He was a team co-captain, proof that one can lead from a point of quiet strength. Coach told me that Austin was already selected to enter the United States Hockey League, which was a real honor. Most players have to try out to get in. I asked Austin if he was excited. He quietly replied, "Yes." Then he added that there was work to do here first.

I told Austin and Coach that I would be at a game just as soon as I returned from a business trip. We parted outside the building, eager to get to our cars to escape the bitter winter wind.

I dashed home and perused the feedback forms. The results were very positive. I had included both quantitative and qualitative questions. I had asked the boys to rate their experience from 1 – 5, where 1 = Strongly Disagree and 5 = Strongly Agree. The results are provided on the next few pages.

Summary of Qualitative Feedback from the Cranbrook Hockey Team

Quantitative Questions	Average Response
1. The Success Workshop for Cranbrook Hockey Team was a valuable exercise.	4.9 (Strongly Agree)
2. I have a better understanding of my strengths.	4.7 (Strongly Agree)
3. I have a better understanding of the strengths of my team.	4.6 (Strongly Agree)
4. I understand the connection between my strengths and my success beyond the ice rink.	4.4 (Agree)
5. I believe this exercise will make our team more successful on and off the ice.	4.5 (Strongly Agree)

I was pleased to see that the response to my question about value was nearly unanimous. One fellow was not sure it was all that helpful, and he even signed his name, which took a lot of courage. Otherwise, they all chose "Strongly Agree." I noticed the gradual drop in numeric value that corresponded with a more sophisticated use of the strengths knowledge – from self to team to success beyond the ice arena. It was a lot to ask after a 2.5-hour workshop. Even a 4.5 response meant that half the team selected "strongly agree" when asked if they believed that they could be more successful on and off the ice.

I asked four qualitative questions and included a few of the responses in the following tables.

Question 1: What is one thing you learned about yourself?

- That I could use my strengths to overcome my deficiencies to help the team in many ways.
- That a strength can have a negative effect if it is not used properly.
- I gravitate towards people who speak truthfully when I ask for constructive criticism.
- I am capable of so much more than scoring goals and I have a better understanding of myself as a person.

- That mediocrity is not okay. I have to push myself and others to achieve the common goal.
- I learned that being a futuristic person, I can help others see the common goal.
- I strongly apply the past. I had inklings to my strengths but had never fully harnessed what they meant or the power they had.
- The restorative theme allowed me to get a realization of how sometimes I strive to compete so much I hurt others.

I was touched by their heartfelt comments. They had definitely climbed the learning curve of self-awareness. Then I asked them about others on the team. The comments were filled with admiration for Jake Nestell's previously undetected intellectual horsepower, and each one made me smile.

Question 2: What is one thing you learned about a teammate?

- I learned that my teammate Jake is way smarter than most people. Give him credit for that, and he is very good at seeing problems that others don't see. (There were other statements like this about Jake.)
- That many of them have very apparent and useful traits, however, they are easily overlooked.
- Everyone has something valuable to offer.
- Mason talks to strangers in the checkout line (Woo).
- I learned that the team is lacking Positivity and Empathy, and that we can fix that with our strengths.
- One guy needs positive reinforcement to help him prevent from giving up.
- That their strengths can intertwine with mine to make for a stronger bond.
- Generally, everyone has a different personality and they would all look to be handled differently.

I focused on what they found most valuable about the experience of understanding their strengths. I was eager to hear how high school athletes might react to this knowledge.

Question 3: What did you find most valuable about learning your strengths?

- It helped reinforce my strengths and encouraged me to put them to use for the betterment of the team.
- When in synch, everything has the potential to be amazing.
- This allows you to perform in a role.
- This will help me for the rest of my life.
- The more I focus on them, the more successful we will become.
- Not only what they are but how to apply them for the betterment of myself and teammates.
- Just how I can apply it to everyday life, not just hockey.
- I found that my awareness of others as individuals is very important.
- Gives me a mission statement to success.

The comments were insightful and more mature than I would have expected. Finally, I offered them the opportunity to provide open feedback.

Question 4: Do you have any other comments?

- It was an enlightening experience. Thank you.
- Loved the workshop. Thank you!
- This was pretty cool.
- Thank you for the time spent. I thought it was very worthwhile.
- Thank you for coming and helping us better ourselves, not only as a team but as individuals.

I received an email from Red Fox, forwarding me a note that Coach Weidenbach had sent. He said the workshops were a great success, and he thanked the Fox family for sponsoring it. I was thrilled. Coach was happy. He certainly was gracious after the workshop. I could tell the process and content had reached him and that it was well-connected to his vision of success.

Once I had completed the feedback analysis, I conducted a self-review of the workshops, leveraging my Maximizer strength to search for improvements. From a content standpoint, I had only one thing I would have done differently. I would have simplified the Secret sauce exercise. I pulled up the form on my computer and fixed it right then. I combined a few of the questions for simplification purposes, and then I was done.

The feedback from the players was excellent, and I knew the team chemistry had improved, but the real proof for the Cranbrook hockey team would be in their response to being tested – on and off the ice. Would they play like a team? Would they be less selfish? Would Coach observe less conflict? Would all the talent in the room be put to good use? Would they refuse to let each other fail? I had never seen my approach fail, but I really wanted this to succeed. Of course, longing for something does not accelerate Father Time. In fact, the opposite is true. I would have to be patient because I was headed out of town

I sat back in my chair, tired but happy. What a week! It felt great to be doing what I do best. It seemed that as I helped the Cranbrook boys hockey team achieve their dreams, they were helping me achieve mine.

Chapter 7: Viva Las Vegas

“Things won are done, joy's soul lies in the doing.”

William Shakespeare

* * *

I pondered how to remain engaged while respecting Coach Weidenbach’s need to focus on the task at hand: winning with character, brotherhood, and refusing to let anyone fail. I would miss their next games because I was traveling to Las Vegas for a week, supporting The Company and my strategic partners who were all attending our enormous technology conference. I considered reaching out to Coach Weidenbach to ask how things were going and to see if I could help in any way, but decided not to. It was his team, and he was the Maestro. I was cautious about inserting myself where I was not wanted or needed.

I decided that the best strategy would be to rely on my friendship with Red Fox.

I emailed Red Fox, explaining that I would be unavailable to see any games until after I returned from Vegas and asked if she’d be my on-location reporter. Her response was immediate, declaring that keeping me informed would be personally delightful. Red Fox’s emails were consistently full of energy and emotion. I was pretty sure she had Positivity because every conversation was permeated by an air of optimism.

It was time to pack up my duds and head west to Las Vegas. I was dismayed that I would not get to see the fruits of my labor firsthand. Perhaps the indicators of success would be immediately discernible from the hockey bleachers! My work with corporate teams is less tangible and direct, so watching a client perform was a rare and precious opportunity. It was not fair that I had to do something I dreaded and miss something that meant the world to me. I realized that this must be how parents feel when a business trip keeps them away from their child's dance rehearsal or sports events. It is depressing. Of course, pay checks matter, but a bank account does not feed one's soul like watching young people grow and learn and work so hard to do their best. I had invested in this team. I believed they were about to demonstrate the powerful advantage that a strengths-based approach brings to an organization. I wanted to be there to see it!

I imagined a conversation with My Boss. "Gosh Boss, I am so sorry to miss the conference in Vegas, but I simply must attend two high school hockey games!" That was a non-starter from the get go. Like it or not, I was leaving on a jet plane. The only good news about the trip was that I would escape the hideous Michigan winter weather, and I would see My Boss and my teammates. It had been over three years since I'd seen a particularly close colleague, and I was looking forward to a fun reunion. Whenever our team meets face-to-face, I realize how much human glue and sense of fun is lost in a virtual, work-from-home environment.

I checked my email one last time before I headed to the airport. There was an update from Red Fox!

Hi Maureen!

During both games they played, one of the parents said. "Wow, I can't believe how well they're playing together with two key players missing."

First game we played verses Wisconsin team:

Coaches said they played the BEST OVERALL GAME OF THE SEASON! They came out hard and played hard the entire game. They worked well together and kept up the level of intensity throughout the entire game. We lost 2-1, but they were amazing – the coaches were praising their teamwork!

Second game verses Rochester United:

We played them at the beginning of the season where Cranbrook lost (and deserved to lose!) They played terrible as a team and blamed each other. Then, they played them again yesterday. They started out slow, but after the first period, they played hard together as a team and looked like a different team. We ended up winning 6-2! I know the boys are excited about what they did!

Red Fox

My heartbeat quickened as I read the note from Red Fox. These were the first two games after the team's training on strengths and success. How exciting to hear about improvements that were visible even to the parents sitting in the stands! It indicated significant progress towards Coach Weidenbach's goal of having the young men play like a team. After all, that was the main problem we were trying to solve. Beating Rochester United, after losing to them earlier in the year, was also a positive sign.

What was behind these improvements? Were the players and coaches able to apply what they had learned as individuals and as a team? Was brotherhood on the rise? Were they refusing to let each other fail? I was dying to know. I also realized for the first time how rewarding it was to have immediate, visible and measurable feedback on the work I had done with a client.

In business, my methodology is the same. The improvement in the human system is immediate, with a visible boost of energy and increased collaboration on the team, but success takes longer to measure. Business metrics such as increased sales, productivity, and profit are lagging indicators of success. It is not the same as sports, which has an immediacy associated with it, such as a win/loss column and a fan base to judge change for the better on the team.

I dialed my brother and shared the news from Red Fox.

"Really?!" Marty exclaimed.

"Can you believe it?"

"No," he admitted, "but I think it's great!"

"Me, too. I'm enjoying the immediate, measurable results. And I'm thrilled that Coach said they played as a team, which means more to him than winning."

"This could become a great story," Marty said.

"Can you imagine if they achieve their goals outlined in their success statement? If they win the state championship by leveraging their strengths, delivering full effort, brotherhood, and refusing to let anyone fail?"

"That would be incredible."

"I know!" I replied. "I wish I didn't have to go to Vegas. I'm dying to see these guys play."

"Sure," he said. "But, you'll be getting out of this weather."

"That's true," I agreed, grimacing at the snow whipping past my window. "But, I'd still rather be here than there."

Before long, I was on a flight to Sin City. I settled in on the plane, glancing at those around me who had their laptops on, earplugs in, or movies playing on their phone. I wanted no part of it. I had four hours of thinking and writing time ahead of me, and I welcomed it.

A tall gentleman with silver hair moved down the aisle and lowered himself into the seat next to me. Even dressed in casual clothes, he possessed the mien of a CEO. I smiled at him. He offered a warm nod. I made sure I wasn't trespassing on his territory and slid my slight frame a smidge closer to the window.

A mental image from my past floated forward. Many years ago, when I was a young engineer at The Company, I had taken a business trip to New York City and sat in a seat a lot like the one I was in now, with an older, more experienced gentleman next to me. It turned out that the gentleman was also with The Company. We chit chatted. I enthusiastically shared my creative efforts to improve the client experience and explained how we were building a services offering with pre-tested software, installation services, and user training. It was a Band-Aid applied in the field, but it was resolving dozens of customer complaints. He listened patiently and politely, nodding from time to time. When I was done, he smiled, leaned toward me and said, "You are a wild duck, aren't you?"

I paused. I was young and was unfamiliar with that business term. "Um, I'm not sure."

"You are," he said confidently, with a matter of fact nod of his head. He let a few moments pass.

I was puzzled, but respectful. I waited for him to continue.

"You know what they do to wild ducks in The Company, right? They shoot them."

"You know what they do to wild ducks in The Company, right?"

I shook my head no.

He turned his head ever so slightly to make direct eye contact with me. "They shoot them."

My eyes widened, and I laughed. I thought he was kidding. He let my chuckle run its course.

"Whatever you do," he continued, in a tone of utter seriousness, "don't ever be the first duck in the V. All they have to do is shoot the first wild duck in the V, and the rest are lost. Problem solved."

Initially, I did not believe him. I thought he was trying to scare me. It would not have been the first time. When I joined The Company, I was the lone woman on a team of 90 people, in a field bereft of female engineers. I had experienced intimidation tactics. One man, upon being introduced to me, shook my hand. He kept a forced smile on his face as he gripped it harder and harder and harder. It hurt. We never lost eye contact. I did not flinch, but I got the message.

It turns out my colleague on the plane was not trying to scare me. He was trying to warn me, and he was right. My career with The Company was a long series of wild duck initiatives, powered by my personal rocket fuel of Ideation, Strategic, Maximizer, and Individualization. I was an intrapreneur – a term used to describe an entrepreneur operating within a company – long before the term was popularized by business journalists. As a result, I was repeatedly and publicly shot, hung, or whacked by leaders who did not want a wild duck in their midst. I was also deeply valued by my clients and even, once in a rare while, rewarded for it by The Company. It was weird to be hung by one executive and then rewarded by another – for the same act!

Once I was presenting at a conference in Colorado. There were many clients and colleagues there. I was sitting in a session when a stranger tapped me on the shoulder and said that one of The Company's executives wanted to speak to me. I had never met this VP before, but I figured he had heard about my creative initiative to solve a big client problem and wanted to thank me. I eagerly followed the guy to a conference room. The executive was there, along with a large army of supporters. As usual, I was the only woman in the room.

The exec motioned me to sit in the empty chair at the very end of a long, oval table. He perused some documents that were sitting in front of him for what felt like minutes, lifted his gaze to meet mine, and gave me a rigid stare. Then, he pulled the trigger. "There are assholes in Detroit who have a dim-witted misunderstanding about the quality of one of my products!" He ranted and snarled and pounded his chest for about ten minutes.

My knees began to shake under the table. When it was over, there was utter silence. I glanced at the others in the room. Eyes were lowered in embarrassment, sympathy, or fear. I swallowed, and swiftly considered my options. I could sit silently and wave the white flag, appearing guilty as charged. Based on my lowly position in the universe, he probably expected me to do that. However, I was not guilty. In fact, once I realized that I was being ambushed by an executive I had never met before, I was angry. I chose to meet fire with fire. I looked at the Big Man in Charge, and said, "Well, since I'm the only asshole from Detroit, why don't I start?"

I proceeded to walk through what we had done and why. Every action I took had the blessing of *my* vice president and *our* customers (we worked for the same company, did we not?). When I was finished, I asked him for advice on what I should have done differently. He huffed and puffed a bit more and eventually backed down, as all bullies do. Here is the funny part. Later, for the same project, I was named Systems Engineer of the Year by my vice president. One vice president's problem employee is another vice president's rock star. Go figure.

This dysfunctional system taught me that I could not judge my human value based on the point of view of an executive from The Company. Instead, I boiled it down to one thing: How do **I** measure **my** success? I measure my success based on the positive impact I have on my clients in the process of accomplishing goals. I was the face of The Company to them, and it was important that I represented The Company well. How they felt about working with me was as significant as the outcomes we achieved. As a result, my clients and strategic partners valued me for being valuable to them. That was success in my book.

I could not judge my human value based on the point of view of an executive from The Company. Instead, I boiled it down to one thing: How do I measure my success?

I sat back in my seat, reminiscing about one client out of Pennsylvania. He was British and was the information technology director for an automotive supplier. He had given me the moniker of Joan of Arc because I made multiple runs at The Company's support organization, determined to get them to do the right thing. It took time, but we persevered. Finally, I was given permission to build a system that resolved their issue. I know how much he valued my efforts on their behalf. It also landed me an overseas stint in Paris, and that experience had changed my life. That looked like success to me.

In the process of solving the recurring software quality problem with this same software solution, I had spent multiple nights – and when I say that, I mean *all* night – at a tiny tool and die shop in a very dreary part of Inkster, Michigan. The story played out the same way every time. The client would call. We had sold him a bunch of crap, he would say. I would listen. He would ask me to come out and help. I would agree. He would add, "Don't forget to bring the razor blades." It was our running joke. It was painful, no question about it. When the computer system they purchased was down, he was judged harshly by his management for spending money on a computer solution that wasn't reliable and delayed their projects. They were a supplier to the automotive industry, and project delays come with financial penalties. When I helped my client fix the problem, his life was better. That looked like success to me.

My mind ticked through my professional ups and downs, and the experience of being repeatedly called out on the carpet. I realized there was a book in that journey. Someday, I would share what it was like to be a wild duck at The Company. For personal preservation sake, I would wait until I was gone. There was no benefit in poking the corporate hornets' nest at this point.

After an easy flight, we landed. I grabbed my luggage and with long, eager strides, headed for the doors. I longed to feel warmth and sun for the first time in months. When I hit the hot, dry Nevada air, it was like someone had wrapped me in a warm and rejuvenating cloak of bubble wrap. I felt my shoulders melt. It was heavenly.

In a rather reckless, mad dash from the airport, the cab driver dropped me off at the New York-New York hotel. The rejuvenating bubble wrap was instantly ripped off me as I walked inside. The smoky casino, ubiquitous screeching of people, one-armed bandit machines, and inebriated human beings, shouting to one another in all languages, assaulted my senses. I had forgotten how obnoxious Vegas was and I instantly hated it. I am a person who treasures silence. It helps me think.

I asked the lovely hotel check-in person if I could have a room in the quiet part of the hotel. She couldn't have been more accommodating, assuring me with a warm, "Of course! Let me see what I can do!" She fiddled around with her computer for some time.

"I have the perfect spot!" she said. "It is far away from the elevators, and tucked back in the corner of our hotel. It's a higher cost room, but I've given it to you at your corporate rate."

I was very grateful, and took her name so I could properly thank her. I am big on acknowledging excellent customer service. I make sure that their boss knows, and I also put reviews on the web and include the first names of those who made a difference.

I headed up a set of escalators to the elevators and made my way to the 23rd floor. I found my room. It was indeed tucked back in a corner away from the other rooms. As I unpacked, I suddenly heard a loud roaring noise, as if an 18-wheeler truck was racing by, followed by what sounded suspiciously like the screaming of people in distress. Puzzled, I walked to the window, pulled back the curtains, and discovered the source of the disturbance. It was a freaking roller coaster.

My eyes traveled the perimeter of the giant steel mechanism. I realized, in utter disbelief, that the hotel was completely surrounded by the beast, like a vertical moat. There was no escaping it by moving to another room. Noise from the hallway or the elevators would be the least of my troubles. I was at this particular hotel because my colleagues were staying here. If anyone had mentioned that we were in the center of a rollercoaster ride, I would have booked a different hotel. Oh well, I had ear plugs. Maybe it would rain. Maybe it would snow. Maybe it would be closed for maintenance.

My team was meeting for dinner that night, right in the hotel. Before I headed to the restaurant, I stopped by the front desk.

"So, tell me about the rollercoaster," I said, as pleasantly as possible.

"Oh it's delightful," said the nice man.

I offered a frozen smile.

"You can get a Scream Pass and ride it all day long! "

I was ready to scream, alright. At that moment, someone hit a jackpot on a hideous electronic casino device. Bells and whistles and lights went off at a decibel level akin to a fire engine's horn blaring directly into my eardrum. "How late does it run?" I screeched over the din.

"Fridays and Saturdays, it runs through midnight!" shouted the clerk with his cheerful, hospitality smile. "The rest of the week, until 11!"

I stared at him and momentarily considered explaining that I have six thinking strengths in my performance toolkit, and that I need lots of quiet time in order to be effective. But, I didn't. I would sound a little silly talking about my performance toolkit to a hotel desk clerk. And besides, who comes to Vegas for quiet time? Nobody.

"Thank you, sir," I said, turning on my heels. I waved my hand in annoyance at the invisible, revolting smell in the air. It was a combination of smoke, alcohol and some sort of god awful air freshener. I suppressed an urge to engage in a public swearing fit.

Maybe I could switch hotels. I circled back to the front desk area, banking on the fact that I wouldn't get the same fellow. I ended up with a very nice lady. I explained that I was not aware that the hotel was blessed with a roller coaster and asked if I could possibly switch to one of the other hotels. Alas, there were no rooms available at our discounted conference rate. If I wanted to move, I would have to pay nearly $100 per night out of my own pocket. I gave up.

I headed in the direction of the restaurant, eager to meet my team and forget about the rollercoaster for a while. I strolled into the dining and drinking establishment and discovered them sitting in the back.

I was truly glad to see My Boss, whom I had not spoken to since my performance review, and I gave him a big hug. I couldn't be mad at him over my B grade because he was caught in the trap of bureaucracy and a broken system. Plus, My Boss had been really good to me during some hard times the previous year. A rather difficult sales leader objected to a creative, cloud-based solution that I had built with one of my strategic partners. He went to My Boss behind my back and claimed that I was giving leads to the competition. This was untrue. My Boss calmly stood by me, which was a rare occurrence at The Company, because at The Company, sales leaders have the most power. In the big scheme of things, that meant more to me than money or grades. The grade would fade, but I will never forget that My Boss had my back.

My Boss calmly stood by me, which was a rare occurrence at The Company.

I moved around the table, saying hello to each colleague – one from New Hampshire, one from California, two from Boston, and a new teammate, a fellow from Austin, whom I had never met before. It felt wonderful to see them face-to-face.

I was the only woman on my team, but that was nothing new to me. Again, it has been that way since the beginning of my career. It did not matter – I think of people as individuals. I had never been much of a "rah rah women!" person. I was more of a "rah rah excellence!" person. Excellence is not gender specific.

I settled in directly across from My Boss, happy that I would get to easily chat with him. We all caught up on each other's lives. We drank and ate and laughed and teased My Boss about paying the bill. I heard the thunder of the roller coaster as it zoomed past. This time, I smiled.

* * *

The long week began. My responsibilities included manning our pedestal on the conference room floor, which highlighted the value proposition of our strategic partners. The conference was held at both the MGM and the Mandalay Bay, which are quite a distance from one another. Lots of walking was involved, and even if an event was in the same hotel, the hotels were so large I had to allow a good 20 minutes between meetings simply for travel time inside the building.

The best part of the week for me was the face-to-face time I spent with my strategic partners. I adored them. We had both work and social time together, and I was present when they received their awards. I was proud and happy for them, for the wins were well-deserved. Naturally, I had conducted StrengthsFinder assessments and training with employees from both companies. This had fortified our partnership because the process of sharing our likes and differences builds human glue.

One of the employees, a very petite, young marketing professional from Germany, had just received her StrengthsFinder results. She had Competition and Harmony in her top five strengths profile. She may hate to lose and would also have a deep need to avoid conflict and find common ground. It felt incongruent to me. I am low in both strengths, so I was curious to see how they manifested themselves in her.

"With both Competition and Harmony, do you ever feel bad when you win?"

"That's a good question," she said, pausing for a moment. "I want to win, but it must be fair."

"I would never gamble, because the win is not fair. It is luck. That isn't winning fairly. Gambling hurts people."

"Interesting," I said, processing that information. "Can you give me an example?"

"Yes," she said, in her charming accent. "It's perfect for Las Vegas. I would never gamble, because the win is not fair. It is luck. That isn't winning fairly. Gambling hurts people."

What a great example! It provided insight into how her blend of strengths manifest themselves in her.

"But," she added with a sweet smile that belied her inner warrior, "if the competition is fair, I always want to win!"

I laughed, happy to be indulging in my favorite pastime: understanding what makes people tick.

That night, when I returned to my hotel, I fired up my computer. In my inbox, I found an update from Red Fox. I clicked on that email first.

Maureen!
We just won a HUGE game with Brother Rice. They WERE ranked #1 … BUT NOT NOW!
Cranbrook is now ranked #1 in the State of Michigan! There are a couple great articles – links attached. Blake Rogow was interviewed. It was neat – he spoke of the team and how they're coming together. I thought he had some great quotes!
I truly believe your impact was HUGE! It looks like we're going to go into the playoffs playing like a team – which is the only way to win!
THANK YOU SO MUCH!
Red Fox

I was overjoyed with the news. They were winning as a team. It is important that the leader speak about winning as a team, but that does not always translate to changes in behavior in the ranks. When the players start talking about playing as a team, it is an indication that the culture is changing. Being ranked as the number one hockey team in the state of Michigan was an impressive milestone.

I clicked on the link to read what Blake Rogow had said. I scanned the article. Cranbrook had beaten Brother Rice by a score of 4-1. I found Blake Rogow's name and read:

Senior Blake Rogow scored a pair of goals in the victory, both coming in the third period as Cranbrook pulled away.

"We played as a team tonight, and I think that's going to help us come playoff time."

"It feels great coming out here and playing a good game against a great team," said Rogow, who now has five goals and 12 points on the season. "We started off a little slow but once we established our forecheck, worked as a team, pressured their defensemen, I think we got stuff going. We played as a team tonight, and I think that's going to help us come playoff time." [4]

Deeper in the article, I saw that Mason Schultz, the young man with Woo and Includer strengths, had also scored. It was fun to read about the players' successes.

Blake Rogow had more to say.

"Every day we work on D-zone. We have great structure implemented by coach (Andy) Weidenbach and coach (Scott) Lock," Rogow said. "We always do battle drills with no sticks, keeping in front of all three forwards. That's helped a lot because we stifle them, and they can't get any shots."

I respected Blake's maturity – seasoned athletes give credit to the opposition first, and speak about themselves or their team second. Blake's summary indicated that the players were achieving what they had described in their success statement. Blake's description of Coach Weidenbach's structured approach to the physical aspects of the game was interesting. If you can rebuff the opposition with no hockey stick, imagine how much better and confidently one would perform with one.

I was so pleased for the team! I replied to Red Fox and thanked her for keeping me in the loop, reiterating how eager I was to get home and watch the team play.

The rest of the week passed relatively uneventfully. I spent lots of time with my colleagues and strategic partners but did not see much of My Boss, who had big meetings with executives from The Company.

On my last full day, I went searching for some souvenirs. I crossed the bridge between the New York-New York and the MGM hotels. Homeless people crouched along the walkway, asking for money. As I approached, one stood up, walked over to the edge of the bridge, and

---

[4] Jason Schmitt, "Cranbrook takes down Brother Rice in battle of top ranked teams," (http://www.miprepzone.com/oakland/), 21 February 2015.

promptly relieved himself. Dozens of people walked past, with nothing more than a sideways glance at what was happening. I stopped in amazement. How does one properly respond to such a situation? I truly did not know. I considered the perspective of the cars passing underneath and wondered if they understood what had just hit them.

"Only in Vegas can you pee on the traffic from a bridge and nobody cares," I said to no one in particular. I gave him a wide berth, and moved on. Between that and the roller coaster, I was ready to leave.

I tracked My Boss down, and discovered he was in the Mandalay Bay hotel. I headed back over there to say goodbye. I wanted to see My Boss, for a small part of me feared that I would never see him again. My stint with The Company was over at the end of December. Even though it was only February, there were no more face-to-face team meetings planned and no large events that would pull us together. It was more than likely the year would pass without us meeting again.

We chatted briefly about his week. I provided a swift update on my strategic partners, and that was it. I gave him a quick hug, thanked him for dinner earlier in the week. He thanked me for my hard work with our partners. I did not mention my fear of never seeing him again. I did not want to turn into a maudlin mess. Plus, just as there is no crying in baseball, there are no feelings allowed on The Company time. Execution, execution, execution was our mantra. With a fond wave at My Boss, I made my way out of Mandalay Bay, made the trek to my hotel and packed up my stuff.

I flew back to Detroit eager to see my first Cranbrook game.

The following morning, I reached out to Red Fox. Were there any games this weekend?

Red Fox swiftly replied. There were no games over the weekend, but Cranbrook had won the night before. Red Fox also provided the playoff schedule which would commence in just a few days.

I thanked Red Fox for all the details and told her I would see her on Monday at the game. I could not wait to see the team play. Plus, in less than two weeks, we would know the final outcome of our work together. Would we achieve success, as defined by the players?

I had lost track of what had happened since we held our workshop, and I looked online for their record.

Cranbrook's Win-Loss Record After Our Workshop

Date	Opponent	Score
2/13	Notre Dame Academy (WI)	1-2 (L)
2/14	Rochester United	6-2 (W)
2/20	Brother Rice	4-1 (W)
2/21	De La Salle Collegiate	6-2 (W)
2/27	Trenton	6-4 (W)

The Cranbrook hockey team had achieved a 4-1 winning record since we built our success statement and identified their individual and team strengths. That was fabulous, but it was not the whole story. It was one of the metrics-based measurements of success, but I wanted to hear about the human and cultural transformation. Were the young men skating the talk and playing unselfishly? Was there compounding interest in the team trust bank? Were the wins a direct result of doing things differently? Was the atmosphere improved in the locker room? Were the players showing respect for one another, and listening to the co-captains? Or was Lady Luck playing a joke on me? It was hard to know without being there. In two days, I would be able to judge for myself.

Chapter 8: Watching the Boys Play

"Greatness is a road leading towards the unknown."

Charles de Gaulle

* * *

I entered the ice arena to watch a game against Royal Oak Shrine. I started out at the wrong end of the chilly stands because I did not know which side supported Cranbrook. I spoke with a few lovely ladies, mothers and grandmothers of players on the Royal Oak Shrine team, who were convinced that Cranbrook would win because Shrine had experienced personnel troubles. I eventually moved to the correct end of the rink, but not before wishing them well.

I waved once at Coach Weidenbach just to let him know that I was there. I did not want to be seen as hovering or interfering in any manner whatsoever.

What I saw amazed me. Cranbrook dominated, winning 11-0, and it was over before I knew it. The game ended after the second period because the mercy rule was intact. The mercy rule is engaged when one team is ahead by more than seven goals after two periods of play. They end the game rather than continue the lopsided battle.

I saw the boys fight hard and play well, but was that due to the personnel troubles of the competition, or were they higher performing as a result of our project? It was hard to tell.

Two days later, they played against Pontiac Notre Dame Prep, and handily won that game in a similar fashion, 8-0.

The following game was at Cranbrook against the dreaded Detroit Country Day school. The Regional Championship was on the line. The two schools have a historic rivalry. The campuses are so geographically close to one another, that it might as well have been a home game for

Country Day. Country Day seemed to have a much larger number of students and supporters than Cranbrook. They were vocal and practicing a form of youthful rebellion called "I refuse to sit down." This was unfortunate for us, because our view of the far end of the rink was completely blocked by the students. The kids from Country Day School were not exactly picture windows.

One of the Cranbrook parents took charge. He stood up and bellowed, "On three! One! Two! Three! SIT!" The kids sat. I thought it was a fine example of situational leadership, and wondered if the man had Command in his StrengthsFinder profile.

Cranbrook won 4-1, but the game was much closer than the score indicated. Both teams played really hard. The Cranbrook boys were tested and appeared to responded well. I did not observe any negative behavior on the bench or on the ice. With that win, the Cranbrook hockey team became the Division III Regional Champions. I was enjoying being a fan, cheering with the best of them, and meeting some of the parents of the Cranbrook hockey players. I am not the most social person ever born, but connecting with people over something I take pleasure in, like the StrengthsFinder and hockey, makes it easier for me.

The quarter finals arrived with Cranbrook paired against Wyandotte. Wyandotte is located in a place we call "down river" because it is located down the river from Detroit. If I thought the Country Day crew was rowdy, I received a new view of the sports universe when we faced Wyandotte. Wyandotte's parents and fans seemed to think that if they swore, abused the referees, or chanted "Bullshit!" it would change the numbers on the scoreboard. It did not. It was high school hockey, for God's sake. When Wyandotte scored a goal, their fans screamed, "Over-rated! Over-rated!" implying that the Cranbrook hockey team did not deserve its #1 standing in the league. Cranbrook won 9-4. Later, I would learn that the Wyandotte cheer fired up some of the Cranbrook players and likely contributed to the wide margin of victory.

Most of us, including me, let the Wyandotte folks leave the building first. There was no need for a ruckus in the parking lot. With that convincing victory, Cranbrook had won the State Championship Quarter Finals. The celebration was short, for there was a championship to win.

I began to observe some discernible disparities between the Cranbrook team and the opposing teams. The Cranbrook team was operating on a different level. They simply competed with greater focus, discipline, and effort. Cranbrook had many seniors, so they were physically larger than some of the others.

When I watched the games, I had my strengths chart handy which showed me the top five StrengthsFinder results for each boy. But, because the jerseys were unnamed, I really did not know who was who. Plus, I got caught up in the excitement of the game. Hockey is fast paced; one cannot really examine strengths charts and watch the ice at the same time. Besides, what I most wanted to know was this: What was happening in the locker room? What did Coach and his team do after our workshops?

The Cranbrook hockey team had racked up seven wins and one loss since they learned their strengths, recommitted to playing as a team, and refused to let one another fail. That was a mere five weeks ago. I was beginning to think Lady Luck had long ago left the building and that Cranbrook's hockey team was performing like a finely tuned engine.

I was beginning to think that Lady Luck had long ago left the building, and that Cranbrook's hockey team was performing like a finely tuned engine.

Next up? The Semi-Finals against Riverview High. This school was also down river, not very far from Wyandotte, so I feared a similar experience in the stands. It was not so. In fact, the opposite was true. Everyone was gracious and exhibited good sportsmanship. It was impressive considering that Cranbrook played with intensity and purpose, outshooting Riverview 53 – 2, and winning by a score of 8-0. The game ended early with the mercy rule in play. As I left the arena, the reality of the situation hit me. The Cranbrook hockey team was now one single win away from becoming the Division III Michigan State Champions!

The day of the big game arrived. Our heroes were pitted against the mighty Houghton Gremlins.

Houghton is a small town in the Upper Peninsula (UP) of Michigan, a good 11-hour drive from Detroit. Houghton's claim to fame is being the place that professional hockey began with the launching of the very first professional hockey team. There is a very rich history of hockey success in Houghton that extends back to the 1800s. The Copper County Hockey Museum has an interesting collection. For example, the first skate blades were made of wood! Then leg bones from deer, then iron, then steel. Skates made from wood go back to 200 A.D. and were used by hunters. Ice hockey began as ice polo in the late 1800s, and then the rest, as they say, is history. In short, Houghton had legend and legacy on their side.

The state final began with the Compuware Arena filled with well-wishers from both sides. A lot of folks had made that long drive down from the UP.

Almost from the beginning, the ending was never in doubt, simply because the hockey puck seemed to be permanently stationed near the Houghton goalie. Mason Schultz scored 42 seconds into the first period. It turned out that Mason's goal was the winning goal, yet Cranbrook relentlessly swarmed the Houghton goalie, scoring two more goals, and outshooting Houghton 19-5 in the first 17 minutes of the game.

When Houghton did manage to cross the blue line into Cranbrook territory, the defensemen covered Houghton like a wet blanket. Cranbrook remained focused, never celebrating too much when they scored. They appeared to have that "next play" mentality.

The Houghton goalie was phenomenal. He made valiant save after save, blocking 46 out of the 50 shots he faced from Cranbrook. As the clocked ticked down in the third period, with a score at 4-0, it was clear there would be no comeback. Cranbrook outshot Houghton 50-13, and became the Michigan Division III State Champs.

I couldn't believe it. The boys had done it! The hard-won celebration began.

The bench emptied as the players piled upon the Cranbrook goalie. Then, they hugged every teammate in sight. There were helmets and sticks and gloves strewn all over the ice. The players, red faced and drenched in sweat, had achieved their goal. Coach Weidenbach and his coaching team congratulated one another with a lot of enthusiasm and big smiles.

The teams lined up and shook hands. Pictures were taken, the trophy delivered, medals dispersed. The boys' faces beamed with joy.

The team headed off to the locker room, where I am sure a wonderful speech was made by Coach and, perhaps, his co-captains.

I waited in the lobby, passing the time by chatting with the parents I had become acquainted with. When the boys eventually made their way out of the locker room, I made eye contact with the same fellow who spoke up first when I met the boys for the very first time, co-captain Cooper Stahl. I grinned and waved. I was so pleased for him and the team. He motioned me over, his eyes wide with excitement, and he said,

"You were right. It worked! That was the turning point in the season for us!"

In that single instant, I received what I had been seeking for some time, and it came in the form of a compliment from a high school hockey player. Cooper Stahl valued me for being valuable. I was thrilled.

In the moments that followed, I thought about the journey we made. With the exception of the exercise where the young men committed to refuse to let anyone fail, I did not do anything differently than I had done with dozens of other clients. The difference was that these boys and Coach Weidenbach were deeply motivated to succeed, which made my value proposition more potent. Plus, it was my good fortune that Coach Weidenbach had Individualization, which is the strength that most enjoys understanding what makes each person tick. The odds were high that he made effective use of the team StrengthsFinder results – a premise I still needed to validate. Finally, the timeframe was compressed; success was achieved more swiftly. It was gratifying.

I spoke to a few more boys without being a pest – I wanted them to enjoy their celebration. All thanked me for my work with the team. Mason Schultz, who had Woo, Communication, and Includer in his top five strengths profile, was swift to give me a hug and was kind in his praise for me. I congratulated him on scoring the winning goal. He looked tired, happy, and relieved. The long season was over.

With the exception of the exercise where the young men committed to refuse to let anyone fail, I did not do anything differently than I had done with dozens of other clients. The difference was that these boys and Coach Weidenbach were deeply motivated to succeed, which made my value proposition more potent.

One of the parents invited me to the post-game dinner at a local restaurant. I was pleased and joined the group. Three or four of the boys shared that the time we spent together was a really great investment and said that the players just treated each other differently after our workshops. This difference made its way to the ice.

One could argue they were the best team in Michigan because during the season, Cranbrook beat the Division I (Catholic Central) and Division II (Brother Rice) State Champions. Even the Houghton hockey coach acknowledged Cranbrook's prowess, quoted by the newspaper,

"They are one of the best teams in the state, regardless of division. They are the standard you measure yourself by."[5]

I did not see Coach Weidenbach after the game. He and his coaches have a post-game ritual that includes a particular restaurant, separate from the team. I figured that they were celebrating in their own way, debriefing on the game, and perhaps even planning what next year would look like. I sure had a hankering to know what the experience had been like for Coach and how he had helped the team understand and leverage their strengths. What did Coach Weidenbach do after we worked together six weeks ago?

When I returned home, I shared the news with Marty, including remarks from the players. He was really excited for me. I was excited for myself, too! It had been an amazing experience from start to finish.

Reveling in the joy of the moment, I opened my computer, and pulled up the Cranbrook hockey team's success statement.

The 2014/20015 Cranbrook Hockey team is determined to win the state championship by recommitting to unselfish play, discipline, focus, trust, respect, team chemistry brotherhood and by caring for one another, on and off the ice. We refuse to let anyone fail.

They had the trophy to prove one part of our success statement. The second part, the human journey, well, it would not be fully understood until I had a chance to speak with Coach Weidenbach. I found the win/loss table I had started a few weeks back, and updated it.

---

[5] Farrell, Perry. "Cranes outshoot Gremlins 50-13 en route to 17th state championship at Compuware Arena", Detroit Free Press, 14 March, 2015.

Cranbrook's record after our strengths-based success engagement

Date	Opponent	Win/Loss
2/13	Notre Dame Academy (WI)	L
2/14	Rochester United	W
2/20	Brother Rice	W
2/21	De La Salle Collegiate	W
2/27	Trenton	W
3/2	Royal Oak Shrine	W
3/4	Notre Dame Prep	W
3/7	Detroit Country Day	W
3/11	Wyandotte High	W
3/13	Riverview High	W
3/14	Houghton High	W

The team was 10-1 since we first met six weeks prior, resulting in an impressive win rate of 91%. Not a single tied game in sight. In fact, with the exception of the one loss, they had largely crushed the competition.

What role did the human system play in this amazing outcome? Did we achieve Coach's goal of the team playing as a team, and caring more about the outcome than the coaches? Had the players become greater young men as a result of the journey? Did knowing their strengths help them value one another, care for their teammates on and off the ice? Did they refuse to let each other fail? I had so many questions!

Wound up from the win, I still had energy to spare. For kicks, I entered Coach Weidenbach's name into my web browser and clicked on the first link that appeared. It was a bio of sorts that included a timeline of his coaching career. As I scrolled down the page, my jaw dropped. I could not believe my eyes.

- Head Coach, Detroit Junior Red Wings / Plymouth Whalers
- Head Coach, General Manager, Detroit Compuware Tier II Junior A. I90 wins, 37 losses, 18 ties
- Skating Coach, Detroit Red Wings Rookie Player Development Camp: 2008-2012
- Coach of the Year

- National League Champions
- USA Olympic Sports Festival Gold Medal
- Cranbrook … 22 years, 10 Division III Michigan State Championships, 440 wins, 149 losses, 38 ties

I was stunned. I had been blessed to work with one of the most experienced and successful coaches in the country, and I did not even know it.

I clicked on other links and discovered more articles and web pages that supported my first impression. Each nugget was fascinating and fed my hungry Individualization strength.

Suddenly, I was glad I did not know anything about Coach before working with him. Our runway was so short that I was more focused on how to work with the team than digging into Coach's background. It was a divine intervention of sorts, because while I am confident (high Self-Assurance, from a StrengthsFinder standpoint), knowing this information about Coach beforehand might have messed with my head. Reviewing his history in the rearview mirror made me appreciate him even more, not just for his accomplishments and experience, but for his willingness to place his trust in me and for allowing me to work with his team. I was truly fortunate.

I was struck by the sudden realization that our strengths-based success journey made Coach Weidenbach even more effective than he already was. Coach Weidenbach was a world-class coach. Had the opposing coaches known that Coach Weidenbach had a new weapon in his arsenal, they probably would have been frightened to death.

A few days later, I emailed Coach Weidenbach a note of congratulations and asked for time in the near future to debrief on how he used the success statement and StrengthsFinder results to help shape the team. He replied with a nice note, expressing his gratitude for our work together and agreeing to meet me for lunch. I could not wait to hear about the journey from his perspective. He was the final arbiter. Or, was he? Later, I would realize there were more points of view to consider.

PART 2: WHAT COACH SAW

Chapter 9: The Maestro's Methodology

"At Facebook, we try to be a strengths-based organization, which means we try to make jobs fit around people rather than make people fit around jobs. We focus on what people's natural strengths are and spend our management time trying to find ways for them to use those strengths every day."

Sheryl Sandberg

* * *

Coach Weidenbach and I settled across from one another at a comfortable restaurant a short drive from our respective homes. Our booth was off the main pathway so it was not too noisy. We could have a deep conversation without yelling over the restaurant din.

He gave me some guidance on which salads were the best, we ordered, and then the conversation began. It was fascinating.

I started the dialogue with how fun it was for me to work with the team, to watch them win, and to imagine how satisfying it had to be for him. I added, "I've been dying to hear what you did after we finished our workshops."

Coach replied with something unexpected. "I've been conducting exit interviews with each boy, and...."

"Wait," I said, interrupting him. "Exit interviews? At the high school level? All the boys? Even those who are returning next year?"

"Yes," he replied, his dark eyes unwavering. "I always conduct exit interviews."

"Wow," I said, absorbing the fact that this was business as usual for Coach Weidenbach. "What did you learn in the exit interviews?"

"I've interviewed 14 or 15 of the boys so far. Each one said that the StrengthsFinder workshops made a difference," he said. "A couple didn't mention it, so I brought it up, and they were quick to agree that it had impacted the team in a positive manner. I'll finish the rest this week."

My curiosity was already piqued by the beginning of our conversation, and I wanted to know more. I asked Coach to describe why he thought this strengths-based approach had been so successful.

He took a walk back through the season. "This state championship should have been a no-brainer," he began. "We had 14 seniors on the team, and most of them had experienced both losing in the quarter finals last year and winning the state championship the year before that. We had 16 kids returning from the 2013-2014 season. We had good captains. The kids were good kids."

He paused for a moment to dig into his salad.

"We started the season, and everything was great. The captains were leading well and managing the seniors. Some of the seniors had the expectation to be on the first lines, and sometimes, it doesn't work out that way. The team was winning. We lost only one game before Christmas break."

I commented on how amazing it must have felt.

Coach nodded, and went on to list the struggles that plagued the team in January. "I let it go on until I felt we couldn't find our way out of it without me taking charge. I intervened and called people out."

I thought about his top five strengths profile. Even though Coach had Command, which would make it natural for him to take charge, it does not mean it was easy to do when it was not how he wanted the team to operate.

"I started with myself. I said that I am the Maestro of this group, and if they didn't play music, then it was my fault, not theirs. Then I went to each boy and clearly conveyed what I wasn't seeing in practice or on the ice during games, told them what was wrong, and how to correct it. And," he admitted, "it probably felt like a kick in the groin for each player."

I could only imagine the dead silence in the locker room as Coach was providing a course correction for each young man. However, he had not just corrected the players. He had also provided instructions on how to improve.

I mentally compared Coach Weidenbach's approach to the typical feedback process many employees experience in a corporate environment. One might hear a lot about what was wrong and receive very little practical guidance about how to fix it. Clear expectations, like those provided by Coach, are rarely established. It also proved to me how much Coach cares. It is easy to pick someone apart; it is more difficult to glue them back together again so that they feel whole and can perform effectively.

It is easy to pick someone apart; it is more difficult to glue them back together again so that they feel whole and can perform effectively.

Coach continued. "I didn't like what I was seeing on the ice, so I changed the practice. We did a lot of battle drills. The drills force the players to get in front of the opponent's net, where the action is. This can cause chaos for the other team. But, I still felt like we were missing something."

I understood. Coach had made adjustments to the formal system (hockey drills, practice) but the human system had yet to be addressed.

"Is that when you found out about me?"

"Yeah," he replied. "I asked one of the parents if they knew anyone who did team building. She was aware of your work and recommended that we speak with you. After we spoke, and I learned more about your approach to success, I was all in."

I told Coach that the day we began to work together was one of the happiest days of my life. Then, I asked what he had done with the team after our workshops.

Coach spoke about a turning point for the team. "After we'd just played so well against the #1 team from Wisconsin, we played Rochester United, the only team we lost to in the first half of the season. We were down 2-0 after the first period, and we'd just taken a 5-minute major penalty. When we got into the locker room, there was no energy. Everyone looked disengaged and drained. The team captains weren't fired up, so they couldn't fire up the others. Because I am the Maestro of the team, I took over."

I recalled being in Vegas, and wondering what had happened in the locker room after the first period of the Rochester United game. Now I knew. Coach had taken control of the wheel. I asked him what it meant to take over.

"I put on my cheerleader outfit, grabbed my pom poms, and I cheered them up."

I burst out laughing. That was not what I had expected to hear.

"Then, I yelled at 'em. Then I hugged 'em. Then I kicked them out of the locker room and told them to give it their all. They went out and crushed Rochester United, 6-2. I did all the things I needed to do to help the team win." He paused for a moment. "But, that's not the way to build a winning team. I needed the boys to take on some of those roles, so they could do these things themselves."

I recalled that one of Coach's goals was to build great men. Helping his team self-lead themselves to success sounds easy and logical, but it is a difficult resolution to adhere to, especially if the leader knows what needs to be done. A leader can fall into the trap of believing it is simply easier to do it themselves. However, that is not leadership; it is a high-performing individual contributor. It also does not develop your followers. They learn nothing from a leader doing it themselves, and they will expect you to do it for them next time.

This scenario rears its head in the business world. Managers and leaders are often promoted to those roles after being strong individual contributors. However, the critical success factors for high-performing individual contributors are different than those for high-performing managers and leaders. Great talent ends up in the wrong role, and that hurts the organization. Working for a manager or a leader who is poorly suited for the role is demoralizing and often results in underperforming, disengaged teams.

However, the critical success factors for high performing individual contributors are different than those for high performing managers and leaders. Great talent ends up in the wrong role, and that hurts the organization.

"What did you do to help them own their roles?" I asked, curious as to how he solved this challenge.

"I always say there are three kinds of people. There are people who make things happen, watch things happen, and wonder what happened. I needed to find a way to help the boys make things happen. So, I did. This is where the StrengthsFinder results were so useful to me."

I waited impatiently for him to tell me more. He pursed his lips and appeared lost in thought. I could see he was trying to determine where to begin.

"I had to work to make their StrengthsFinder results tangible to me. I'm the Maestro, so I needed to understand what each boy could bring to help the team, beyond Competition. One day I sat down, looked at the team strengths profile, and began to assign roles for each boy."

I leaned in, eager to hear more.

"So Mason has Woo, right? And that brings energy to the room, right?"

"Right," I replied, marveling at Coach's recall. I had talked about the influencing category bringing energy during our workshop two months prior. We had not spoken since then.

"Well, once I'd figured out a role for each boy, we had a team meeting. I reminded them of the Rochester United game where I had to take control, and I said that was no way to win. I said that we were going to do things differently going forward. Then, I went around the room and talked about each player. I started with Mason Schultz, and I asked him if, when the locker room was down, his Woo *could* bring energy. He said it could. I pushed him further and asked him *would* he leverage his Woo to help? Mason said he would."

A strengths-based success journey is not a pill. It is a process which requires constant feeding.

I was trying to picture this moment in my mind. Coach described the strengths-based role and asked the player if he could perform in the role. If the answer was yes, then the player was asked if they would adopt the role. It was genius. Coach had extended and underscored the secret sauce exercise we did in the workshop. A strengths-based success journey is not a pill. It is a process which requires constant feeding. I asked Coach if he conducted this conversation in front of the whole team. Public commitments take on a life of their own. He had.

"Then," Coach continued. "I moved to Nolan Rogow. He's our backup goalie. He's unlikely to see a lot of ice time, so maybe he can't do much on the ice, but I wondered if there was something he could do off the ice."

I loved this. Coach was honoring the holistic view of talent and supporting the success statement, where the team had declared that off-ice success was as important as on-ice success.

"Nolan is the guy everybody loves," continued Coach. He's the guy you want to go on a fishing trip with. Yeah, he has Competition, but he also has Harmony and Relator – that human glue stuff. He's also younger." He paused to see if I understood the importance of that point.

I was puzzled. "What does that mean in terms of leveraging his strengths?"

"Well, here's the thing. There is always a hierarchy on a team. There are boys fighting to be on the first line, or the starting goalie. There is a hierarchy in terms of seniority. There is a hierarchy in terms of age. There's a hierarchy in terms of performance. Nolan is lower in a hierarchy constructed under those terms. He's young. He's the backup goalie. He won't win games from the bench. Therefore, the odds of him having the guts to assert his strengths, on his own, from the lower end of that hierarchy, are slim. I called him out," said Coach, "and asked him if he sees two players going at it in the locker room, can he do something about it? Nolan said he could. I asked him, you can do it, but will you do it? He said he would."

Interesting. Coach had eliminated the power pyramid so that Nolan could make a difference to the team. Going forward, when Nolan stepped up, the stars or senior players could not push back on him as a little nobody.

"I can't be in the locker room babysitting these guys all day long," explained Coach. "I needed to show the team that Nolan had my permission. In fact, it was my *expectation* that Nolan intervene if things got heated in the locker room. It was his role on the team, and I needed him to have the courage to play that role."

I was stunned by the simplicity and clarity of Coach's leadership. It sent a message to everyone that all talent was valuable and that each player must use his talents to support the team. It also contributed to player engagement. Research shows that when we know what is expected of us in a role, we are more likely to be engaged. Engaged teammates bring higher energy, productivity and performance.

Contrast Coach Weidenbach's approach with that with the general experience of a player, vaguely wondering if there was something they might do to help the team win. If one did speak up or leverage their strengths on their own, the others on the team might think they had a dumb idea or that nobody asked for their lowly opinion. That would be hard. It would take exceptional courage. It is no different than a highly talented intern having the courage to speak up or ask a question in a meeting that includes a vice president. When is the last time you saw that in the corporate world?

"I did the same thing with 8 or 10 other guys," continued Coach. "I said to each one, 'If the situation is X and we need Y, you are Y.' In that locker room conversation with each player, they had to tell me and the others what strengths they would bring, with *specific actions*, to help the team win. Eventually, everyone had a role."

This was a key part of Coach's success with the StrengthsFinder tool. Specificity of impact was critical for clarity, personal ownership, and team accountability. Each boy had to describe what strength they would bring, and describe how his choice would support the success of the team. This helps people internalize their strengths and connect them to team goals and objectives. By implementing this process, Coach had added structure to the human system, just as he did to the hockey system. He had demonstrated his ability to leverage the players' StrengthsFinder results. Later, I would learn more about how that ability comes so naturally to him.

Coach dug deeper into his tactics to intensify the commitment of the team to their success statement. He said he focused on their refusal to let anyone fail and reminded the team that walking the talk was essential. "Between that, the workshops, and me finding a role for everyone, it was the convergence I was looking for. I was the Maestro, and with all our work, we were able to hit the perfect high note at exactly the right time."

"Between that, the workshops, and me finding a role for everyone, it was the convergence I was looking for. I was the Maestro, and with all our work, we were able to hit the perfect high note at exactly the right time."

I recalled UCLA Coach John Wooden's remark about greatness being at your best when your best was needed. Coach Weidenbach was on that page, too.

"And that," said Coach Weidenbach with great emphasis, "is what we were missing the year before. We didn't peak at the right time. We struggled, and couldn't figure it out. This year we did. Timing is everything. We did the right things at the right time, and the guys just got better and better."

I sat back in my seat and studied Coach. My hunger for the details was satisfied, and I held him in more esteem than ever. He was indeed a Maestro, for he had figured out how each player could contribute to the team by using their strengths. He saw the need for thinking, relating, influencing, and executing, and filled that need with the person who had the talent to deliver. A goalie wasn't just a goalie. A goalie could also be an effective peace-maker with the gift to build human glue. A forward could skate fast, shoot the puck, make fancy moves and bring energy when there was a low point on the ice or in the locker room. I was in strengths heaven talking to Coach.

Exploring Coach Weidenbach's Strengths

Coach Weidenbach
Individualization
Responsibility
Activator
Command
Relator

It was time to turn the tables. My Individualization strength wanted to know more about how Coach's top five strengths manifested themselves in his universe.

"Let's talk about you," I said, which frankly, was more of a question than a statement.

"Okay," agreed Coach, between bites.

"Individualization is your number one strength. You see each person as a human snowflake and are interested in their strengths fingerprint." I paused and looked at him with a twinkle in my eye. "I think you have a pretty good handle on that one, don't you?"

"Yes. I've used it a lot over the past few months."

I smiled at his understatement. "Number two is Responsibility. In a nutshell, that means you like things done right or you don't want to be associated with it."

"Absolutely," agreed Coach. "I always say to my team, why be just regular Navy when you can be a Navy SEAL? Be the best. I always tell people, 'Labor great or small – do it right or not at all!'"

Coach had an amazing ability to come up with a quotable quip for just about any topic. In that sense, he reminded me of Yogi Berra, the great New York Yankees catcher who was effortlessly funny.

"Responsibility is also a crossover strength," I continued. "When you are responsible, you build trust. Trust is the currency of all relationships, so it creates strong bonds. People know that they can count on you to do what you say you will do. In that sense, even though it is an executing strength, Responsibility builds human glue."

Coach agreed that he was of the reliable sort.

People high in Responsibility generally hate it when things are not done correctly or in an irresponsible manner. It is a huge strengths violation and frustrates those with Responsibility to no end. I decided to see if Coach felt the same way. "Does it bother you when people don't do things the right way?"

Coach rolled his eyes. "Opposites attract, right?"

I nodded.

"Well, I think things should be done in an orderly way. When my wife buys groceries and puts them in the cupboards, she doesn't really care where things go as long as they fit. I am the opposite. I like the canned goods with the canned goods. The crackers don't belong with the canned goods. So, after she's finished putting them away, I go back and reorganize them. Then, we're both happy."

It sounded like a successful marriage to me.

"And the other day," continued Coach, "I was at a friend's house for a small party. I went in the bathroom and saw that the toilet paper was not coming off the top of the roll. In my opinion, this is the wrong way to hang toilet paper. I took the liberty to fix it for them. Then, when I rejoined the group, I confessed to them that I couldn't leave it alone. I said I'd be glad to go back and change it back if they'd prefer, but in my opinion, it was correct now. They told me not to worry about it."

I burst out laughing, thinking what a wonderful party conversation that was.

"There's a right way to do things and a wrong way," declared Coach, reaffirming his position on the matter.

I wondered if by chance Coach had Arranger in his top 10 strengths profile. Arranger is the conductor strength, and it can also manifest itself with symptoms of tidiness and organization. If we unlocked Coach's complete StrengthsFinder results, we would know for sure. I continued with his top five strengths.

"Activator," I said, with a knowing grin. "Mr. Impatient?"

Coach confirmed his need for action. "I am not patient, and anyone can tell you that."

I pitied the man who stood on the ground between Coach and the start of one of his projects.

"Command," I stated, in a tone that implied that no further commentary was required.

"Yeah," said Coach Weidenbach. "The coach is the field general. The dictator. The person making the decisions. Leading the drills. I'm good with that."

"You know when I saw your Command?" I asked.

"When?"

"When I screwed up the exercise of splitting the team into small groups of three. I didn't give them very good directions, and it was all messed up. You had to intervene, take command, straighten it out, and then all was well."

"Right," replied Coach, with no hint of apology.

To be clear, I wasn't seeking one. Coach's takeover of my exercise that went awry is simply the natural use of his strength. It is no different than saying to a great accountant, "And then you straightened out the accounts and everything was fine."

"Right," they would reply, "that's what I do." I did not resent Coach's intervention. I valued it.

"Coach, do you remember that I said that Command is the least common top five strength in the data base of 11 million people?"

He nodded.

"Less than 5% have this strength. This is one of those talents I talked about in the workshop. It's a blessing because it is rare. Because it is rare, it is difficult for others to understand. It is incumbent upon us to communicate these rare strengths, and talk about their value in helping you be successful in your role so that we aren't misunderstood by the rest of the world."

"Less than 5%, huh?"

"Less than 5%," I confirmed. I paused for a few moments to let him process the information. Then we explored the possibility that Coach might have colleagues who did not understand him and might resent his confidence, command, and success. He confirmed that he had seen it. It did not bother him (and with his strengths profile, it wouldn't), but at least now we understood why that might be. He had an uncommon set of strengths.

I moved on to his next talent.

"Relator," I said, "is the last strength in your top five profile. You probably have a small, but very tight, circle of friends. Depth is more important than breadth for Relators."

"That's true," said Coach.

I knew it was true as well, because even though I was spending time with Coach, I was not quite sure where I stood with him. I did not feel part of the in-group yet. That might be a correct read, or it might be that I did not know him well enough to come to such a conclusion. These things take time. I was also eager to err on the side of not bugging the man.

"We should unlock your 34 profile, Coach," I said. "I think you'd really enjoy it, and I'd like to take a deep dive into this with you."

"I'd like that," he said in a positive tone. "I love this stuff. I want to know more."

"What would you like to know?" I asked, figuring he had a specific question or two.

"Everything."

"Everything?" My tone was incredulous. I had been at it for ten years, and I did not know everything.

"Everything," he confirmed with an emphatic nod for punctuation.

"Okay!" I chuckled, delighted by the scope of the assignment. "I'm all in. I'm heading out to Omaha in a few weeks for some additional training. Maybe we can take a deep dive into your strengths after that? How does that sound?"

Coach was pleased with the idea.

The moment I was dreading had arrived. I desperately wanted to ask Coach if he would like to work with me to build a strengths-based sports platform. Between his history and mine, we had a strong foundation of experience. However, I am not gifted with the art of self-promotion. I can sell the heck out of someone else's talent but have a terrible time selling my own. Searching for the right words to start the conversation, it was a huge relief to discover I didn't have to.

"I'd also like to do more of this somehow," added Coach.

I nearly stood and high-fived the man. He had voiced my exact thoughts.

"Me, too!" I agreed, trying not to sound overly excited. "I think we have something here, Coach. Between what you know and what I know, and the business of success in sports, it could be great."

We agreed that we could create a platform to build strengths-based teams in the sports world. I offered to begin by documenting the Cranbrook hockey story from start to finish. We could use that to get started. Coach thought it sounded like a good plan

We paid the bill and headed out to the parking lot. I shook his hand and thanked him for his time. We agreed to speak again in a few weeks and take a deep dive into his strengths. I knew how much fun that would be, and I was eager to see what his entire StrengthsFinder profile looked like. I knew that we would discover something very unusual and very exciting!

I headed home to start documenting our story. I was thinking maybe a short paper comprised of ten pages or so, something we could share with other coaches or leaders. Well, I clearly missed that estimate by a mile. It is not my fault. The deeper I dug into the team's journey, the more interesting it became.

Chapter 10: Coach's StrengthsFinder Profile

"Keep away from people who try to belittle your ambitions. Small people always do that, but the really great make you feel that you, too, can become great."

Mark Twain

* * *

Within a few days, I had Coach's complete StrengthsFinder profile, all 34 strengths from top to bottom. It was fascinating to gain further insight into the patterns of excellence that made him the remarkable individual that he was. Before I dig into it, I want to illustrate an important point about our strengths-based success journey.

I had been pretty sure he had Arranger, remember? He did not. I am sometimes wrong when I guess people's strengths. However, the process of trying to figure out their strengths is fruitful. I am observing their patterns of behavior, looking for likes and dislikes, and there is value in that. I am more likely to be curious than furious with a frustrating colleague because I know they are giving me insight into their strengths lens. Their strengths lens will never be the same as mine. What makes perfect sense to them may not make sense to me at all. I have become less likely to judge people through my own lens. Instead, I become a human detective, gathering clues about them so that I can maximize my effectiveness when engaging with them. Let me offer an example.

My dear friend, Joanie, is not one to rush into things. In fact, she does not wish to be rushed, ever. I would have bet my 401K that she had Deliberative (the foot on the brake strength). We made the strengths-based success journey together, and voila! Joanie did NOT have Deliberative. She had Intellection (think and think and think – a processor in the brain that needs to complete its task before moving on) and Input (seeks information, may research things to death). Plus, she had Achiever at the bottom of her profile. She is not driven to a level of burnout like many of us are. Her strengths, in combination, looked like Deliberative to me, because deliberative people do not like to be rushed and rarely race out of the gate. My guess on the strength was wrong, but the impact is the same: Do not rush Joanie. Give Joanie time to think before asking her to act or make a decision.

Coach describes himself as a Maestro. In his role of head coach, he conducts the hockey team like an orchestra. That is one of the classic definitions of the Arranger strength. What is wrong with my guess? Nothing. He has other dominant strengths, that, in combination, look and feel like Arranger, and generate the same results. With the Maestro, the team moves from making noise to making music.

Our StrengthsFinder Profiles

Note: visit my website at www.maureenmonte.com to see a color-coded version. It's much easier to digest.

Coach Weidenbach		Maureen
Individualization	1	Ideation
Responsibility	2	Strategic
Activator	3	Learner
Command	4	Achiever
Relator	5	Individualization
Belief	6	Input
Achiever	7	Activator
Self-Assurance	8	Responsibility
Connectedness	9	Self-Assurance
Learner	10	Relator
Analytical	11	Maximizer
Significance	12	Context
Focus	13	Command
Context	14	Intellection
Discipline	15	Connectedness
Futuristic	16	Belief
Deliberative	17	Positivity
Arranger	18	Arranger
Restorative	19	Developer
Woo	20	Deliberative
Communication	21	Significance
Competition	22	Competition
Strategic	23	Focus
Includer	24	Analytical
Ideation	25	Futuristic
Harmony	26	Communication
Intellection	27	Adaptability
Input	28	Woo
Developer	29	Discipline
Positivity	30	Restorative
Maximizer	31	Empathy
Adaptability	32	Harmony
Empathy	33	Consistency
Consistency	34	Includer

Before we dive into Coach's strengths, it is possible that you dropped right to the bottom of our profiles to see our lesser strengths. This is human nature, particularly in the United States, where we have academic, business, and media empires that focus on what's wrong with us. I might as well address the result of this weakness expedition right now: neither Coach nor I are going to win the Miss Congeniality award at the beauty pageant. We are both low in the more emotionally potent human glue strengths, such as Empathy, Includer, Positivity, and Harmony. I am not upset by this fact, and I doubt that Coach is losing sleep over it, either. Why? They don't contribute to our performance strategy. How do we manage to be successful without those amazing, beautiful human glue strengths?

We do what other high performers do. We find success via other means – using our top 10 to 12 dominant strengths. We are not bereft of feeling. We are not cold-hearted. We are not negative. We just don't melt with emotion. In fact, one of the goals of making the strengths-based success journey is to embrace your lesser strengths (some will call them weaknesses) with the same joy you embrace your dominant strengths. Then, seek the presence of your lesser strengths in the dominant strengths of other people, and embrace those people as strategic partners. You can ask them for help. They will love you for honoring what is great about them and for fully utilizing their talent to make the team or organization more productive. Don't ignore your weaknesses. Find ways to mitigate them.

I know this works because I practice it daily. Notice that my Restorative strength lies at #30. People high in Restorative remove roadblocks like human bulldozers. I hate obstacles, especially nonsensical ones. In my role with The Company, roadblocks are the norm. Remember I spoke about building strategic partnerships and overcoming resistance? There is a roadblock at every turn – legal, sales, support, awareness in the field – nothing is easy and forward progress is slow. To cope, I have Restorative partners who will help me remove roadblocks. For example, mindless bureaucracy drains the life right out of me. I like to run fast and free on the road, helping people and teams achieve success. If I were a horse, I would be a thoroughbred, running in the Kentucky Derby. I would not be a draft horse, slowly, methodically plowing the field, digging up rocks, and pulling heavy loads. Don't ask a thoroughbred to plow the field, and don't ask a draft horse to run the Kentucky Derby. Pair them up to make their weaknesses irrelevant.

In addition, we can leverage our top strengths to achieve the same outcome as our lesser strengths. I guarantee you I can leverage my Ideation strength to come up with ideas on how to get around roadblocks. That's my other survival strategy. I'm not a bulldozer. I'm a ninja warrior and I use my Ideation and Strategic and Achiever to accomplish the outcome of bypassing the roadblock.

However, having low Restorative has not been my biggest personal challenge during my career. My biggest personal challenge has come from my low Harmony.

In the corporate world, it is important to be tactful. Therefore, I have had multiple Harmony partners. One of those Harmony partners was a wonderful information technology architect, Jeff, who once said to me, "Microsoft Word has a grammar checker and a spell checker. It doesn't have a diplomacy checker. You need a diplomacy checker." I was uncertain at first, but after a few mishaps, I realized that Jeff was right. I invited him to play that role for me. I often introduced him to new team members as my Diplomacy Checker. This served two purposes: a) it honored Jeff's amazing abilities, and b) it informed the newcomers that I was not diplomatic. This is a good survival strategy.

Performance Strategy vs. Survival Strategy

I recommend this rule of thumb with my clients: Invest 80% of your resources in your performance strategy, which is your top 10-12 dominant strengths; and invest 20% in your survival strategy to manage your bottom 5-6 strengths. Don't confuse a performance strategy with a survival strategy. They each have a place in our success arsenal, but one is far more important than the other. Why?

When you invest in your strengths and develop them with intent, guess what you get? Excellence. When you invest in your weaknesses and develop them with intent, guess what you get? Average.

When you invest in your strengths and develop them with intent, guess what you get? Excellence. When you invest in your weaknesses and develop them with intent, guess what you get? Average.

This is actually good news. We get to choose between excellence and average. Average doesn't pay very well emotionally, physically, spiritually, or monetarily. What manager proclaims, "We need an average team!" No. They say, "We need a high performing team!" The surest path to high performance is to understand, develop and utilize your employees' strengths.

Remember my Harmony example above? Send me to diplomacy school, and I will become slightly more diplomatic. However, I will never be as skillful in finding common ground as Jeff is. Not even close. He does it like breathing. I labor away and barely earn a "C" grade. For me, diplomacy training is a survival strategy that feels like reform school. For Jeff, diplomacy school is a performance strategy that feels like perform school. Same class, two different tactics for people with vastly different StrengthsFinder profiles.

On the other hand, if I were to spend that same energy at brainstorming school, investing in my top three strengths, which are Ideation, Strategic and Learner, I would be higher performing, happier, and more engaged. I would drive more value for my clients and colleagues. I would maximize my contributions to the team. Attending brainstorming training feels like perform school and is a viable success strategy for me.

I'll brainstorm with Jeff, and he can be my diplomat. We'll both operate within our sweet spot, our strengths zone. We can trust one another and believe in our abilities because they are founded in our natural talents. We can refuse to let another fail.

Choose excellence over average by investing a majority of our precious resources in our performance strategy. In doing so, we will find success and effectiveness. We will be better equipped to face the challenges of life.

There. Now that we have the important weakness discussion out of the way, let us get back to exploring Coach's performance toolkit. This is one of my favorite things to do as a leadership and team consultant – explore the greatness of other people.

Coach has a lot going for him with his top dominant strengths. My observations include:

- His top 12 strengths are quite evenly divided between Influencing (four strengths), Executing (three strengths), and Relating (three strengths). His profile had two thinking strengths, Analytical and Learner. I was reminded of his remark that he wanted to know everything about my strengths-based success philosophy. That sure sounds like Learner. His Individualization would drive his thirst for knowledge about the unique traits of each person.

- I was surprised to see Competition come in at #22. This indicates that Coach does not hate losing as much as his players with Competition in their top five StrengthsFinder profiles hate it.
- With Significance at #12 and Responsibility at #2, Coach is driven to make an impact and help the players on his team become the very best men they can be. His StrengthsFinder results supported the conversations we had shared about why he chose to coach high school versus professional hockey. He is not in it for the win; he is in it to develop leaders and guide them to success. For Coach, this is simply the right thing to do.
- With Command at #5 and Self-Assurance at #8, Coach takes charge with ease and pursues decisions with complete confidence. I know from experience that this powerful combination of Command and Self-Assurance might look like arrogance to others. This misinterpretation is often the consequence of filtering the behaviors of others through the lens of our own strengths. It may also be the result of strengths envy. Both are mistakes and should be avoided.

I summarized Coach's performance toolkit and its impact.

Summarizing Coach's Performance Toolkit

	Influencing (Horse-power & Energy)	Executing (Task Orientation)	Relationship-Building (Human Glue)	Thinking (Navigating & Solving)
Dominant Strengths	Activator + Command + Self-Assurance + Significance =	Responsibility + Belief + Achiever =	Individualization + Relator + Connectedness =	Learner + Analytical =
Resulting Outcome of Dominant Strengths	Achieve impact and results through swift, confident leadership	Personally productive, value-based and responsible execution	Understand what makes each person tick, easily sees connections between people, and has a tight circle of trusted, close friends.	Navigate problems by weighing facts/data over emotions, with a deep commitment to learning to achieve excellence

Summing the horizontal impact statements into one paragraph, I crafted a personalized strengths profile:

When Coach Weidenbach leverages his strengths, he is a confident leader who executes tasks with high standards and speed. He motivates players by learning and appreciating their unique abilities, connects their strengths to their role, and analyzes how each can align and contribute to the success of the team. Coach Weidenbach builds a high-trust environment, resulting in relationships that last long after the players graduate.

I like to be really prepared when I meet clients to talk about their StrengthsFinder profile, which is why I go through the steps above. Now there was nothing left but to have a deep dive conversation with Coach. That is where the real learning occurs on both sides.

Deep Dive Strengths Conversation

I arrived at the ice arena promptly at 8:00 am. I lugged all my coaching materials into Coach's office and sat in a chair adjacent to his desk.

"This is going to be the most fun EVER!" I announced.

"I can't wait," replied Coach, in his typically dry tone.

"Any questions before we begin?" He told me he didn't have any.

"Okay, let's get started," I replied, eagerly rubbing my hands together. I was full of energy because I was doing what I do best – helping talented people understand their strengths and determine how to better leverage them in their roles.

I noticed Coach's StrengthsFinder Insight Guide sitting on his desk. "I see you highlighted key statements in your Insight Report."

"I did," said Coach. "There's some good stuff in here."

We walked through the customized report for Coach's top five strengths, starting with his first strength, Individualization. Coach read the highlighted statements aloud.

Coach's Individualization description made note of his ability to go to great lengths to understand why things happen. Once discoveries are made, the report described how Coach has the gift of streamlining complex information so that it is easily understood by others. It also identified his ability to set up systems for repeatable tasks. Coach read lines about his patience being put to the test by people who do not follow his program, fail to meet deadlines, waste money, or deliver in a shoddy or incomplete fashion. These specific patterns of excellence were evident in Coach's leadership of the team and in his ability to transfer knowledge of the intricacies of drills, systems, and strategies. There was also a quote regarding Coach's talent for helping a team discover ways to perform together in a way they had never previously considered.

"Wow," I said, "doesn't that exactly describe what you did with the hockey team and the StrengthsFinder information? You used it to help them perform together in a way they had never done before."

He agreed. We both marveled at the accuracy of the information and acknowledged how hard it would be to describe, in such rich detail, his unique value proposition associated with the powerful strength of Individualization.

We continued the journey of exploring Coach's report. His Responsibility strength description spoke about honoring commitments and speaking in a forthright manner. I asked Coach for an example of that behavior because I know straight talk can be viewed by some as harsh or unkind, especially if kids are involved.

"Well, when I have a guy who has a terrible slap shot, I tell him it is terrible. However, I also tell him that we can fix it, and I will help him."

This was a good example, because such conversations can go one of two ways.

First of all, the player can hear the truth, absorb it, and perhaps even feel a sense of relief. He probably knows his slap shot is not as good as it needs to be. Along comes Coach, validating the player's understanding, but also saying, "I can help." If the young man listens and practices, he is very likely to improve. Problem solved.

Of course, everything that Coach did with his team can be related to business. Coach's example helps us understand that investing in the human system by conversing frequently and honestly with the people who work for you is a manager's job. Those who do it, and do it well, are beloved by their employees. It is a powerful performance accelerator because we all want to be as effective as possible. Straight talk followed by support, helps us get there.

Investing in the human system by conversing frequently and honestly with the people who work for you is a manager's job.

However, there are very few managers in the business world like Coach Weidenbach. Many are walking around on egg shells, hoping their employees can decode a very subtle or soft suggestion for how to improve. One can be both direct and kind in their feedback. Many others simply do not have time to provide feedback because they are running like hamsters on a wheel, focused on execution and metrics. Others do not have the talent or experience to do it well, so they avoid it. This is a common issue in the workplace, and it hinders the performance of individuals and teams. Other factors can also contribute to the problem.

Some managers have teams that are too large or are globally dispersed, making direct conversation difficult. I once had a manager who had 70 employees reporting to her. We had quarterly team meetings that were held via conference phone. She was 600 miles away, even though her entire team was located in another city. We did not have one-on-one conversations unless there was a customer problem or the calendar indicated that it was time for our annual performance review. She was not present to see how well or how poorly we were doing, so feedback on how to improve was impossible. As you might imagine, morale and engagement was pretty low. The sad part about this scenario is that this problem is preventable.

What would our world have been like had the manager scheduled monthly discussions with us to understand what we were doing, and how the customer felt about it? With 70 employees, she could conduct three or four 30-minute employee conversations a day, and repeat that monthly. Many organizations would say that it is the employee's responsibility to schedule time with their manager. Okay, I will accept 50% of the responsibility for not setting those up. However, every single quarterly team phone call began with a long, dramatic story about how busy she was. When she finally got around to asking what was going on with us, the oxygen had been sucked from the room and very few employees responded with anything of substance. I do not believe she intended to shut us down. I do not believe she tried to be a bad manager. She just did not know what to do differently. The awkwardness of the calls made it even more difficult to ask her for one-on-one time. We did not have direct conversations.

On the other hand, in the world of high school hockey, the consequences of a direct conversation with a young hockey player might head in the other direction. The player might be hurt by direct conversation about his or her talents. There are two parts of coaching high school sports – the players and the parents. Like it or not, players come with parents. If Billy went home and complained, "Coach says I have a terrible slap shot!" well, let's just say there are parents who may be offended. That is unfortunate, because high school is not the last time a young adult will be criticized. It happens in the workplace all the time – most often without supporting information on how to improve. Therefore, learning to respond well to criticism is an important life and business skill. Thick skin is useful in the workplace.

Learning to respond well to criticism is an important life and business skill. Thick skin is useful in the workplace.

When an athlete is provided feedback for improvement that may be a hard pill to swallow, parents have two choices. One, parents can intervene on the player's behalf. (If you think this is a good idea, read Mike Matheny's book called the *Matheny Manifesto.* He makes a strong case for why this is not a wise tactic.) Two, parents can support the student on the difficult journey, encouraging him to practice and play hard, and demonstrate that they love him no matter what. Unless someone's safety is at risk, adopting a behind-the-scenes approach is often more effective.

Another line in Coach's Responsibility strength description talked about the consequence of his honesty. It helped people believe in themselves. If the parents intervene, the player may not get the chance to truly believe in himself. Wouldn't it be a shame if a young man or woman was robbed of that gift by a well-intentioned parent?

Coach had additional content in his Activator & Command strength descriptions that reinforced his bent towards honest conversation. It described him as helping people reach goals though direct orders, calling out slackers, or driving the performance of people who are not passing muster. It went on to talk about these conversations being flavored with enthusiasm for what is possible, which helps people achieve goals they may have believed were out of reach. Coach Weidenbach's ability to lead with swift action and understanding of talent helps his team play with more energy and confidence. It also acknowledged that such power requires regulation so that his high-octane approach would not intimidate others. This last statement could be more applicable in the world of business, but one can see how it might benefit parents who are eager to support their children.

Coach Weidenbach's ability to lead with swift action and understanding of talent helps his team play with more energy and confidence. It also acknowledged that such power requires regulation, so that his high-octane approach would not intimidate others.

His Relator strength could help temper that forcefulness, and his report spoke about building and sustaining bonds with people who have shared their goals and who often come to him for advice. I realized that I was rapidly becoming a member of that camp. Frankly, that felt great. He always gave me a straight answer, no sugar coating. It was said without malice, and I did not feel stupid. I decided to acknowledge it right then and there.

I reminded him that when I had tossed out the idea of approaching the new head coach of the Detroit Red Wings and sharing our program with him, he had given me a straight answer about the importance of timing. Coach said that the new leader was likely dealing with issues that would require his immediate attention.

"Right," replied Coach. "For this sort of thing, timing is everything. If the timing is wrong, then they will reject it."

"We want them to say 'Yes!'" I said, with a smile.

"We do," agreed Coach.

"So, direct conversation is always best?"

Coach hesitated. "It's what I do best," he slowly replied. "It's why I don't work with young kids. I'm not a warm, fuzzy guy. I'm demanding. My approach works for older kids who are truly interested in greatness, can take straight, hard talk, and will put in the effort required. It's a commitment that few young kids can make."

"They have to want to be here."

"Yes," said Coach. "But, I also know the importance of the warm, fuzzy stuff. That's why I have Coach Ronayne. He's great at that. When I've been hard on someone, I'll tell Coach Ronayne to go give them a hug. I know they need it, but I'm not great at doing it. Coach Ronayne is great at it."

"When I've been hard on someone, I'll tell Coach Ronayne to go give them a hug. I know they need it, but I'm not great at doing it. Coach Ronayne is great at it."

This was a perfect example of Coach leveraging his Individualization strength and building a success partnership. Notice that Coach does not imply that players do not need kindness and encouragement. Coach knows they need that. He also knows that delivering it is not his forte. He gives what he gives well and empowers others to provide what he does not give well. Notice also that Coach does not ignore his weaknesses; he effectively manages them. We reach strengths maturity when our strengths are understood, embraced, and well regulated. We reach weakness maturity when our weaknesses are understood, embraced, and well-regulated. We must do both to reach our full potential as people.

Coached glanced down his strengths profile and asked, "What is Connectedness?"

"Connectedness is someone who connects people to one another. You can see that Joe needs to meet Mary, because they have something in common. It happens naturally, like breathing."

"Oh yeah, I do that," agreed Coach. "I'll be on a fishing trip and meet someone, hear what they do for a living, and then I'll say, 'Oh, you need to meet this other guy I know. You're in the same business.'"

It was apparent that Coach consistently formed human glue between two people who did not previously know one another. That is the power of Connectedness. Because both parties knew Coach well, they accept the connection without question. People high in Connectedness often believe that everything happens for a reason. Coach simply sees connections that are not obvious to others, and then he builds a bridge so that all parties can benefit from each other.

"It's interesting that you have Connectedness and Individualization in your top 10," I said.

"Why so?"

"Connectedness is seeing the forest, and Individualization is seeing the trees."

Coach returned to his strengths profile. "Here's something I don't believe."

"What's that?"

"Positivity. Number 30 out 34! I am the most positive guy I know!"

I thought for a moment about my friends who have Positivity in their performance toolkit, and Coach did not behave like them at all. Knowing Coach, I knew he would need proof. I realized that he had already provided an excellent example.

"Coach, remember when you told me that you speak plainly when a kid has a bad slap shot?"

"Yeah…"

"You don't go out there and say, 'Oh, Honey! Don't worry that you didn't come close to the net! You'll get it next time!'"

Coach looked mortified. "I would never say that!"

"Right. You don't have Positivity. And Developer is right next to Positivity at #29. These are lesser strengths for you. They require more time, energy, and concentration for you to access. Remember you said you don't like to work with young kids? You have to slowly develop young kids. Teach them their ABCs before they read, and every inch forward is celebrated like it is a mile. That is the strength of Developer. You don't have that."

Coach agreed.

"It doesn't mean you aren't of a positive frame of mind," I added, wanting to clarify the point. "It means that you don't lead with it. For you, positive things happen when you do the right thing, work hard, and be a Navy SEAL, not regular Navy. In the StrengthsFinder world, Positivity often looks like someone who is brimming with optimism."

Coach continued to study his list of 34 strengths. I gave him a few moments, because I am fully aware that the strengths-based journey is full of unexpected vistas, detours, and even some backtracking. It takes time, and there are no short cuts. After a while, he nodded, and I could see we were ready to continue.

"Belief is #6 for you," I observed, "Belief is your strong value system – you know what you believe in – and it drives what you do and how you do it. Achiever at #7 is personal stamina. You must be productive every day. Self-Assurance at #8 is simply another word for confidence. It's an influencing strength because teams and peers will follow confident people."

Coach Weidenbach reeked of confidence, from his ramrod straight posture to his intense gaze to his walk that has a bit of pop to it. There were all kinds of body language signs that supported this strength. He had honed his confidence with the experience associated with a long, successful coaching career, which made his Self-Assurance strength even stronger.

We moved on to Coach's most dominant thinking strengths, Learner and Analytical.

"Yeah," agreed Coach. "I like data."

"Can you give me an example?"

"Well, for one thing, I weigh the guys every day."

"Every day?" I asked incredulously.

"Twice."

"Twice??"

"Every day, twice. I weigh them before and after practice. The reason is this: if a player weighs less today than yesterday, then he isn't hydrated. If he isn't hydrated, then he doesn't think well. If he doesn't think well, he's not going to succeed in school. Plus, he'll drag on the ice. I weigh the guys so they stay hydrated. They will be more successful at everything if they stay hydrated. We track it on a chart."

I stared at Coach, wondering what kind of talent management phenomena I was looking at. Who does these things, especially in high school sports? I found myself searching for words to adequately describe my admiration for him and then asked if he had considered sharing his methods with other coaches.

"I've shared all my ideas, techniques. But the reality is that very few high school coaches are willing to do what I do."

"Oh sure," said Coach. "I've done that. I've shared all my ideas, techniques. But the reality is that very few high school coaches are willing to do what I do."

I could believe that. I also believed that the same statement could be made for leaders in business.

Coach had repeatedly talked about the importance of discipline in his work, and I asked if he had an example of where he had applied that strength.

"For sure," said Coach.

"Can you give me an example?"

"We've got one right here."

I looked at him, puzzled. "Where?"

"Right here," he said, tapping a cup on his desk.

There were three cups. One had pencils in it. One had highlighters in it. One had ink pens in it. They were entirely uniform in how they were placed in the cups. I looked back at Coach, wondering where the conversation was headed.

"See how all the ink pens are placed with the ball point down?"

I nodded.

"One day, I noticed that one of my pens was ball point up and I knew somebody had been in my office. I questioned one of my coaches because I knew he was the culprit. He confessed. Then we had a conversation about the importance of putting the pens with the ball point facing downward."

My attempts to stifle a rising chuckle were largely unsuccessful. He continued, unfazed.

"I said to him, 'Look, you've got an MBA from Michigan, and someday, you're going to be working with a client, and that client is going to be ready to sign a huge contract that would make you a lot of money, and because you didn't store your ball point pens with the ball point down, there won't be any ink left in it, and they won't be able to sign. You'll lose the deal.'"

Coach spoke with the conviction of someone who believes deeply that a disaster would be avoided by proper pen management. By the time he was done, I was doubled over in laughter.

Coach nodded with all the confidence in the world, and added, "I've got another example."

"I don't know if I can handle another example," I teased.

"There's no fighting on my hockey team."

That stopped me in my tracks. If you know anything about hockey, you know that, at least in the National Hockey League, fighting is associated with honor.

Coach explained. "I tell my kids this: 'I don't care if your life is in danger. I don't care if there is a gun pointed at your head. I don't care if somebody is about to step on your neck with their skate. There is no fighting on my team.'"

I stared at him in disbelief.

He wasn't done. "There hasn't been a kid on any team of mine in a fight since 1993."

I calculated the numbers inside my head. Twenty-two years.

"Now," said Coach, "I know that if there is a terrible situation like I described, the kids will defend themselves. A person can't help it, we all have reflexes. But, on my team, on my ice, on my bench – no fighting."

In that moment, I realized I was learning more from Coach than he was learning from me. His depth of understanding and commitment to his craft rivaled that of great musicians or writers or scientists. He knew who he was, and he was unwavering in his approach to success. It was a great lesson about the power of self-awareness, reflective learning, and the results possible when one dedicated themselves to their purpose.

"I want the boys to be great men," said Coach. "Having an impact on their lives and helping them become the best person and hockey player they can be, means more to me than winning."

"Well, Coach, I think that is a perfect lead-in to your # 12 strength, Significance," I said. "Significance is the deep desire to make an impact, to leave a visible dent in the universe." I looked at Coach with particular meaning. If he wasn't the epitome of Significance, I don't know who was.

"I want the boys to be great men," said Coach. "Having an impact on their lives and helping them become the best person and hockey player they can be, means more to me than winning."

I was stricken and touched by this statement. It was such an emotional and heavy sentiment, especially coming from a man. A man who coached a boy's varsity team. A hockey team. From anyone else, his words may have sounded soft. But, we both knew he wasn't soft. He cared immensely about the young men on his team, probably more than they knew.

Thinking back to what makes a great manager in the workplace, Coach was modeling excellent leadership behavior. He judged his success based on how much he was able to give to the team so that they were successful. He valued the importance of developing great leaders over awards or numbers in a win/loss column.

I observed that many want to help build men of character, but that Coach's process was different from most.

"That's probably true," said Coach. "I do it for the kids. I love what they learned this year, and I think they'll be more successful in life. I don't need another state championship," he declared, in a calm, deliberative tone. "I don't coach to win another trophy. I do this for the kids and their parents. The parents love their kids more than anything in the world. When their kids bleed, their parents bleed with them."

He paused for a moment, collecting his thoughts, and then described the difficult job of being a parent. "It shows up most in the losses. The kids get over a tough loss in a week, maybe a little longer. As the maestro, I struggle with it longer. I run through scenarios in my mind – we might have done this, we might have done that. But parents," Coach said, shaking his head, "it takes them forever to get over it. It affects them more because they want so much for their kids. So, I do it for those reasons."

His motivations ran deeper than the trophy experience. They were founded in the human experience.

I mused over his remarks, realizing that the motivators for Coach were connected to impacting the lives of kids and parents in a positive manner. He wants to win, and he wants the boys to develop, which is why they work so hard and do things the right way. But Coach had just won his ninth state championship since 2000. He had been there and done that. Therefore, his motivations ran deeper than the trophy experience. They were founded in the human experience. He enjoyed pulling the best out of each boy, finding a contributing role for them and helping them feel connected to the mission and to the success of the team. He was building great men. In his own firm but caring way, Coach was nourishing character, confidence, and connections. I was pretty certain those connections were the kind that lasted a lifetime.

Suddenly, I was struck by a thought. There was another important avenue to explore. I understood my journey. I had explored Coach Weidenbach's journey. What about the players' journeys?

"Hey, Coach, I have an idea," I exclaimed, excitement welling up inside me. "What do you think about me interviewing some of the boys?"

"I think that would be interesting," replied Coach matter-of-factly.

And with that one sentence, I was on to yet another mission. What did the boys see?

PART 3: WHAT THE BOYS SAW

Chapter 11:
Mason Schultz – The Energy Guy

"You've done it before and you can do it now. See the positive possibilities. Redirect the substantial energy of your frustration and turn it into positive, effective, unstoppable determination."

Ralph Marston

* * *

Executing Strengths (Get it done!)	Relating Strengths (Human Glue)	Thinking Strengths (Navigators)	Influencing Strengths (Energy to Move People)	Roles on Team
Restorative (solve prob-lems)	Includer (social inclusion)	Strategic (connect dots)	Communication (gift of gab)	First Line Forward
			Woo (social courage)	Energy Guy

I was excited to have a deep conversation with a player to learn firsthand what the six-week journey was like. Coach and I certainly had a plan, but the young men had to execute the plan, and they would view the experience through the lens of their strengths. As such, the team journey would be experienced differently by each player.

Before I dialed the phone to speak to Mason Schultz, I looked at what Coach had asked of him, his role on the team both on the ice and off, and his top five strengths.

Coach had put Mason in the Energy Guy category, which makes sense with two Influencing (red) strengths. Glancing at his top five StrengthsFinder strengths, I saw that Mason could help keep the team engaged and encouraged. This would be a valuable contribution to the team, on and off the ice.

The strengths of Woo and Communication gave Mason social courage and the gift of easy conversation. It was no big deal for him to meet and talk to strangers. During and after the games, I had observed him chatting it up with the referees. He was the first person to speak to me in the locker room when I first met the team. There was a social ease about Mason. He also had Restorative – he would feel satisfied when he helped solve a problem. With Includer, it would be natural for him to be a team player, focused on leaving no one behind. I had seen his Includer in action when he offered to share his snacks with others in the room during our workshop. And finally, Mason had the thinking strength of Strategic. Give him a destination, and he could connect the dots and build the best path to get there. Looking at his strengths combination, I knew my conversation with Mason would be easy and fun.

I dialed the phone. Mason answered, and we chatted for a moment. He told me about his work as a summer intern for GOJO Industries, the makers of PURELL instant hand sanitizer.

I asked Mason what his job was.

"I am working in the e-commerce and consumer division. It's a lot of online market research. I focus on competition pricing, as well as where we stand. We want to ensure we're doing the right things to make sure that our sales increase. 70% of business now is e-commerce. Everyone orders online through a warehouse, so we're trying to be as efficient as possible," explained Mason.

When I looked at my summer internship, I also reviewed my strengths to make sure that I did something that fits me well, rather than take a role where I might not be as strong."

"Wow, that sounds interesting," I said. "Are you using your strengths in your new role?" I couldn't help myself. While I know that not everyone remains lodged in the strengths-based success world as I do, I am compelled to remind people that they do have a performance toolkit.

"Actually, yeah, I am," said Mason. "I knew that when we did it (the StrengthsFinder exercise) I could also take the information to the business world. When I looked at my summer internship, I also reviewed my strengths to make sure that I did something that fits me well, rather than take a role where I might not be as strong."

I praised him for that decision. Mason shared his excitement for heading to Miami University in Oxford, Ohio in August. He also stated that he planned to use his strengths forever. I chuckled and told Mason that he had permission to contact me directly if he had any questions about his strengths during that forever time period. Then we dove into the hockey team conversation. I asked him if he had any comments regarding the journey of the hockey team before and after we focused on the team's strengths.

Mason paused for a moment. "Actually, I don't have comments about it, it's more praise for it. Once we finally captured our thoughts about what we wanted out of the team, things went so much better. Everyone said they wanted success, but until we got that statement pinpointed as to what we were going to do to succeed, I don't think anyone was on the same page. Then, we created the statement and we were able to say, 'That's our success statement, and here is what we are all going to do to win the state championship.' It helped us focus our energy."

Had the team's energy been channeled differently in the past?

Mason spoke about how knowing their strengths had provided direction. "Knowing our strengths went hand-in-hand with knowing what you want out of them. Identifying our success statement, then looking at our strengths, we could each say, 'Strength X can help me achieve our main goal, and this is how I'm going to use it.' Without the success statement, it wouldn't have been as effective."

I was pleased to hear this. Mason's remarks confirmed my belief that knowing what success looks like before asking a team to invest in their strengths is an important milestone in the journey. Otherwise, we have a high-powered motor with no rudder, and this undermines the effectiveness of the program. The success statement provides direction.

Unfortunately, getting business organizations to complete this step is a challenge, and that increases the difficulty of building a winning team. At the root of the problem is most business workgroups are focused on getting their work done, and they overlook the opportunity to maximize their success by beginning with the why. Why are we doing this? What does success look like? Can we measure it? Where will we land? Does how we get there matter? The Cranbrook hockey team began by building the success statement, and it served them well.

The strengths-based success journey is one of peeling back the onion. Questions over time are the norm, just as they are when learning any other subject. I asked Mason if he had any questions or thoughts about his top five strengths.

Mason confessed that he had struggled with being one of the rainbow people. Mason was one of the few people on the team who had one strength in each category, with a second influencing strength. I recalled him asking about it in the workshop. Most people are flavored in one or two categories of strengths. They might lean towards building relationships or executing. Mason had a profile that extended across all four categories.

Mason shared his struggle with knowing what strength to focus on. "For me, it was both a good thing and a bad thing," he said. "It was good in that I could contribute in multiple ways. I could bring human glue. I could bring energy. I could help execute. At the same time, being a little bit of everything, it almost kept me from focusing on one certain strength."

That made sense. If you were being asked to focus on a strength to help the team win, it might be difficult to pick only one when you could choose from each of the four categories.

"Because I had one of everything, I couldn't naturally lean one way or another," he added. "I had a hand and foot in each basket. I wasn't sure what to do until Coach gave us guidance."

I made a mental note to be sure we had multiple meetings with next year's team. The reality is that Mason could wear multiple hats, and Coach and I could have helped Mason be a jack-of-all-trades on the team. If he saw someone feeling down or left out, he should act (Includer). If he had a chance to encourage them, he should act (Woo, Communication). If he saw a problem, or someone on the team came to him with a problem, he should act (Restorative, Strategic). To maximize his contributions, we could have given him permission to do those things. Next year, we would do better.

Humans are messy. Teams are messy. Life is complicated. Give guidance, but also empower them to act on their own.

"What did Coach ask you to do?" This was an important question because while Coach had a clear role for each person, each player also had to accept the mantle and adapt as required. It is not like math, where 1 plus 1 always equals 2. Humans are messy. Teams are messy. Life is complicated. Give guidance, but also empower players and teams to act on their own.

"Coach definitely put me in with the Energy Guys, and he talked about my Woo," replied Mason.

Mason was the only guy on the team with Woo, and that talent would be amped up with the addition of Communication and Includer. It was a role where Mason could add a lot of value.

"What did you do differently once you knew your role?" I asked.

"Once I was made aware that I was an energy guy, I focused on that," he replied. "I focused on succeeding in that rather than be a little bit of everything with my other strengths. I put all my focus on being an energy guy."

I wondered what that meant to Mason and asked if it was an internal or external experience for him.

Mason paused, considering the difference between the two. "Well, I think it was more internal. I used it to give more energy to everything. I had more energy to pick up the play, to check someone, or to give energy on the bench. I wasn't extremely vocal about it. There were other guys on the team with Command, etc. I let them be the verbal and vocal leaders. I did it my own way."

Clearly, he felt empowered by Coach to leverage the strengths in a manner that was most natural for Mason. That is a critical success factor in the process because it delivers lasting and repeatable results.

"How did it feel to have a role to live up to?"

"It did feel good to have that goal and focus. It was amazing to have something that you know that if you did this, you could contribute to the team."

This is an important point. Research indicates that when people know what is expected of them in their role, they are more engaged and higher performing.

Mason knew what was expected of him, which relieved him of the burden of figuring it out himself, and hoping his choices would make a difference. Hope is not a strategy. Coach's guidance gave Mason the confidence he needed, and because he was using his natural strengths, he knew he could deliver on the expectations.

Coach's guidance gave Mason the confidence he needed, and because he was using his natural strengths, he knew he could deliver on the expectations.

I wanted to turn the conversation to others on the team and asked him how he felt about learning the strengths of the other players.

"It was great," responded Mason, without hesitation. "Once we all knew our strengths, we were able to pinpoint what we could do to help the team do better. There were people who were trying to be leaders or be motivational because they thought it was the right thing to do, but it wasn't easy or natural for them. Once they got their results, they focused on what they do better, like long-term vision or human glue. It was, I don't want to say, shocking, but in a way, eye opening. For some of them, once they learned their strengths, they backed out of their old role and assumed the new one."

How interesting! Imagine being a high school hockey player and thinking that you must do anything you could to help the team win, even if it is not natural for you. I had seen the same thing in the workplace. It drives well-intentioned, but unnatural, behavior. Scream at a turtle to run faster, and neither the screamer nor the turtle will be satisfied by the results. But, because they do not know what else to do, they just keep doing it.

Scream at a turtle to run faster, and neither the screamer nor the turtle will be satisfied by the results.

I wanted to hear more about it from Mason. "So, you had observed people trying their best to do something they can't naturally do well?"

"Right. And it didn't work," he said. "Once we got that out of the way, and people settled into their role to help achieve our overall success goals, I think we flourished."

His word choice was interesting and important. Don't we want our corporate teams to flourish? What about our volunteer teams? Of course we do. I asked for more detail.

Mason spoke about the intensity gained by investing in all the strengths on the team. "We had a team meeting and shared which strength we were going to relate to hockey," he explained. "I loved it. It brought another level (of intensity) to the StrengthsFinder. It took it even deeper because we put into words what we could do. Everybody heard it. Then, everybody succeeded in their goal of playing to their own strengths and developing their own role on the team."

I again felt a sense of deep admiration for Coach Weidenbach. Imagine what a corporation could do if they had leaders and managers like Coach Weidenbach who were willing to invest in the strengths of all the talent in the organization – and ask them to bring them to bear to solve business problems. It is not an easy journey, but it is a worthy and fruitful one.

"Plus, there was that 'I refuse to let you fail!' exercise," he added.

My ears perked up.

"Once everyone bought in that we are a team," he explained, "and that we could use our strengths to succeed together or fail together, that was huge."

I asked him how it was huge.

"Well, not to throw anyone under the bus," said Mason, hesitating slightly, "but there were some guys on the team who were problematic earlier in the year. Once everyone realized that we are all in this together, everybody picked up the slack of, 'Well, I'm just doing my part and that's it.' If there were people who wanted to back off and be detrimental to the team, it was our job to bring them in. Succeed together, fail together. We said, 'I refuse to let you fail,' so we are in this together."

I could hear Mason's Restorative, Woo and Includer strengths in his statement. He was not about to let somebody be problematic by distancing themselves. He would take action and influence them to make a different choice so that they were included in the success plan. I wondered if Mason realized what a nice combination of strengths that was and how well they could serve him over his lifetime. And, best of all, he did it like breathing.

I asked Mason how long he had played for Coach Weidenbach and whether there were any particular lessons that stood out in his mind.

Mason shared that he had played on the Cranbrook varsity hockey team for three years. In that time, the values instilled in them by Coach were the main takeaway he'd gained. He said they made him a better human being, and then dug deeper into what those values were. "Coach asks guys to work their hardest and respect one another. He is really creating better men rather than just better hockey players."

I asked Mason if that goal of becoming better men was something the players appreciated when they started the journey of playing for Coach Weidenbach.

"No," he laughed. "I definitely grew into it. At the beginning, I thought he made us do some things that were very mundane and unrelated to hockey. But, what Coach was really doing was helping us take things to the next level."

I liked that. Next level is a description of relentless forward progress resulting in maximized effort, energy, and results.

Mason had more to say about the topic. "For Coach, everything is next level. Here's the bar set by normal high school students and normal high school hockey players. We are Cranbrook. We expect more out of you, and we're going to get more out of you. Now that I'm back in Ohio," Mason reflected, "I can see that my experience was completely next level in every sense of the word."

"For Coach, everything is next level. Here's the bar set by normal high school students and normal high school hockey players. We are Cranbrook. We expect more out of you and we're going to get more out of you."

I asked him to tell me more about that.

"I've been comparing my experiences with my friends in Ohio who didn't go to Cranbrook," explained Mason. "When I say 'next level,' I am speaking about the experiences I had and the standards I was held to at Cranbrook."

"Academic or hockey standards?"

"Both. Cranbrook has high standards in academics. They expect more – you're there for an excellent higher education. Coach takes that to another level. On Coach's hockey team, you're held to even higher standards in almost every way."

We agreed it was a marvelous life lesson to receive. I knew we were running short on time, so I thanked Mason for the insightful interview and for making the effort to speak with me. He expressed his gratitude for the work I had done with the team.

It was really satisfying for me to hear about our journey from the point of view of a player. I was delighted that Mason had bundled up his strengths-based knowledge and leveraged it in his summer job. It was also rewarding to hear Mason echo Coach's own words and purpose. There was a monumental business lesson in Coach's approach to leading the team. What he wanted the players to experience was aligned with their reality. He wanted them to be great men. They learned what that meant for each one of them and started down the lifelong journey to that end. This is an important success factor because it is very difficult to form a strong connection between what the leader wants the follower to experience and what the follower actually does experience.

In the corporate world, one of the immense challenges facing leaders and managers is that the way they experience the workplace is completely different from how their employees experience the workplace. There can be a massive disconnect between what is said and observed at the top and what is felt at the bottom. Without malice or intent, there can be a "Let them eat cake!" situation, with executives living in an ivory tower and employees feeling undervalued and undernourished in their role. Organizations have to work relentlessly to be sure that the gap is minimized. This requires time and resources, which may be scarce to begin with. It also requires that the folks at the top understand and agree that the employee experience gap exists. Denial must be defeated because that gap will kill the success of an organization.

There can be a massive disconnect between what is said and observed at the top and what is felt at the bottom. Without malice or intent, there can be a "Let them eat cake!" situation, with executives living in an ivory tower and employees feeling undervalued and undernourished in their role.

Defeating denial is not for the faint of heart. It takes someone with a lot of courage to speak the truth to leaders. Hearing the truth about the realities of the workplace can be disruptive and annoying to company executives. That leads us full circle back to the wild duck discussion. The outcome of an attempt to defeat denial is either gratitude or punishment for the disruptor. It is a pivotal moment.

If gratitude is shown to the disruptor, more disruptors will have the courage and confidence to help improve the company. Disruptors will flock to the corporate leadership with ideas on how to make the organization more successful and effective. Momentum is built and generates compounded interest.

If punishment is the outcome, it is bad news for all involved. That is basically what happened to me when my strengths-based success movement was flattened inside The Company. After it was shut down, the whisper campaign began. All the people connected to the movement (and remember, we had over 6,000 people sign up for one of our events) were concerned and dismayed. Word spread like a virus in all directions: Disruptors suffer capital punishment. The other disruptors who had connected with me – some of whom had great ideas of their own about how to improve the workplace and had the will to implement them – were taught that it was not worth it. So they shrugged their shoulders and said, "Never mind." How many burgeoning business benefits were lost because one wild duck was shot?

Missed opportunities to defeat denial about the employee experience are difficult to measure in dollars and cents. The human system is undermined, even if it appears that the formal system is flourishing. Morale drops off a cliff, prospects and competitive advantages slowly sink under the weight of fear, and the organization's soul dries up like a dead raisin. Momentum evaporates. People disengage from the company and from one another. They do their work – and nothing more.

Attacking this problem is a worthy endeavor because when it is minimized, and the talent is valued and aligned behind what success looks like, teams are high performing and happy. The human system and the formal system flourish equally and work in harmony. Everyone is having the same experience at the top and at the bottom of the pyramid, which not only feels hopeful and stable but also builds trust. People perform well in hopeful, stable, and trusting environments. Sometimes they even win state championships.

Attacking this problem is a worthy endeavor because when it is minimized, and the talent is valued and aligned behind what success looks like, teams are high performing and happy.

Chapter 12: Jack Blumberg – The Learner

"I'm still learning."

Michelangelo (at age 88)

* * *

Executing Strengths (Get it done!)	Relating Strengths (Human Glue)	Thinking Strengths (Navigators)	Influencing Strengths (Energy to Move People)	Roles on Team
Achiever (personal productivity)		Learner (loves to learn, enjoys new environments)	Command (comfortable taking charge)	First Line Defense
			Competition (hates to lose)	Energy, Leadership, Inspire Followers
			Activator (sense of urgency)	Observe attack points on the opposition, and prevent germs from spreading

I was excited to speak with Jack Blumberg for a couple of reasons. When I was in the locker room speaking to the boys about defining success, I recalled observing a very serious looking young man studying me. I glanced at the name above his locker – Blumberg. He listened intently, and I wondered what he was thinking. I also remembered that he played well in the semi-final game, earning a hat trick. He was also the only person with the Learner strength on the team, which, statistically speaking, was completely off the charts. There should have been seven players in the room with Learner in their top five strengths profile.

We texted one another and arranged to speak. Once we connected via phone, I asked him what he was up to for the summer.

"Actually, I'm headed to Canada for hockey camp," Jack said.

"Really! Where are you going?"

"It's near Ottawa."

"Are you there all summer?"

"No, just for three days. I'm a little nervous because my goal is to play Junior Hockey. This is where they pick the teams."

"Oh my goodness," I said. "No wonder you are nervous. How does it work?"

He explained that players must be between 16 and 20 years old. Junior Hockey, he said, is the feeder to the farm systems for the National Hockey League.

I wondered how that might impact his plans for school and asked if he planned on attending college.

"Yeah," replied Jack. "I graduated from Cranbrook this year and got accepted into the University of Michigan. If I play Junior Hockey, I can defer school a year without losing my acceptance at U of M."

"Couldn't you just play for U of M?"

"Actually, you have to play Junior Hockey to play at U of M."

"Oh!" I said, entirely confused by the process.

"Junior Hockey is the entry into a college, or the OHL, or AHL. Only Austin Alger (one of the team captains of the Cranbrook hockey team) had a commitment previous to his graduation."

I pondered the hockey hopes and dreams of these young men at the camp, which are entirely dependent upon their performance on the ice over a three-day period. I wished him good luck.

Jack thanked me. He had been terribly polite in all our exchanges – text, email, and now on the phone as well. I admire good manners in others and believe it is an overlooked proficiency that differentiates the best from the rest, especially in young people. My brother Matt once hired a young man partly because his manners were impeccable. Good manners make a great impression and leave the interviewer with the sense that you are likely proficient other areas, such as engineering or software programming.

I asked Jack if he had a particular career in mind.

"I wouldn't mind studying a variety of things," said Jack. "Science has always interested me. Or maybe microbiology or infectious diseases."

I couldn't help but chuckle. The words hockey, microbiology, and infectious diseases do not often share the same space in a sentence. Jack was a classic Learner, interested in multiple disciplines. Learners have a big knowledge spectrum. The world is their educational oyster. Only a Learner would make it possible for me to have a conversation with a defenseman who was trying out for Junior Hockey and whose plan B was to study medicine at the University of Michigan. I shared that observation with him, and he laughed, agreeing that it was unusual.

Learners have a big knowledge spectrum. The world is their educational oyster. Only a Learner would make it possible for me to have a conversation with a defenseman who was trying out for Junior Hockey, and plan B was to study medicine at the University of Michigan.

It was time to focus on the team, and I asked if he had any observations about his own journey.

"After figuring out that our team had all those reds (influencing strengths), it explained a few things," said Jack. "We all like to compete, even in practice. Sometimes we would get into it with each other and fight a little. And we weren't even playing against the opponent yet."

I recalled wondering about that when I saw all those players with the strength of Competition. Who was the real opponent? I glanced at his StrengthsFinder profile. Jack was one of those with multiple red strengths, including Activator, Command, and Competition.

Jack shared his viewpoint on the team's influencing horsepower. "Seeing all of the reds," he continued, "in everyone from coaches to players, well, it helped the team's perspective. We learned that it's good to have it, but we had to harness it the right way. We couldn't abuse it. Once we understood that, it helped us stop bickering in the locker room or on the ice."

I asked how that change in behavior had impacted the team.

"Before the seminar, certain players who had a lot of the red strengths would get into it, and it would cause problems here and there," said Jack. "After the seminar, we understood it better. Things ran more smoothly in practice, and that made its way onto the ice."

"You actually observed a difference?" I asked. It is one thing to believe something will help; it is another thing to watch it help.

Jack confirmed that he had and added that the lower-friction practice sessions allowed Coach to keep the pace going and get more done with the team. The players were more engaged. "We weren't distracted by someone cross checking someone and the other guy slashing back. We kept our concentration. It helped with games too. The more focus you have in practice, the better you play in games."

I appreciated the domino effect that Jack was describing. Know your strengths, use your strengths, appreciate the strengths of others, reduce conflict, become a well oiled machine, and achieve higher performance. This process was directly aligned to the one I intentionally create when I work with teams in the corporate world. The positive outcomes are energizing to employees and managers, especially if the team was struggling. And what team isn't? My approach accelerates and ignites the talent on the team, which helps unify and align them. Unified and aligned teams will always outperform those who are distracted by silos, pronoun trouble, and unproductive conflict.

Know your strengths, use your strengths, appreciate the strengths of others, reduce conflict, become a well oiled machine, and achieve higher performance.

Jack had more to say. "This information didn't just impact the players with red strengths," he told me. "It was a relief to a lot of people. The players who were more human glue, those who had more green strengths, it was a huge benefit for them to understand the other players' strengths. It made their job easier and helped bring the team together more effectively."

This was an important point. In a world of sports slogans focused on getting it done now and full effort, it would be easy to overlook the importance of the people who build strong personal connections. That human glue keeps the team together. It was also interesting that Jack appreciated the human glue because he did not have any of those strengths in his top five profile. This is an additional benefit of a strengths-based success program – understanding and valuing the strengths of others who possess talents that are different from ours.

"Have you used your strengths since the hockey season ended?"

"Yes, not only did I use them throughout the hockey season, but I even used my strengths as a lacrosse player. We won the state championship in lacrosse, too."

I congratulated him on the double state championships and remarked that it had to be a blast.

"It was," agreed Jack. "We had some similar problems on the lacrosse team, but not as bad as the hockey team. Mark was on both teams, and he used his strengths as well. When any skirmish or argument happened in the locker room or on the field, we used our strengths to settle people down and remain on the same path."

I loved hearing this. As a result of our workshop and the structure provided by Coach Weidenbach, the hockey players were equipped to be better leaders. Within a short period of time, Mark and Jack had transferred their knowledge to the next team they played with. They already had the confidence to take action based on their experience and understanding.

I looked at my team Strengths chart. Mark, the other player mentioned by Jack, had Competition, Achiever, Self-Assurance, Focus, and Discipline. I could see how having fewer distractions on and off the ice, resulting in greater order and improved results, would be appealing to Mark. Between the two StrengthsFinder profiles, keeping teammates on the same path would be both natural and productive, resulting in an internal "all is right with the world" feeling for them. It is also likely that the other lacrosse players appreciated the guide rails provided by Mark and Jack, because they want to be successful, too.

My experience in the corporate world has taught me an interesting fact about humanity, and this fact was validated by the Cranbrook hockey team. There are some people who want to be seen as nice. There are some people who want to be seen as right. But a vast majority of individuals do not care about being liked or about right or wrong. They care about being seen as effective and successful in their role. The strengths-based approach removes the nice factor or right or wrong factor from the equation and focuses on effectiveness. Nearly everyone can agree that effectiveness in a role is a worthy goal, and that is how I obtain buy-in from hard-wired, high-powered executive teams. Focusing on being well liked or doing the right thing may not persuade them. Speaking to their innate talents and finding ways to leverage them to achieve the desired outcomes is a success strategy. This relieves people from the burden of trying to be something they are not. Instead, we give them permission to leverage their unique patterns of excellence to be the best person and leader they can be. Mark and Jack understood and leveraged their strengths to help new teammates be more successful.

I was curious about which strength Jack enjoyed most.

"During school, I really liked my Learner strength," replied Jack. "Not just because I was the only one on the hockey team who had it, but I had viewed myself as a learner for a long time. To actually see that it was one of my strengths was exciting."

I could hear Jack's enthusiasm in his voice. I asked why he found that exciting.

"I have known for a long time that I do things that an average 18 year old doesn't do."

"Can you give me an example?"

"I watch things like the National Geographic Channel and find different topics that interest me. I've learned to embrace being a Learner, but this experience has helped me enjoy it more."

As a fellow Learner (it is third in my StrengthsFinder profile), and in an effort to support his future journey, I shared information about a recent engagement.

"Last month I worked with a whole herd of doctors," I said. "Jack, 80% of them had Learner in their top five strengths, and 90% had it in their top 10. With your interest in science and medicine, owning the Learner strength will really help you." I paused, thinking about it a bit further. "In fact, you'd fit right in with this group, except they don't have your influencing strengths. They could really use you to help move things forward!"

Jack laughed. I explained that there was a marvelous Gallup scientist named Shane Lopez who was doing a lot of StrengthsFinder work with college students, focusing on success and hope. I offered to send a link to a webcast I had just seen because I thought it would feed Jack's Learner talent. Then, I shifted my focus and asked if he had enjoyed learning the strengths of others on the team.

"Yeah, for sure," replied Jack. "Some people who I have been closer with, I could tell that those were their strengths before, but seeing their StrengthsFinder results solidified my perception of what they see (their lens). Blake is one of my close friends. He was one of two people who had Analytical. I could have said that would have been the case, but the other person who had Analytical – Jake – I don't think anyone on our team would have said that."

The value they are providing is occurring inside their head, and we can't see what is happening inside someone's head.

I reflected back on all the remarks in the feedback forms pointing to the general astonishment associated with Jake's thinking power. This is the conundrum linked to the strengths in the thinking category. Unless a clue emerges, like a thinker shouting, "I love analysis and numbers!" that person is often overlooked. The value they are providing is occurring inside their head and we cannot see it as it happens. Plus, when a thinker is busy inside their own head, they are not talking. This leads people to believe that thinkers have little to say, do, or feel. Jake's fateful decision to raise his hand and speak up about my rounding error had left a lasting impression on most players.

"I realized that you never really know," continued Jack. "I realized that if you make Blake do all the analytical stuff, then you're not letting Jake try to help or work with Blake. No one realized that Analytical was a strength for Jake. With the people who did not have red strengths (influencing) or who also had greens (relationship building) or blues (thinking), we figured out how to bring out those strengths in people and utilize them for our team. All the strengths could add value. I didn't know that before."

Bingo! Jack had just articulated the ultimate goal of harnessing the talent on a team. Identifying and honoring the strengths of others allows them to provide value, perhaps in ways that had not previously been considered. This helps maximize the contributions of each person on the team, and not only do they deliver, but each person feels understood and valued. When people feel understood and valued for whom they really are, they will run through fire and ice for the team and the leader.

Identifying and honoring the strengths of others allows them to provide value, perhaps in ways that had not previously been considered.

Jack spoke about the team meeting where Coach asked each player to select a single strength to help craft their role. "We went around the locker room, and Coach had everyone share their preference on which strength the person thought would most benefit the team. If one guy has Competition and another person does, we don't need them in competition when maybe the other person can add Woo. We got to see how each individual could help achieve our common goal – become state champions *and* become a more connected team."

"What strength did you choose to add beyond your Competition strength?"

"I told Coach I would use my Learner because other people had already taken Competition and Achiever. I knew it could be valuable since no one else has it. Coach also said we had to give an example. I said that if there was a player on the other team who wasn't so strong or fast on the outside, I would tell one of the forwards to drive wide. That would help the team learn and adapt to our situation."

I thought that was genius. Jack could leverage his ability to learn and focus it on the opposition. He could identify weak links in the chain with his power of observation. Looking at his other strengths, I asked if having Command and Activator helped him motivate the team with the information he provided.

"Yes, it did," said Jack. Then, he returned to his Learner value proposition. "I gave Coach another example where I would use Learner to help the team. I said that if someone on the team was sick or had a runny nose and they touched or drank from one of the water bottles, I would take the water bottle and put it on the side. That way the cold and infection wouldn't spread around the team. I liked this idea because it combined my interest in science and hockey. I could help the team stay healthy."

Jack's example embodied what happens when you give people the permission and the power to do what they do best! Imagine helping keep the team healthy over the long season, on top of being a great defenseman, a wonderful leader, and acting as a scout to pick out chinks in the armor of the opposing team. Seriously? I wanted to cheer.

"I love that you added value in ways that are unique to you and your blend of strengths. Doesn't that feel good? Doesn't it feel better than trying to wear a shirt that doesn't fit?"

"It does."

"I bet Coach loved it, and it's not something that he would have come up with for you to do on his own."

"Correct."

Coach created the opportunity for each person to contribute but put the onus on each player to determine what that contribution would be. This approach resulted in ownership and buy-in from the players, making it more likely to stick.

Sharing our specific value statements is not easy. It requires internal work and the courage to overcome feelings of vulnerability. It only works when people know they won't be judged harshly. I asked Jack if it helped that Coach created a safe space for players to share their value statements.

Sharing our specific value statements is not easy. It requires internal work and the courage to overcome feelings of vulnerability.

"Yes," said Jack. "I really like what we did that day. For me, it was a relief."

There was that relief word again. I was learning just how important it was to the team when they were able to let go of the struggle and embrace the team's strengths. I asked Jack to describe how it felt.

"Personally, when we had that meeting, and after we had learned our strengths and saw how we fit in, I thought it was a relief. I could do my job and not be worried about being the superstar or the guy who gets all the glory."

I asked how that was different from his experience on the team before we held our workshops.

"For example, my job on the power play is very specific. Stand in front of the net and create chaos, like Tomas Holstrom."

Tomas Holstrom was a professional hockey player for the Detroit Red Wings, known for driving the opponents crazy by stubbornly refusing to leave the sacred space in front of the opponent's goalie. If the goalie cannot see the puck, the goalie cannot block the puck.

"I think after my role was clarified on and off the ice, I really could accept that role on the power play and focus on that aspect of it as much as I could," said Jack.

I continued to probe, asking about his experience on the team before the roles were refined.

"I used to do too much," answered Jack, matter-of-factly. "I might go to the side boards and make a skill play or a pass like that, etc. The most effective power play we were going to run was if I just did my job in front of the net. I could do that, and be more comfortable with that on the ice."

Jack's observation was similar to the one made by Mason, and resurfaced the importance of well-defined expectations. In the corporate world, knowing what is expected of you at work is a foundational component of an individual's emotional commitment to a role and a team. Coach Weidenbach had helped simplify and clarify the expectations of Jack's role. This was a relief to Jack because he was no longer racing all over the ice trying to solve as many problems as he could.

I asked if the exercise where the players committed to refuse to let others fail was helpful to him.

"Absolutely," said Jack. "Even if it wasn't said before every game or practice, it was in everyone's mind. It's true, these are your teammates, but they are more than that. I realized that for a period of four to five months, these are your brothers. You wouldn't let your family fail."

"I realized that for a period of four to five months, these are your brothers. You wouldn't let your family fail."

Gosh, that was an additional dimension I had not previously considered. Would you let family fail? No, you would do something about it.

"Coach said it before big games to remind us," said Jack. "We held it high. We didn't want to let anyone fail. Our locker room is our home. It is where our guys feel safe. I don't think there was anything more that could have been said. That 'I refuse to let you fail' statement covered a lot of the problems we were having."

I noticed how different the Cranbrook hockey team's commitments to one another were from commitments made in the corporate workplaces. I had been exposed to many companies, both as an employee and as a consultant. A very, very small number spoke about their colleagues as family. Those that did use that term were not in large organizations. Maybe it's not possible to have a family feeling in the workplace once a company reaches a certain size. Or maybe, once a company reaches a certain size, they no longer focus on making it a place that feels like family.

"Last question, Jack," I said, glancing at the clock, wanting to keep my commitment to a 30-minute timeframe. "You've played for Coach for some years now. What are the one or two key things you've learned from him?"

Jack paused, giving the question proper consideration. "Two things," he replied. "From the whole coaching staff, but especially

Coach Weidenbach, he taught me to hold myself accountable. He always talks about discipline. It's his thing. It is how he runs his teams, and that goes along with accountability. That has helped me more as a person than as a hockey player. It helped me with hockey too, but to hold myself truly accountable was a big lesson for me."

"Was there a day when you weren't accountable?" After all, teens aren't generally known for being focused on responsibility, accountability, or discipline.

"Well, from age 15, when I started playing for Coach, through age 18, I can really see the change in myself," observed Jack. "When I was 15, I was goofing around and saying 'that's not my fault, or 'that wasn't me.' Now, I hold myself responsible and accountable for whatever I do. There have been some things that weren't all my fault, but I accepted responsibility. Accountability is the biggest life lesson I learned from Coach Weidenbach."

I tried to process the magnitude of this particular life lesson and Jack's timing for learning it. Think of all the sports figures, or Hollywood figures, or business leaders, or political figures, who will not accept responsibility or hold themselves accountable for mistakes or unethical behavior. Sometimes I think society teaches us to *not* accept responsibility for our actions. Jack listed it as the number one lesson he learned from the coaching staff at Cranbrook.

Jack had additional thoughts on the importance of structure. "I really think that playing on the team is a life lesson. I joined the varsity team in my sophomore year, and it really helped me in school. The structure on the hockey team is always there, and it helped me set my time priorities academically."

I asked for an example.

"Well," said Jack, "we had to be at practice from 5 pm to 7 pm, so I couldn't do homework then. I had to figure out when I could do homework, and then get it done. I like to be very organized, so the structure around hockey gave me a set schedule and a routine. I learned how to manage my time to get a lot done."

I glanced at Jack's top five strengths again. He had Achiever, which values personal productivity. Being personally productive, every day, would be one measure of his success. It would be difficult to be productive in a tight schedule without structure.

"It really benefited me," he added. "I like that life lesson. As I move forward, I will always have to manage my time and set goals. Now I know how to do that, thanks to playing for Coach Weidenbach and the Cranbrook hockey team."

I was amazed at Jack's maturity and how much he had gained from the journey we had made together. I asked if he had anything else he would like to share.

"I just want to thank you for taking the time to come help the team and help us achieve the final goal of winning the state championship."

We parted with my promises to send him more information on strengths and Shawn Lopez, and I wished him well in Ottawa.

Jack had described some important points about building a high-performing team. Identify the talent, develop the talent, empower the talent, and leverage the heck out the talent. Let them define their path to achieve goals. Build a well-rounded team around sharply focused individuals, not the other way around.

I glanced over my notes. I suddenly realized that I had overlooked a question that I had added at the last moment. I meant to ask Jack about the hat trick he scored in the semi-final game. His performance helped give Cranbrook the opportunity to compete in the state championship game. That had to be an awesome highlight of his hockey career, yet Jack did not even mention it. What a great kid.

Identify the talent, develop the talent, empower the talent, and leverage the heck out the talent. Let them define their path to achieve goals. Build a well-rounded team around sharply focused individuals, not the other way around.

I looked forward to watching what these amazing boys would achieve when they made their way out of college and into the workforce.

Chapter 13: Austin Alger – The Constructor

"The road to success is always under construction."

Arnold Palmer

* * *

Executing Strengths (Get it done!)	Relating Strengths (Human Glue)	Thinking Strengths (Navigators)	Influencing Strengths (Energy to Move People)	Roles on Team
Consistency (stick to the process)	Harmony (find common ground)		Competition (hates to lose)	Co-Captain, Forward
Arranger (productivity through others, a conductor)			Significance (make a meaningful impact)	Leading by example on and off the ice
				Determine how to motivate and create structure to bring out the best in individuals and the team

I was eager to have my interview with one of the co-captains on the Cranbrook hockey team, Austin Alger. I wondered what the co-captains' experience was like as the team traveled the path to the state championship. In addition, I had learned something else about Austin, and I wanted to incorporate it into our discussion.

Coach Weidenbach had sent me home with a copy of the 2014-2015 Cranbrook Hockey yearbook. It contained an article about Austin.

He had been voted "Mr. Hockey" by the high school coaches in Michigan. That is a big honor, often associated with being identified as the best hockey player in the state. Austin had finished the season with 27 goals and 64 points. He finished his high school career with 86 goals and 196 points.

What strengths had he used to fuel his motor? Austin's StrengthsFinder results included Competition, Consistency, Significance, Arranger, and Harmony. At a high level, he would be happiest competing (Competition), making an impact (Significance), sticking to the process or system (Consistency), driving team productivity (Arranger), and finding common ground (Harmony). He was likely a winner who valued team success over personal success. Indeed, Austin's unique lens to the world was present from the first moment of our conversation.

"Austin, I have to begin our conversation by congratulating you for winning the Michigan Mr. Hockey award! How did that feel?"

"Awesome!" he replied, with a chuckle. "I didn't know if I would win it or not. My brother, Alex, was supposed to win it a few years ago, and he didn't."

"You have an older brother who also plays hockey?"

"Yes. Alex was captain when I was a sophomore."

I asked if there were any other family members climbing the ranks.

"My little brother plays tennis," said Austin, with pride in his voice.

I noticed that Austin did not dwell on the Mr. Hockey award. He might have said it was the best thing that ever happened in his life or shared stats associated with it. He did not. We were done with that part of the conversation.

I asked him some questions about his summer plans. Austin told me he was working at a hockey clinic coaching young players both in groups and one-on-one, which he found very enjoyable. I had also read in the Mr. Hockey article that he'd been selected to play for the Omaha Lancers.

"When do you head west?"

"In August."

Did he feel nervous?

"I'm nervous, but excited. It's a bigger, faster, and stronger game at that level, but the great part is that hockey is everyone's passion. In high school, players can engage in multiple sports. The US Hockey League is a feeder into the college programs. If all goes well, I'll play with Omaha for a year or maybe two, and then join the Miami University hockey team," said Austin. "I have to get bigger and stronger."

Bigger and stronger is the mantra of talented athletes on the journey to the professional leagues. I inquired about his living arrangements in Omaha.

"I will have a billet family, probably with another kid from the team. The season is from mid-August until late May or early June, and we have long road trips."

It sounded both exciting and nerve-wracking to me. All roads leading to the Land of Hopes and Dreams will have peaks and valleys. Austin had led the team to the state championship, and that journey certainly had its share of ups and downs. I wondered how it had shaped his role as team co-captain.

Austin emphasized the human management aspect of leadership. "The role of captain has a lot to it. We're responsible for many things, but in my mind, it is most important not only to be a leader on and off the ice and always lead by example, but it's also really important to learn about managing people and determine what kind of structure certain people respond to the best."

I was instantly impressed. Here was a high school student creating a personalized feedback process for each player so he could get the most out of them. That was probably his Arranger strength speaking. I decided to dig into it further by asking what he meant by the word structure.

"Some people respond best to hard criticism; others need it to be softer or nicer. But, those two things, managing people and being a leader, are most important for the role of captain."

"That's very different from scoring all the goals," I said, indirectly referring to his Mr. Hockey award.

"Yes, anyone can do that."

That reply caught me off guard. I expected Austin to say that scoring goals was another part of his responsibility – and clearly it was – but he did not see that as the most important part of being captain. They were separate roles. Constructing team success requires the artful arrangement of player roles and the management of player emotions to achieve the desired outcome. Austin was prepared and equipped to do that by leveraging strengths, like Ar-

Constructing team success requires the artful arrangement of player roles and the management of player emotions to achieve the desired outcome.

ranger, Consistency, and Significance. The team's success was his success. His "we before me" philosophy is essential to great leadership. Unfortunately, society doesn't offer up many role models for us to emulate.

How many Hollywood movie stars say, "I worked hard, but my success was possible only because every other actor was also able to deliver their best work in our scenes together. Ditto for the lighting and camera crews." I really liked where Austin was headed, and I was eager to learn more. Unexpected detours can be the best part of an interview.

"What was bugging you about your team before we built the success statement and held our workshops?"

Austin disclosed that he had felt both confidence and doubt in the team. "We weren't as close as we'd been in previous years. Younger guys and older guys were clashing. Veterans had entitlement issues and thought they were owed stuff. They demanded respect that the rookies weren't giving them. On top of that, some of the veterans didn't want to listen to Coop (Cooper Stahl, the other captain on the team) and me."

I asked for more information about that behavior, and Austin shared what most frustrated him.

"They put themselves above the team. The rookies had entitlement issues, too. They wanted to play, and yet they hadn't done anything to prove themselves. I couldn't side with either the veterans or the rookies because they were both being ridiculous."

This situation was clearly a strengths violation for Austin. He had Harmony, and being unable to find common ground in a sea of ridiculousness would antagonize him. In addition, trying to lead people to achieve maximum impact when both sides were acting silly would not be fun.

"Once we did the Strengths workshop and had the team meeting with Coach," recounted Austin, "the team got a lot better. Attitude issues declined."

"Strengths helped level the playing field. It reminded people of who they are and what they needed to do."

I asked what the team looked like once attitudes improved.

"Strengths helped level the playing field. It reminded people of who they are and what they needed to do. It helped them focus on doing their own thing rather than being someone bigger or different than who they were."

Austin's remark struck me. Great teams are comprised of great teammates. Great teammates are unselfish. They realize that there is a give and take in building a winning team. What old mantle will you relinquish? What new mantel will you embrace? These are tough choices.

I recently read an article that described this process perfectly. The flashy Detroit Tigers shortstop, Jose Iglesias, was challenged by a teammate for not hustling, which resulted in a brief brawl in the dugout. The shortstop looked bad. Later in the season, Iglesias approached his coaching staff and asked how he could become a better teammate. In that single moment, he moved from being a highlight reel player to a consummate professional. Iglesias redefined what success looked like for him, and it has transformed his game. His consistency and reliability have improved. He relinquished the highlight reel and embraced the mantle of being a great teammate. There is a world of difference between the two.[6]

I realized that Austin Alger had already made that choice because he didn't focus on his Mr. Hockey award. Being a great teammate and winning games meant more to Austin than personal achievements. He went on to describe his thoughtful approach to constructing team success. "I thought I was pretty good before the StrengthsFinder test, and my results made sense to me. It wasn't so much about me. When the other players learned their strengths, and responded to them, it made my job easier. They were easier to talk to and easier to tell what to do in a good way. Peer-to-peer dialogue was more effective."

Effectiveness is the ultimate goal of my work with individuals and teams. It is the most compelling reason to pursue a strengths-based approach to success because it improves understanding and collaboration between colleagues. People feel valued for being valuable. This improved atmosphere positively impacts so many business metrics, including engagement, retention, productivity, and profitability.

I asked if he saw a difference in how the team behaved.

"Yes," agreed Austin. "There wasn't any lashing out anymore. At the beginning of the year, I constantly had to step in and break up bat-

---

[6] McCosky, Chris. "Iglesias Shows Signs of Growth On and Off Field." The Detroit News, April 22, 2016.

tles. After we worked with you, there wasn't as much confrontation and that made us a better team."

Again, I could see that the immense influencing horsepower in the group, behaving like race cars roaring around and crashing into one another, on and off the ice, had really frustrated Austin's Harmony strength. That made it more difficult for him to effectively leverage his leadership strengths to motivate his teammates.

In addition, Nolan Rogow, the other person with Harmony on the team, probably did not feel he had the street credibility or authority to intervene and help Austin. He was not a captain. He was not a senior. He was not a starter. Only after our workshops, when Coach asked players to bring other strengths to the equation, was Nolan's secret sauce recognized. Before then, Nolan's talent sat on the sideline, largely unnoticed and certainly underutilized. How many people on your team are sitting at your conference table with untapped and undervalued strengths? Is it you?

Resource Management

I have worked in the world of technology, and when we deploy a computer server that is underutilized, it is considered poor resource management. You are paying for a resource that is not well utilized. The same applies to people management. My program helps identify all the human talent on the team, and with the right leadership, fully utilizes that talent to bring success to the organization. The additional benefit is how great Nolan felt when his talent was both valued and leveraged.

My program helps identify all the human talent on the team, and with the right leadership, fully utilizes that talent to bring success to the organization.

I asked how Coach Weidenbach helped refine his role on the team.

"I don't remember the strength," he said, "but when we had that team meeting, I talked about pushing the pace of practice, and by pushing myself, I would push everyone else around me to be better."

I glanced at his top five strengths again, and said, "It's probably Arranger, which is the 'team productivity' strength, and maybe Significance, helping the guys realize their full impact."

I was not concerned by Austin's inability to remember which strength it was. It had been months since he had been exposed to the StrengthsFinder. To focus on naming or memorizing the strengths would be to miss the point. The point is that Austin used his strengths, with intent, to help him and the team to become more productive. He knew what success looked like and how he could impact the team.

Austin appreciated the requirement that players step up and take ownership of their roles. "The key thing about that meeting," continued Austin, "was that people actually had to verbally commit to what they were going to do. Once we knew what their commitment was, it was easier for Cooper and me to hold them accountable. We could go to players and say, 'Remember when you said this in the locker room? You're not doing it.' It made it easier for me to construct everything. It helped, as Coach said, 'Make music, not noise.'"

I glanced again at Austin's strengths and concluded his Consistency strength was likely engaged. I have seen the Consistency strength appear with regularity on teams working in the world of regulatory compliance. Austin was forcing the players to comply with their public commitments. Their commitments had been based on their strengths. Therefore, it was easier to lead and construct success for the team when the other players were committed to doing what they do best. That does not mean that it is easy. It requires a great deal of relentless effort on everyone's part. But, the results speak for themselves.

Austin told me he had played for Coach Weidenbach for four years, since he was a freshman, and I asked him what his biggest takeaway was.

Austin reflected upon the formal system Coach had in place. "Coach was big on knowing your place. It's a system. You have to buy into it; you have a job in the system. You're not going to come in as a freshman, no matter how good you are, and change the system. No player is bigger than the program or the system. If you're asked to pick up pucks, pick them up. It's part of contributing to the team. Coach says that everything starts with discipline. That's what the program is built on."

No player is bigger than the program or the system. If you're asked to pick up pucks, pick them up.

He paused. I let the silence lie, sensing that Austin had more to say.

"We won games because we were disciplined," he said, thoughtfully, "more than because of the talent we had on the team."

I thought that was a pretty powerful observation from Austin. Talent needs structure and guidance. This important principle applies to talent in the office as much as it does to talent on the ice.

Austin added his perspective on the team's strengths-based success journey. "I found this experience to be very useful. I talked to Coach about it. We lost a lot of guys this season, so I think it would be very beneficial for the team to do this again next year, even for those who have already been through it."

I was pleased that a high school senior, co-captain, and Mr. Hockey was suggesting that our exercise was fruitful enough to repeat. I wished him well in Omaha, and he thanked me.

I looked over my notes, and realized that Austin had chosen the path less travelled. He valued being a leader over being Mr. Hockey. He wanted team success more than he wanted personal success. Austin had all the goods to just be another individual contributor, a rock star who was eager to beat the competition. And he was that. But that alone was not enough to motivate him to achieve his very best performance. Austin's secret sauce included his Significance and Arranger strengths, which fueled his desire to help the team reach maximum productivity and impact. The discord on the team had felt like an anchor, pulling on the team and on Austin. Once that drag was removed, he was able to run on all cylinders as a leader, a constructor, a great teammate, and as a great hockey player. He helped other players own their place in the system, encouraged them to follow the system, and to deliver on their commitments to the team. They complied, and as a result, the goal of becoming a high performing state championship team was achieved.

Anyone can score goals. Leadership, for Austin Alger, was much more than that.

Chapter 14:
Jake Nestell – The Thinking Man

"What you have, what you are – your looks, your personality, your way of thinking – is unique. No one in the world is like you. So capitalize on it."

Jack Lord

* * *

Executing Strengths (Get it done!)	Relating Strengths (Human Glue)	Thinking Strengths (Navigators)	Influencing Strengths (Energy to Move People)	Roles on Team
Restorative (loves to solve problems)	Adaptability (go with the flow)	Strategic (best path to strategic outcome)		Forward
		Futuristic (sees over the horizon to solve problems)		Help with data and analysis during games
		Analytical (values data, numbers, facts over emotion)		Observe opponent's anomalies or patterns and share them with the team

I was eager to interview Jake because he truly was the star of the show during our success workshop. The feedback forms were filled with remarks related to Jake's previously unknown brain power. When he identified my rounding error, I was pleased that he had the courage to speak up and that a human thinking machine was demonstrating his value to the team. In my interviews with the players over the summer, each mentioned Jake by name. The Jake Nestell lesson had stood the test of time.

If one were to strictly look at the top five strengths of the players and coaches on the team, it would be easy to say that Jake was the odd man out. He was the only player with three thinking strengths in his profile. In addition, he was one of only two people in the group without influencing talents in his strengths profile. He was a thinking man surrounded by a sea of influencing and executing strengths. The only other fellow who stood out like Jake was co-captain Cooper Stahl. He had three relationship-building strengths, which was also unusual. In total, Jake had 13% of the thinking strengths on the team, and Cooper had 13% of the relating strengths on the team. They offered a unique value proposition with Jake's bent towards navigating, and Cooper's bent towards providing human glue.

With that in mind, there is another important StrengthsFinder point to make. It is never a good idea to judge anyone simply by reviewing their top five strengths. For all we know, Jake's next three strengths were influencing talents. Nonetheless, it was a visual anomaly on the team strengths chart, and a real one as well. The reality is that this hockey team did not sit around and think; by default, Jake's three thinking strengths could add a lot of value to the team.

Jake's top five strengths include Strategic (connecting the dots), Futuristic (looking over the horizon), and Analytical (likes numbers, math, data). He is energized by removing roadblocks and solving problems (Restorative) and could go with the flow (Adaptability). The combination of the three thinking strengths and Adaptability, which rarely resists changes in a program or agenda, probably made him one of the least vocal people on the team and more likely to be overlooked and undervalued.

Employees with multiple thinking strengths in their top five profile are often overlooked by leadership because they do not make waves.

In my corporate engagements, especially in STEM-related fields (Science, Technology, Engineering, and Math), employees with multiple thinking strengths in their top five profile are often overlooked by leadership because they do not make waves. They do not generate a ton of energy like the influencers, and they are not surrounded by the drama and activity associated with executing tasks. They may not hang out at the water cooler with the human glue people. Thinkers may absorb and process information before relating, influencing, and executing. They think first, often observing the landscape and then mentally plotting their next steps. When given permission, they help navigate the ship to the right spot on the map.

With this analysis in mind, I began to speak with Jake about his experience on the Cranbrook hockey team. We started with the usual questions about graduating, working, and getting ready for college. Jake was helping some friends who owned a power washing company and working in landscaping. He was headed to Adrian College in the fall. I asked what he was planning to study.

Jake's Futuristic strength showed up immediately in his choice of career. "I am interested in eco-friendly and green engineering, more on the marine side. I like the idea of finding new energy forms from the waves or thermal vents in the ocean. I am also interested in deep sea fish farming because shallow ocean fish farms are polluting the shallow waters … things like that."

Well, that sure sounded like a strategic thinker focused on the future and solving problems. I made a mental note to introduce Jake to Shawn Patterson, my friend at DTE Energy in Detroit. They are always seeking good engineers interested in new ways of generating power.

"I'd like to minor in entrepreneurship so I can sell whatever solutions I design," Jake added.

I was excited by his plans. "We need more engineers that are start-up minded. And I can totally see your strengths reflected in what you just said – coming up with creative and future-minded solutions to solve problems. I've worked with a lot of entrepreneurs, and many of them have Futuristic as a strength in their profile. It makes sense." I went on to mention that Gallup has an entrepreneurial assessment tool, and I promised to send Jake more information. Then I returned to the topic at hand.

"Before we go much further," I said, "I want to share that the feedback forms from our workshops were full of admiration for you because you identified my rounding error."

Jake chuckled, and acknowledged that plenty of the guys talked to him about it after the workshop. "They said they never knew I was analytical. It was just a coincidental moment, really. I happened to notice the error, and it was due to one of my strengths. I always felt that on the team, I noticed things. I don't usually voice my opinion, so the fact that I noticed your mistake and said something was ironic."

I told him that acting on our strengths takes courage.

Jake acknowledged that he learned a life lesson from the experience. "Previously, I didn't mention stuff that I noticed, mostly because I assumed others noticed it, too. So, why say anything? However, once the team knew I was analytical, I understood how important it was to share things that I notice. The moment in the workshop helped me understand that."

I shook my head out of frustration over the lost talent of thinkers. My mind went to my experience with corporate teams, and I had the feeling of déjà vu all over again.

Because our top five strengths come so natural to us, we assume that everyone else sees, does, thinks, or feels the same way we do. Not true. The strengths-based success approach is compelling because we get insight into the lens of our teammates or our colleagues. In Jake's case, much of his power was invisible to the group because it was happening inside his head, making it even more difficult for us to understand his value proposition. Until he spoke up, and exposed his lens to the rest of us, he was unaware that his strengths lens was unique. Once he became aware, he took action that proved valuable to the team. In doing so, he felt understood and appreciated by his teammates. Imagine this process repeating itself with every member in your family, with every member in a church, and every employee in a company. It is a positive, joyful experience that generates real impact.

In addition, my approach of revealing and capitalizing upon all the talent drives self-awareness and others-awareness. It harnesses the power of the collective and maximizes the potential of the team. In organizations that have not adopted this success strategy, there are talented people who run silently beneath the radar of the group, entirely unnoticed. The outcome is a sub-optimized workgroup or corporation. The outcome of a sub-optimized corporation is sub-optimized results. Look around you in your own world. Which strengths are lying dormant on the bench? Do you know? Do you want to know?

Look around you in your own world. Which strengths are lying dormant on the bench? Do you know? Do you want to know?

Why does a strengths-based approach help optimize teams and companies? First of all, it identifies talent, and some of that talent is not visible to the human eye, like Jake's thinking horsepower. But the real bang for the buck lies in the hands of the manager or leader of the team because it helps eliminate a chronic problem with performance management by feeding them previously unavailable information.

"Walk a mile in his or her strengths." Only then will we understand how that person sees the world.

Managers judge their employees through their own strengths lens. It is human nature to do so. We have all heard the old adage, "Walk a mile in his shoes." I would convert that to: "Walk a mile in his or her strengths." Only then will we understand how that person sees the world. When managers make the mistake of judging the talent of an employee through their own strengths lens, the employee is instantly sub-optimized. When that happens with each member of the team, the team is sub-optimized. When that happens across an organization or company, the entire organization is sub-optimized. Maximum success is out of reach, and the company relinquishes a competitive edge.

Conversely, when the manager understands his or her own strengths, and then understands the strengths of their team, they move from being self-aware to team-aware. They have key insight into each employee's secret sauce. They are enabled, and hopefully empowered, to do what Coach Weidenbach did. The manager can have a conversation with each person, and ultimately, the team, to bring all strengths to bear. The odds of reaching full potential increase. The manager does not even have to figure it all out on their own.

Coach had instructed each player to select a strength beyond Competition with which they would help the team win and then state how they would use that strength to add value. The onus was on each player. Coach simply supported and guided them through the conversation and offered encouragement. Isn't that a manager's role? In this manner, the team moves towards the state of being maximized and optimized. Players and employees get to do what they do best, every day. Goals and tasks are accomplished with more energy, in less time, and with greater momentum. This momentum perpetuates more success, and when supported by leaders, it can become the new normal. The new normal delivers a sustainable competitive advantage.

Jake brought me back to reality, answering my question about being a silent observer.

"Right," replied Jake. "Instead of mentioning it, I focused on other things. What I realized was that even if what I notice is minor – that mistake on your chart was minor, but no one else noticed it – it could make a big difference. In a game, I might notice something that I believe is minor. Maybe it is minor, or it could be game changing. If I speak up about it, it could potentially help the team."

This was huge. At all times, Jake was observing and processing information that others were not, and there is value in that. Even small observations can have a big impact when shared with the team. The workshop had given Jake courage to voice the things he noticed. It was a way he could add value that did not involve skates and a hockey stick.

Jake had an important observation about the role of Coach Weidenbach in this process. "A lot of the success we had with this is thanks to Coach's tenacity to chase after it and help us take the strengths knowledge to the next level," added Jake. "It was really good on his part."

This took me back to my interview with Mason Schultz, who said that Coach Weidenbach was all about taking things to the next level. That obviously included leveraging the strengths of the team.

"How did you see Coach's tenacity benefiting you?

"Coach Weidenbach wanted us to do whatever it takes to succeed. He helps us through hockey. Hockey helps us develop better life skills."

Coach was helping Jake be more successful on the road of life. Jake was manifesting Coach's reason for coaching. Both were better off for knowing and working with one another.

Jake had also discovered a partnership opportunity in his experience with strengths-based success. "I've thought about it," said Jake. "We did the exercise for hockey, but even outside hockey, for everyday life, I could see it was interesting. Knowing some of these strengths, taking that test, it showed me that because you don't have one thing as strong as one in another area, I either need to improve that area or partner with someone who has it, and become a team."

This was music to my ears. Jake had already established strategies for managing his strengths and managing his weaknesses. I asked Jake if other players felt the same way.

"Yeah, to an extent," said Jake, after pausing to think. "Before this, I sort of had an idea of some of the strengths people had. This helped narrow it down, and revealed that some had strengths I never knew they had. This knowledge helped clarify a lot of roles and showed how we could support each other on the team."

Jake spoke about the importance of off-ice contributions. "Coach basically had us take what the results were from our test, come to the locker room, and select some key points that we could use to help the team. It wasn't necessarily on the ice, but also in the locker room, or things we could do to improve team chemistry."

Coach had mastered the concept of holistic leadership. How the players behave and perform on the ice was only one category of success. Everything off the ice contributed as much, if not more, to their ability to achieve their success statement: winning the state championship, with a sense of brotherhood, and refusing to let anyone fail. I asked Jake if he liked the process.

"I liked it a lot," affirmed Jake. "In my eyes, if you're not helping the team, you're hurting the team. Every player had to take their results and use it to the maximum advantage that they possibly could."

"In my eyes, if you're not helping the team, you're hurting the team. Every player had to take their results and use it to the maximum advantage that they possibly could."

If you are not helping the team, you are hurting the team. It was similar to the trust bank idea. Each interaction with someone else is either a deposit or a withdrawal in the trust bank. There is no neutral value. I asked Jake how his role on the team changed after people began to understand his Analytical strength.

Jake realized that he needed to be as engaged with the team on the ice as he was off the ice. "Before this exercise, I always spoke around the locker room, but at game time, I was in my own zone. I didn't talk to people a lot. What I learned and what I changed, was that during games or after games, I needed to be more vocal about the things that I noticed."

"What sort of things did you notice?"

"I became more observant about seeing things on the ice and watching people's reaction to what happened. I watched what was happening on the ice even when I was on the bench. It's hard to describe, but I would say that I used to have kind of a tunnel vision. After I learned that I noticed things, I looked at the broader picture, and shared what I saw. Then, I went from there."

I heard the similarity in Jake's comment to Jack's remark from our interview, that his thinking strength gave him a special power of observation and that he shared those observations with other players. Harnessing and channeling that observation power helped the team maximize their effort by utilizing information they would not otherwise have had. Coach had empowered these boys to leverage their thinking strengths to add value to the team.

"From a team perspective, how did the team change after you learned your strengths and Coach had the players share what they would bring to the table?"

Jake spoke about the importance of human glue. "I thought it helped everyone understand why they are really there. Besides the on-ice factor, what could we be doing off the ice to help the team? Some were really competitive, and some were not getting along. All that did was hurt the team and damage the team chemistry. It was helpful to have the human glue guys come in, know the mood, solve the problem, and then we could all get on with the hockey side of it."

"Solving some of the conflict made a big difference to the team?"

"Yeah," said Jake. "I noticed that trying to solve the problem right then and there was hard, especially for competitive people."

"Why was that?"

"When they get wound up, they get a hard-headed thought stuck in their mind, and they think, 'I'm not wrong! No way I'm wrong!' You can't budge them. But, the human glue guys helped solve the problem, get to the conclusion, and we could move on with the game."

I thought about all the wasted time and energy involved in unproductive conflict. I had written about this topic for my MS in Leadership program at Duquesne University. The cost of unproductive conflict in the workplace is significant. Teaching teens that there were people who had the talent to diffuse conflict, and to lean on those people for help, was a valuable lesson for business and life.

"Who were the human glue guys on the team who could help solve the problems?"

"Nolan and Danny," replied Jake. "Nolan really had a significant role, and he wanted to be a part of the team more than ever. We had two goalies plus Nolan, so it was hard for him to get ice time. He made a big difference to the team with his human glue."

Jake had an important observation about expanding the view of success beyond oneself. "The 'I refuse to let you fail' exercise brought it to our attention that you're not doing it for you. Everything you do impacts the team. It also made me see that if one guy isn't performing, I could help pick up the slack. Everyone could use their strengths from the test and use them the best they can so that nobody fails."

Hardly any of the players had talked about actually winning the state championship, so I decided to ask what it was like.

"I was on the varsity team last year, and we didn't win it. I was surprised that the last games were as easy as they were; I thought they'd be more difficult. It was great to win. Not many people win that, especially not their senior year. It was a great way to end my last year of high school."

Later, I would measure just how easy those games were to win and use data to connect their success with the team's emphasis on leveraging every talent on the bench. The team was on such a high when they aligned their strengths with their defined role that they played with nearly infinite and unbeatable energy. It points back to that idea of perpetual momentum and mounting success.

Jake had more to say about playing on the Cranbrook hockey team and how he valued one of Coach's key parameters: discipline. "I played for Coach Weidenbach the last two years. What I gained most was learning how the discipline factor impacted the team. If even one person doesn't want to become part of the team or doesn't want to do what others are doing or refuses to listen to who is running it all, then the team fails. We had a couple of players like that the last few years. It hurts the team and causes commotion. If you can't follow discipline, then it's not the place for you."

Jake did not have Discipline in his top five strengths, but that doesn't mean he did not appreciate its value. He was also able to connect the concept to success beyond the hockey team.

"I like discipline because it gets you to perform to your best, both physically and mentally," added Jake. "Enforcing discipline was helpful. It gave us that little push – we need it. When everyone on the team was pushing harder, it created some competition. And we all wanted to do better just because everyone else is. I can see that in business, everyone wants to be their own boss, and maybe they don't want discipline enforced. It depends on the scenario. I definitely understand both sides. Enforcing discipline and following discipline."

Then, Jake spoke about being different than others on the team. "A lot of times I was thinking outside the box. I'm not your average mainstream guy. I like to think of other ways to do things. That's why I'm interested in entrepreneurship, especially in engineering. I am eager to come up with who knows what. Nobody got to see that side of me until we learned our strengths. That's why a lot of people were intrigued as to why I was considered the thinking man."

My heart was broken and thrilled at the same time. It is heartbreaking to hear that a young man has gone many years without being thoroughly understood and valued. To hear that the team finally got to know and value the real Jake – and how good that felt to him – was manna from heaven for me. Jake Nestell, The Thinking Man, was understood and appreciated. It doesn't get any better than that.

I thanked him, and concluded with how delighted I was to meet a fellow thinker. As one engineer to another, one entrepreneur to another, I encouraged him to follow the path and told him that I would be watching the Thinking Man!

The lesson of Jake Nestell was bigger than it might appear on the surface. Jake's unique value proposition really helped the team understand that there are many ways to contribute to the success of a team or an organization. I was glad that his thinking prowess was not undervalued on the road to the state championship title. As described in other player interviews, Jake's observations were perceived as useful by other players. Could we have said that before we made the strengths-based success journey with the hockey team? I think not. What an opportunity lost that would have been.

Chapter 15:
Nolan Rogow – The Harmonizer
Blake Rogow – The Team Competitor

"When a person feels appreciated for their infinite and absolute value, you can then communicate about any issue and you will have their cooperation and respect."

Kimberly Giles

* * *

Nolan Rogow
"The Harmonizer"

Executing Strengths (Get it done!)	Relating Strengths (Human Glue)	Thinking Strengths (Navigators)	Influencing Strengths (Energy to Move People)	Roles on Team
	Harmony (find common ground)	Futuristic (sees over the horizon to solve problems)	Competition (hates to lose)	Goalie
	Relator (warm, deep & authentic relationships)		Communication (gift of gab)	Diffuse and resolve conflict, strengthen relationships
				Encourage & challenge other goalies and brother Blake

Blake Rogow
"The Team Competitor"

Executing Strengths (Get it done!)	Relating Strengths (Human Glue)	Thinking Strengths (Navigators)	Influencing Strengths (Energy to Move People)	Roles on Team
Restorative (loves to solve problems)		Analytical (values data, numbers, facts over emotion)	Competition (hates to lose)	Forward
Deliberative (sensitive to risk)				Drive team competitiveness
Achiever (personal productivity)				Consummate penalty killer

On a breezy, warm summer afternoon, I sat down with Blake and Nolan Rogow in their lovely back yard. Their parents lounged by the pool. The Detroit Tigers game played in the background. We gathered around a table, nicely shaded by a large umbrella.

Blake was a forward on the team, and Nolan was a backup goalie. Blake had just graduated from Cranbrook. Nolan was entering his senior year in the fall. I was pretty certain that interviewing two brothers who knew their strengths and played on the same team would make for an interesting conversation.

"As you guys look back on your season in the rearview mirror, do you have any thoughts?"

They glanced at each other and engaged in the secret code that always exists between brothers. Blake spoke first.

"The strengths event was a turning point for the team," began Blake. "It was a relief, a burden off of us. You could see it and feel it. We only lost one game after, and even that loss was one of our best games of the year. We outshot the other team something like 48 to 10."

Right out of the shoot, Blake had noticed a difference on the team. And the word relief was one that was becoming more and more prevalent in my conversations with the young men. I also knew it meant different things to different players. I asked for more detail.

"After the workshop, everybody had a clearer understanding of what their role was. Before that, we had a lot of tension, most of it underlying tension, due to the fact that people were trying to overachieve, do things that didn't come naturally to them, or they were trying to do too much."

"I agree," said Nolan. "And, that didn't work very well."

I had heard about the problem of trying to do too much from Jack Blumberg as well. He realized he was trying to do too much, and the success exercises helped him self-regulate his efforts.

"After the workshop," continued Blake, "people felt comfortable knowing who they are, what they bring to the table and how to play off one another. That was the most beneficial thing that could have happened. Everyone had their identity on the team and knew what to do to help us succeed."

I glanced at Blake's strengths. With his Analytical, Achiever and Restorative strengths, a practical approach to removing the roadblocks to success likely felt very satisfying to him. Blake had opened the door to speak about others on the team, so I followed up.

"What was it like to see the StrengthsFinder results of others on the team?" I asked.

Blake again replied first. "I think that learning about the human glue guys (relationship builders), there were some I didn't expect to be in that category. I expected Nolan to be. He's always lightening the mood when people are tense or down. Even though he didn't have a huge opportunity to go out and play because he had two seniors (goalies) in front of him, he definitely overachieved in the locker room and helped the team that way. He kept us glued together."

I glanced at Nolan and smiled. I had already heard from other players how helpful he had been to the success of the team. He nodded as if to say, "That's just what I do!"

"Danny was another human glue guy," added Blake. "Before we all took the StrengthsFinder, I wouldn't have thought of him as someone who was glue guy. But, after that, I realized he also had a calming presence on the team. It wasn't really vocal, but his actions and his presence were soothing for the team. You could notice it after, once you knew that he was a human glue guy. He and Nolan had different methods to calm and keep the team together."

I glanced at my strengths chart. Danny's first strength was Relator. He'd be likely to enjoy deep and authentic connections. He would have a calming presence when chips were down or when the going was tough. Danny also had Competition, so he wanted to win just as bad as the rest of them, but his Strategic and Arranger would help him see how people could perform at their best. In addition, he had Responsibility in his top five strengths, so it was likely he felt that being calming was not just helpful, but it was the right and responsible thing to do.

"Do you think that Danny might have had that same calming presence all along, but it went unnoticed?"

Blake nodded and said he could see how Danny glued his line together by removing tension and contributing in a manner that would not show up on a statistics sheet. "We played well and overachieved as the 2nd line. Looking back, I understand his calming presence on the team."

It was Nolan's turn to speak up. "What I saw, once everyone found their strengths and everyone knew about it, they started actually working on it and showing it more. They weren't scared to bring it."

"What did that look like to you, Nolan?"

"Well," said Nolan, thinking it over, "if someone was really quiet in the beginning, and then took the test, and we learned that they were a human glue guy, they would start being more of who they are. That helped the team win in ways we didn't know about before."

The Cranbrook hockey team had discovered buried treasure in the locker room and found new ways to win games by leveraging the untapped talent of the team.

The Cranbrook hockey team had discovered buried treasure in the locker room and found new ways to win games by leveraging the untapped talent of the team. With discovery comes use. Use drives value and awareness, making the strength even stronger. This was the beauty of my strengths-based approach to success.

"What did you guys think about Coach assigning roles to people and asking them to reveal those strengths they were going to bring to the team?"

"Coach had us write down what our role should be based on our strengths," said Nolan, jumping in before Blake had a chance to speak.

"For me, #1 was Competition. I am obviously competitive. My role in the team allowed me to be competitive in practice and push the other goalies to play better, but it didn't allow me to be competitive during the games. I wanted to win, but didn't play that much. So, to support the team, I had to go to my other strengths. I became the glue guy in the locker room. I tried to be the best I could be to be a team guy and resolve conflict. My job was to clear the air and help people out."

Nolan's strengths allowed him to diffuse conflict through authentic, caring conversations. In this manner, Nolan helped the team compete more effectively, achieving that winning future and adding fuel to the commitment of refusing to let anyone fail. This was his secret sauce. That is how I saw it. Did Nolan agree?

"Well, I talked to them individually to see what each person thought, what was going on in their mind, and tried to figure out the best solution."

"Did you feel pressured?" I asked, speaking through my own lens. I am not good at helping people resolve conflict. In fact, I make conflict worse. I would definitely have felt pressured.

"No, not at all," replied Nolan with a confident, slow shake of his head. "They opened up to me."

"Coach always said that if he was going on a fishing trip, he was going to bring Nolan," inserted Blake with a grin.

I had heard Coach Weidenbach say the same thing myself. Hopefully, Nolan liked fishing!

Nolan shared some of his conflict resolution techniques. "If two people had tension in the locker room, I'd get to the bottom of it and find a way for them to apologize to each other because it's detrimental to the team when there is fragmentation. I get them to like each other. If that won't ever happen, then I tell them to not let their relationship affect the team and that it cannot impact their play on the ice."

Nolan spoke with the ease of someone who had simply gone for a leisurely stroll along a nature trail and solved a major problem at the same time.

"Did this eliminate the open conflict in the locker room?"

Nolan nodded.

I stared at Nolan as if he were a fish out of water. Was it really that simple? For the answer to that question, I turned to his brother and asked him if he had observed Nolan in action.

"Yeah, I did, a lot," confirmed Blake. "Nolan is competitive too, so it's not like he's a soft kid that didn't have any desire. He wanted to compete. When there's a bunch of competitive kids on a team, there is going to be fragmentation, and Nolan helped soothe it and remove things that were detrimental to the team." Blake glanced at his brother and smiled. "He's such a relatable guy. He knew his role and embraced it, and people responded. Even though he's not making a huge impact on the ice, Nolan made a huge impact off the ice. In doing so, he encouraged others to do the same."

I was impressed with Nolan's impact, and made a note to start sharing his journey with some of my corporate clients, because some of them lack relating strengths on their executive teams.

Blake continued to rave about Nolan's abilities. "Nolan is definitely a Relator. He understands people's feelings – he is competitive himself so he knows where they are coming from. He's had his share of tantrums. He's fiery but he has learned to harness it and control it, so it helps him relate to others when they have their own fiery moments. Nolan gets it because it has happened to him."

Nolan agreed. "Sometimes my competitiveness gets the best of me. I couldn't use it as much this year, so I went to my other strengths."

I was filled with admiration. With all that horsepower in the locker room, having Nolan to smooth things over would be like the importance of adding oil to the moving parts of a high-powered engine. Things only go well if the engine parts are running smoothly. Without oil, the engine self-destructs. Not pretty.

Things only go well if the engine parts are running smoothly. Without oil, the engine self-destructs. Not pretty.

Blake spoke about his strengths-based role on the team. "I actually kept Competition for mine," he said. "In our workshop, we saw that there are a lot of different types of competitiveness. Some people's competition looked like being better than the person next to you, doing your best, and winning the game. Mine was more aligned with wanting to see the team succeed, over any personal success. I have a 'team first' competitiveness. Coach remarked that that role fit me because even though I was one of the smallest and lightest people, I was willing to go out there, block shots, go into corners, do the little things that make a big difference and lead by example. People followed suit."

"So you used your Competition strength to play really hard, to lead and inspire the team?"

"Kind of," agreed Blake. "I was one of the few kids who would rather go out on the penalty kill than on the power play. Goals didn't mean as much to me as preventing goals and putting teammates in a position of success. I'd rather prevent the goal than score the goal."

That was a powerful statement. Most players would rather score the goal than prevent the goal. I glanced at Blake's StrengthsFinder profile again and heard his Restorative strengths in his remarks. In addition, he had Deliberative, which has a special sensitivity for risk. He would see goal prevention as a form of problem solving and risk reduction. Plus, his Analytical strength probably accounted for his reverse preference for preventing versus scoring goals. The glory of hockey is most often portrayed by the hero who scores a goal. Most people who have Analytical in their performance toolkit are not glory seekers.

Blake spoke about the emotional connection between his Restorative strength and his success. "I was the top penalty kill player this year," added Blake. "There is a lot going on out there on the PK (penalty kill). I allowed only one goal on the PK, and I was devastated. It was the game-winning goal when we lost to Rochester United, 5 to 3. That was harsh. After that, I told myself that I wasn't going to let that happen again. I would do whatever it takes to stifle teams and not let them score."

I could hear Blake's determination and a deep personal commitment to preventing such a disaster from happening again. I asked why that particular experience had such an impact upon him.

"A penalty kill can either go one of two ways – you can gain momentum or lose momentum. In the state championships, when we had to kill off a 5-minute penalty, the other team only got two shots off. That gave us a ton of momentum going into the 2nd and 3rd periods. Huge. Usually the team would expect to score during a 5-minute penalty. And they did not," said Blake emphatically, with a clear sense of pride and accomplishment.

"So that was your unique secret sauce, and it was embraced by Coach and the team?"

Blake nodded.

"How did it feel to have a role to live up to and bring your strengths to?" I asked.

"It was a sense of relief to know that one person didn't have to do everything," replied Blake.

There it was again. Relief.

"The captains, Austin and Cooper, used to think that everything was on them," interjected Nolan. "They thought they had to be perfect and do everything for the team. In reality, that's virtually impossible. They have weaknesses, too, and when they realized that people could fill those gaps, they saw that the result would be more of a team effort."

"This team had a bunch of seniors," added Blake. "That meant that there were some egos, and some thought they were entitled to play on power play, or do this or that. The team captains had to handle all those people. As a captain, you have to be team oriented and possess relatable traits. You have to lead by example and not just want the best for yourself. Once they learned their roles and learned the other players' roles, others were willing to fill in, and the captains let them. It was no longer a threat to leadership. There was no friction from people caused by not knowing their identity."

"That's true," agreed Nolan. "There are a lot of expectations put on the captains of the Cranbrook hockey team because you are expected to win. There is a winning culture around you. You play in the best league in Michigan, and you're expected to win that league. If things aren't going right, if we're not winning decisively or not playing well, there is a lot of tension. To deal with that, the high expectations, and being the two best players on the team – that's a lot of pressure."

Blake described the damaging nature of friction and tension. "Tension is contagious," he said. "I was close to Austin and Cooper (the co-captains), particularly Austin, and we would talk a lot. When I listened to what Austin had to deal with, I felt bad for him. He was doing the best he could, but there are some things that are too hard to deal with for just one or two people who are leading a team. And remember, the captains still have school, their own game to focus on, their own issues to deal with, and then they have to deal with the issues of 21 other players. That's a lot of pressure."

I nodded, with new appreciation for the team captains and what it must have been like for them when the team was struggling.

Nolan added insight from his own strengths lens. "The team ran how Austin ran. He's one of the best. If Austin was tense, we were tense. If he was scared, we were scared. If he was playing well, we were playing well. It was nice to take weight off his shoulders and distribute it."

Nolan may have done the most to lift some of the weight off of Austin's shoulders and the team overall. The gift of Harmony is resolving conflict. It is a relief, like having a dull, relentless headache go away, and thinking, "Man, that headache was really bugging me. I feel so much better now." Unresolved conflict eats away at the human glue.

Blake had another important observation. "If there are issues in the locker room, the team wouldn't be as connected on the ice. After our issues got resolved, Austin played phenomenal and showed why he was Mr. Hockey. He is easily the best player in Michigan. The lesson for me was that there is a lot of stuff off the ice that, when it affects one person, can affect everybody."

As I listened to Blake, my mind leapt to a senior leadership team I had worked with. When the leader went south, the team went south. My engagement with the team helped them become a more stable and reliable unit because each person walked away from the workshops with the ability to understand, communicate, and leverage their unique value proposition. As a work group, they appreciated the value of the people around them. It altered their expectations of one another and resulted in higher collaboration on all levels. Team dynamics have more to do with the success of an organization than many corporations recognize. A strengths-based success intervention can help.

Blake spoke about the long run of a hockey season, and the demands it places on the team. "It's a long season. You go to school with them, go to hockey with them, and engage with them every day for six or seven months. There is bound to be tension. There is no perfect team out there. If you can deal with it in a positive manner and relieve some of that, it helps. It is impossible not to have friction. If there are people on the team who can relieve it, you're bound to have more success."

Blake moved to the concept of refusing to let others fail and the difference that made to the team. "It kind of became a motto," said Blake. "In the competitive spirit of hockey, there is a lot that goes right, and there is a lot that goes wrong, too. You have to deal with it. If someone had a bad game, you go over and lift them up. We have your back. We're not going to let you fail or underachieve. We are all there to support you. This approach had a positive impact on everyone in the locker room."

I asked Blake and Nolan if they were givers in the "I refuse to let you fail" endeavor.

"We had a lot of competitive kids," replied Blake. "They wanted to play their best and help out the team. But once they know they have your support, and you have their back, it strengthens the links in the chain. We weren't willing to let anybody break at any point."

Nolan went even further with it. "I thought that motto was good for both camaraderie and accountability," added Nolan. "I refuse to let you fail. This brings everyone together to think about the ultimate goal of winning a state championship. It also held everyone to a high standard. If a teammate played bad, pick them up. If they did something wrong, something they shouldn't have done, tell them they have to be better."

"If a teammate played bad, pick them up. If they did something wrong, something they shouldn't have done, tell them they have to be better."

The notion of playing poorly versus making a mistake was an interesting point of differentiation. For Nolan, accountability was part of refusing to let others fail. I was enjoying this conversation. It was fun to learn from kids who were hardly old enough to drive and had been strengths-aware for only a few months.

I wondered if they had found a way to use their strengths since the hockey season ended.

Nolan was quick to respond. "I use my strengths every day. I know who I am. I use my strengths just doing whatever. Baseball, friends, anything I do."

"It gives you a sense of identity, and you know who you are and what your strengths are," concurred Blake. "You can put them into everyday action. It's not just something you can apply to hockey and be done with. It carries over into everything."

"I'm competitive in everything. I give 110%, and I beat him all the time," Nolan said, with a nod at Blake.

"There's no mercy, either," said Blake. "In horse (a basketball game), I don't even let him shoot sometimes."

This exchange reminded me of conversations between me and my brothers. We were also a sports household. There was more than a little bit of one-upmanship.

Blake remarked on how their competitive nature helped them hold one another to a higher standard. "We always played on the same teams.

If one of us didn't do as well, we would pick the other one up and motivate him. If he's doing well, I want to do well. If I'm doing well, he wants to do well. Even in video games, which are just for fun, it's the most competitive thing ever."

Nolan extrapolated Blake's observation to their behavior on the hockey team. "Between periods, I would go up and give Blake advice. I would tell him what the other team is doing, what he has to do better. I would hold him to a very high standard. I'd tell him to throw the body around, do some cross corner dumps."

I looked at Blake.

"He's not afraid to tell me the truth. I know his advice is meant to make me better, and I accept it."

"If Blake didn't play his best hockey, I would tell him," continued Nolan. "It wasn't to be mean or anything. It was to make him better. It might be okay for someone else, but not for Blake."

"He knows how well I can play, and he holds me to my same high standards," said Blake. "He's going to motivate me to play a stronger period. It is great advice, and coming from him, I know it's going to make me better."

"He does the same to me," chirped Nolan, "if I let in a weak goal or didn't play the puck behind the net."

Their collaboration extended to the practices. "I'll shoot 20 or 30 shots to his glove side to get that better," said Blake. "We don't just say that 'you suck' and do nothing about it. We help each other improve."

Nolan and Blake were able to coach one another to drive performance. This is a sign of a high-performing team, and it contributes to the momentum of the group. It was interesting to me that their conversations did not disintegrate into petty arguments. I concluded that the brothers were mature for their age.

Peer-to-peer feedback is very effective in the workplace when it is done with trust and a positive intent. The Rogow brothers used a particularly direct and instantaneous approach. I wondered if that same approach would survive in a corporate world. In the right environment – with the right culture and a hefty amount of human glue – it might work. It was definitely a powerful tool in the world of sports.

I shifted the conversation to the life lessons gained from Cranbrook and asked about playing for Coach Weidenbach.

Blake spoke to the maestro abilities of Coach Weidenbach, referring to Coach's ability to put people in a position to succeed and orchestrate the team. "He also said he'd rather take less skilled overachievers than the most skilled people out there. That stuck with me and inspired me. I was definitely one of those overachievers. Even though I might not be 6' or weigh 200 pounds or lift the most weight, if I put my mind to something, I can probably do it. As long as I am overachieving, then I am going to succeed."

Blake's observation was important to successful leadership in the business world. Isn't it interesting how leaders often prefer a dedicated overachiever versus a less committed but more talented person on the team? There is a point where the pain of putting up with a brilliant but selfish person is less effective than coaching an overachiever with some of the talent and a lot more desire. The road to success is littered with immensely talented people that have self-imploded and become toxic. The best thing to do is remove them from the team before they poison the water beyond a point of no return. It happens more visibly in sports than in the corporate world, where the problem lies hidden in the multiple layers of a deep organization chart – but the challenge is identical.

The road to success is littered with immensely talented people that have self-imploded and become toxic.

Toxic people often believe they are untouchable, which escalates the negative energy around them. Late in the season, the Detroit Tigers sent a pitcher home, publically and unapologetically citing his poor effort level. Boom. Gone. See ya! Come back when you've grown up. The Detroit Lions traded a star, basically paying him millions to leave. The team trust and goodwill was worn thin by endless conversations, multiple second chances, inexcusable scrapes off the field, and unacceptable personal fouls on the field. Leaders who keep people like that around teach the others on the team that it is okay to be self-centered, have poor character, and flaunt a lousy attitude.

It happens in the corporate world, too. I worked with a talented and knowledgeable customer executive who was one of the most difficult and mean people put on this earth. This person threw things at employees and suppliers, used unimaginable language, and rebuffed peers who tried to intervene. It was like watching a wild dog run around and bite people, with no one willing or able to stop the dog. After years of running unchecked, this leader was finally ejected from the premises. Guess what happened next? The team bought a cake and celebrated. What does that tell you about the emotional impact of this problem? Coach Weidenbach understood the value of talent *and* the value of character. They are not mutually exclusive, and we need both.

Blake offered additional insight into the benefits of a disciplined approach. "Coach is a very systematic guy," he said. "We had a bunch of systems we play with, and that had a huge impact on our success. For example, we allowed only 21 shots in our final two games in the playoffs. Also, during the playoffs, we had a brief moment of adversity. Against Wyandotte, we let in a weak goal due to a system breakdown. The Wyandotte guys yelled 'Over-rated!' That got us fired up, and because we were resilient, we scored 5 goals in a row. The lesson was clear. Stick to the system and stick to your roles in the system. Because we knew our identity in those roles, it helped us succeed in that moment of adversity."

I chuckled. I remembered the "Over-rated!" chant.

"Coach just finds a way to get the best of you and the best out of each player," added Nolan. "He finds a way to make you work harder and want it even more. Those motivators are unique for each person. To get the best out of you, he can be your best friend or worst enemy. He knows which buttons to push to get the best out of each and every player. There were a couple of players that Coach really ripped into. They ultimately played their best hockey once he really pushed their buttons the right way."

Both brothers provided excellent summaries of why the team was successful, and I could not imagine a better endorsement of a leader or a coach. I had excellent content from Blake and Nolan and decided it was time to let them go enjoy their Sunday afternoon. I asked if there were any parting thoughts.

"Yeah," said Nolan. "We're losing 13 seniors, so that's going to be hard. I'm excited to do this (the success workshops) next year because we will have a lot of new faces, new characters, different traits, different abilities. It will be good to learn those. We can do it earlier in the season, get going from the start."

I agreed, cheering internally. We would do this again next year!

"The StrengthsFinder helped me succeed on and off the ice," said Blake. "It is definitely something I can use in the future, in the business world, and at the University of Michigan. It is something I can take with me wherever I go."

I was pleased with the Rogow brothers' awareness of how they could use their strengths beyond the hockey team.

Blake was a young man who provided grit and perseverance, that consummate overachiever who would rather prevent goals than score one. He was more guts than glory, and that spirit would remain with him at the University of Michigan and beyond. His intangible talents proved that he was not like regular Navy, he was like a Navy SEAL. Coach knew he could rely on Blake in tough circumstances and inserted Blake in those situations.

Nolan's name repeatedly came up in the interviews, with each player providing specific examples of how Nolan's human glue and communication talents helped reduce conflict on the team. This removed distractions that were wasting energy on and off the ice. He may have singlehandedly done more to help the team win with his contributions off the ice than any other player. His commitment to the "how we win" portion of the success statement was enormous. He epitomized placing the team first and highlighted the importance of those intangible traits, like being the mayor of the locker room and a trusted advisor to the players. These are traits that the Clifton StrengthsFinder can help us identify and harness for the greater success of the team.

I do not know where Nolan and Blake will be five years from now, but I feel very strongly about one thing: no matter whom they are working for, the people around them will say, "I'm glad he's on my team."

Chapter 16: Cooper Stahl – The Calminator

"The world belongs to the Enthusiast who keeps cool."

William Mcfee

* * *

Executing Strengths (Get it done!)	Relating Strengths (Human Glue)	Thinking Strengths (Navigators)	Influencing Strengths (Energy to Move People)	Roles on Team
	Adaptability (go with the flow)	Futuristic (looking forward to resolve today's problems)	Significance (make an impact)	First line Defense
	Developer (celebrates incremental progress)			Team Co-Captain, Calm the team down when under pressure
	Relator (deep, authentic relationships)			Channel energy into what matters

If I were to summarize my interview with co-captain Cooper Stahl, it would be this: Keep calm and play hockey. Or start a startup company. He's doing both.

A quick look at Cooper's StrengthsFinder results will show you that he is one of those human glue guys, and he used those three relationship-building strengths to create a serene environment, whether it was diffusing drama over a girlfriend or being behind by a goal with two minutes left to play.

However, Cooper was the first to admit that being calm was not easy when the team was rife with tension and struggling to succeed. We will talk more about that in a moment.

I met Cooper for breakfast, inviting him to join me at the tail end of a meeting with my friend Shawn Patterson. Shawn is the Vice President for Organizational Effectiveness at DTE Energy. DTE Energy leverages the Clifton StrengthsFinder to drive employee engagement and performance, so we have been chatting about how we might use that same approach to support the STEM (Science, Technology, Engineering, and Math) movement in Michigan. I have a personal goal for Michigan to become the first strengths-based state in the nation. I am also an engineer, and I know that many technical people are thinkers. As we learned from our interview with Jake Nestell, thinkers are often over looked and undervalued because their talent is manifesting itself between their ears. The StrengthsFinder helps us identify that talent and utilize it. Shawn and I are working on that project separately from the one I am engaged with on the Cranbrook hockey team, but he was eager to meet Cooper and hear for himself what the experience was like.

Cooper began by giving us the quick version of his summer project – launching a start up that would rival Instagram. He was partnering with three other friends, and they had hired a developer who was a student at the University of Michigan. He had also just returned from trying out for a Junior Hockey team on Long Island. One or both would occupy him for the next year, after which, he hoped to enroll in an Ivy League school and study Entrepreneurship. Time would tell what would happen, but he was leaning toward focusing on the app. I asked why.

"I am faced with a tough decision," replied Cooper. "My hockey experience in New York showed me that I'll never have it as good as I had it at Cranbrook. The (Junior Hockey tryout) experience was so disorganized. It was nothing like how Coach would have run it."

There are very few Coach Weidenbachs on this earth.

"Perhaps I will work on the entrepreneurship instead," he continued. "Maybe my desire for business will take over my desire for sports."

We nodded. Life is full of choices, and the road unfolds as it will.

Shawn shared a few details about how DTE Energy uses the StrengthsFinder, citing that it helps employees understand how they fit into their role and the organization. He was then ready to question Cooper.

"Did you see a shift on the team after they experienced the StrengthsFinder?"

"I sure did. I'm a believer now!"

I had been eager to speak to Cooper because I had a question that I had been harboring since the very first day I met the team. "You were the first person to speak during our first team meeting, weren't you?"

Cooper nodded.

"I asked about what makes a good defenseman. Do you remember what you said?"

Cooper paused. "I think I said that responsibility was important."

"Exactly!" I said, triumphantly. "I loved it because as you now know, Responsibility is a strength. Did you speak first on purpose?"

"Well, I had an answer," said Cooper, "but yes, I wanted to show leadership and pave the way for others to speak."

I nodded and asked if Coach had talked to Cooper about what was going to happen before I arrived.

"Yes, we talked about it being a difficult situation. Austin and I were having trouble as captains, having difficulty getting the thread through the hole. At that point, we were feeling desperate and open to anything."

"What had happened on the team?" asked Shawn, seeking some context.

Cooper spoke about the team's history. "The season started strong," replied Cooper. "Our first weeks of practice were great. We were climbing, and then things began to drop. We tied three teams in a row, and it felt like we couldn't win a game. We were underperforming."

How had our workshops changed the atmosphere?

Cooper spoke about revealing the elephant in the room. "I thought the first meeting laid the groundwork – there is going to be change. It was the starting point of our recovery process, and it broadened everyone's mind. It showed that we have a problem, and that we need to get together and work it out. It was kind of like a subliminal message."

I was curious about his role as co-captain. "Were you wondering what the others were thinking about the direction we were headed?"

"I think that the team took the workshop like a class. It was interesting, but it also went in one ear and out the other."

Cooper made an important observation. As in the corporate world, one dose of the Clifton StrengthsFinder is not enough. It must be reinforced by repeated conversation and leadership. It is like speaking a new language. You cannot do it just once. It must be part of a daily dialogue. Your ability grows if everyone else around you is speaking the language, too. Language is an immersive experience and so is strengths-based success.

Cooper acknowledged that Coach Weidenbach catalyzed the strengths dialogue. "That changed when Coach came into the locker room and went around to everyone and asked, 'How can your StrengthsFinder results support the hockey team?'"

I could not wait to hear what Cooper had chosen for his role.

Cooper became the Calminator, and described what that meant to the team. "I said that I could come into the locker room between periods and give advice, tell everyone to calm down, relax, that it was going to be fine and remind the team that there was a lot of hockey to be played. I also told Coach that if there were two guys arguing on the bench, I would calm them down and tell them not to waste their energy on that. I didn't realize that not many people could do that 'human glue' function."

Most people assume that what comes naturally to them is also natural for others, so they do not think of it as anything special. Jake Nestell had the same realization associated with his ability to observe and analyze things.

"Personally, the experience was important. You know your strengths, but you can't label or describe them. I would never have been able to come up with the term 'human glue,' but it describes me perfectly," said Cooper. "This knowledge will help me in job interviews and talking about my strengths."

"Personally, the experience was important. You know your strengths, but you can't label or describe them. I would never have been able to come up with the term 'human glue,' but it describes me perfectly," said Cooper. "This knowledge will help me in job interviews and talking about my strengths."

Shawn Patterson, an expert on strengths-based teams, asked Cooper about the team experience.

"It sounds cliché, but it was monumental," said Cooper with a slightly sheepish grin. "It was monumental not only for the guys graduating like me, but for next year's captains. It gives them the opportunity to realize that if they are not a guy who can stand up in front of the team, maybe they shouldn't force it. If you're really good at it, you should do it. If you're not, you shouldn't do it."

My mind leapt to Hunter Pence, a baseball player who gives crazy, rousing speeches before and after games. I had seen him do it in the playoffs and World Series. They are incredibly effective. But, if I tried to imitate Hunter, I would look like a fool, and it would not have near the impact. To thine own self be true, as Shakespeare said.

"This information helps with actual life," continued Cooper. "People know that if I'm in a business meeting, I can bring people together if they are arguing. I am never going to be the one who stands up and says, 'No that's wrong!' because I don't want to upset people."

"So this experience gave you a new perspective on how to achieve success?" I asked.

"Yeah, it made you think. It moved the rocks around in your head and got them floating."

Shawn and I both laughed out loud. That was a description neither of us had heard before.

"How did it feel to have a specific role to live up to?" asked Shawn.

Cooper spoke about the relief he felt. "Actually, it wasn't my role that was so important. That meeting was crucial because at the start of the meeting, I felt like I had 100 pounds on my shoulders. It was a relief to hear everyone talk about how they were going to use their strengths and describe their role. As each person spoke, 5 pounds were lifted off of me. By the time they got to me, I knew that I could trust the guys to do their job. Before the meeting, everyone wanted to be the leader. After the meeting, when we realized that the other guy could do a better job than I could at something, we just let him do it."

"...at the start of the meeting, I felt like I had 100 pounds on my shoulders. It was a relief to hear everyone talk about how they were going to use their strengths, and describe their role. As each person spoke, 5 lbs was lifted off of me."

Removing the burden off the shoulders of the captains had made a big difference in how they led the team, which contributed to their success as a group.

Cooper referred back to the original question posed when I learned the team's strengths. Who was the competition? "My life was easier because I didn't have to do as much of the babysitting to make kids get along," replied Cooper, sounding exasperated with those who were bickering. "They realized that maybe I'll never get along with you because we're too similar, but we can learn how to coexist and work together. That was our biggest struggle in the beginning of the year. After we worked with you, we stopped competing with one another and began competing against the other team."

The Cranbrook hockey team, under the leadership of Coach Weidenbach, was finally able to harness and channel all the horsepower in the room. Once that was accomplished, the team ran on all cylinders, making them nearly unstoppable.

Cooper underscored the point. "Our team results were amazing. I mean, I expected more red (influencing strengths) or Competition than a business team, but it was still outrageous. And the strengths were dead on."

Cooper's observation mirrored comments I hear often at all levels of the corporation: The StrengthsFinder results nailed the person. This helps drive connections between colleagues. If we resonate with our own StrengthsFinder profile, we trust and embrace the results of others on the team as well.

If we resonate with our own StrengthsFinder profile, we trust and embrace the results of others on the team as well.

Cooper commented on the journey of learning the strengths of the rest of the team, noting that he was surprised by some of the results, especially those associated with players who were more reserved. "I was intrigued to see their results and learn what they were hiding." Cooper mentioned two particular players that he knew would be heavy in influencing. "I knew what kind of color (category) they would be, but not beyond that to their individual strengths."

This is normal. We can observe someone and notice proclivities, but details related to talent are more difficult to discern. This is why the StrengthsFinder is such a useful tool.

"Some were really interesting, specifically Jake Nestell." Cooper made a very important observation about thinking strengths: they eat up time. He talked about how Jake needed time to think, and how that gave people the wrong impression. Others might mistake it for lack of effort or being a bump on a log. "Maybe he's looking at things at a different level, and he's taking longer to process it."

Amen. I asked Cooper if he had seen a change in Jake after the StrengthsFinder experience.

"Yes and no," replied Cooper. "He was always quiet. The change I did see was that he was using more of his analytical skills, telling us what kind of face off the other team was showing, etc. If even one person hears it and remembers it, it can save a goal."

Cooper's observation validated what Jake told me. He was more open to sharing his observations, and it was less about data and more about what he saw on the ice.

"Did you and Austin talk afterwards about how to reach people on the team?"

"I don't think we did, but it was implied. The biggest thing with the whole process was that it channeled everyone's anger. It didn't have to be said. I was willing to be me. 'I'm the green (relationship building) guy, let me step in!' I would joke about it. Others did the same for their role. It was nice for us."

It seemed that the understanding of other's strengths oiled the interactions between teammates. Maybe there was more joking, less poking. I decided to dig into Cooper's strengths a little bit more and asked about his Futuristic strength.

Cooper shared how it alters his perspective of time. "Nothing really panics me in the game. I never think, 'Oh my God, we only have two minutes left and we're down by two.' I always think there is more time. I'm less aggressive than others because I see that there is still possibility in the future."

Eleven people on the Cranbrook hockey team had Futuristic and would understand the possibility inherent in the next moment. There is a coach who has mastered this concept by creating a "next play" mentality on his team. It is an approach developed by the most winning coach in college basketball history, Coach Mike Krzyzewski of the Duke Blue Devils. Coach K (his name is reduced to K for obvious reasons) has his players shout, "Next Play!" on every trip up and down the basketball court, whether they score or not. He was interviewed about this concept and said, "You cannot do anything for the last play. Someone who is always looking in his (or her) rearview mirror will never make the most of the current moment. The next play is the next moment. Why wouldn't you want to be at your best for the next moment?" I write more about this topic in Appendix C.

Cooper's Futuristic strength kept the team focused on the next play and gave the team hope. His Relator, Adaptability and Developer kept them calm as the intensity of the game increased. It is an aspect of human glue that can make a big difference when the pressure is on. And in both sports and business, the pressure is always on.

Shawn Patterson rose from the table. He had to run to another meeting. We shook hands, and he gave me a look that said, "This kid is amazing!"

I explored another of Cooper's strengths, Significance. Significance is one of the least common top five strengths on the planet, and I wanted to hear how Cooper used it to lead the team.

"I have always preferred a teaching coach over a yelling coach," said Cooper, after thinking for a moment. "I would rather have the guy say 'Good job!' and use the sandwich technique. I know what I did wrong, so don't just yell at me – help me fix it."

"I would rather have the guy say 'Good job!' and use the sandwich technique. I know what I did wrong, so don't just yell at me – help me fix it."

I understood him instantly. People high in Significance are not motivated by being yelled at. It is a strengths violation. They need encouragement, positive reinforcement, and assurance that the work they are doing is important and making a difference. Being yelled at minimizes them and undermines their desire to feel elevated. It is not an effective approach to culling the best performance from a person high in Significance.

Then, there was Cooper's knowledge of the sandwich technique, and his ability to communicate how to effectively motivate him by using that process. I found that both mature and amazing. How many high school boys do you know who talk about the sandwich technique in developing talent?

The sandwich technique is used by instructors to drive improvement. Think about it in layers, just like the three layers of a sandwich. The first layer is an encouraging remark about progress the student has made. The second layer is a corrective remark, including what the student did wrong, and how to fix it. The third layer is another encouraging remark. The student hears two positive statements for each correction. This approach to developing others is investing in the human system by helping people feel good about themselves and at the same time, driving improvements in the formal system, like a good grade or successful completion of a task. For someone like Cooper, the sandwich technique is motivational. For others, they might need something a little stronger. Each person is different, but one can hardly go wrong with the sandwich technique, especially in the beginning of a learning journey. It is also a very effective technique in the workplace!

Cooper had more to say about it. "I do better when I'm confident and happy," he said slowly and thoughtfully. "I don't get motivated by guys saying 'You suck!' If I suck, then don't play me. That approach works with some of the red guys (those with lots of influencing strengths) because they'll try to prove you wrong. For some people, it's the way to get to them. It isn't the way to reach me. Coach Weidenbach has the ability to know who he can yell at and who will shut down."

This is why having a leader with the Individualization strength is important. Coach Weidenbach knows who to push – and how hard. He customizes his approach when interacting with his players. He does not make the most common mistakes, which are either treating everyone the same way or treating them as you would wish to be treated. That does not work, because no one is the same, and they are not little clones of you. Instead, treat them as the unique human being they are. We do it in dog training. We do it in horse training. No animal is the same, learns the same, or responds the same. Shouldn't we offer the same respect to people? Focus on what works best for them. Cooper has shown us that people who have the Significance strength want positive reinforcement. Negative approaches demoralize him.

He does not make the most common mistakes, which are either treating everyone the same way or treating them as you would wish to be treated. That does not work, because no one is the same, and they are not little clones of you.

Being a human glue guy, I wondered how Cooper felt about the "I refuse to let you fail" exercise and commitment.

He shared that it did not personally have a big effect on his game, but that it offered relief to know that there were a bunch of guys pulling on the rope behind him. "As much as it was 'I refuse to let you fail,' it was also 'I refuse to let the team fail.' That was the real outcome for me, and I showed that on the ice."

I thought about Cooper's role as co-captain. Captains have responsibility for the team, so he modified the commitment to reflect his role.

He refused to let the team fail. I liked that. I asked if he had used his strengths since the season had ended.

"Nothing really specific," he said. Then, he paused for a moment. "Wait, I take that back. I did use my strengths in school if kids were fighting or there was drama about their girlfriend. I was there to calm them down and find the middle ground. I do it, but I don't notice it."

Cooper, just like the rest of us, uses his dominant talents with the same level of consciousness that demonstrate when we breathe. We just do it, without noticing it.

"Tell me about Coach Weidenbach, and then I'll let you go."

"Playing for Coach Weidenbach taught me that you should make everything have a purpose."

"What do you mean?"

"He does things subliminally," said Cooper. "All the drills in practice revolve around our systems. He'd explain the drill, you learn it, and then he'd go over the d-zone the next day. Suddenly I would recognize that the drill from yesterday was part of the d-zone system. After the four years, I realized this was happening all the time. Now I appreciate that everything he does has a purpose." Cooper named additional examples of lessons learned in mundane or seemingly disparate activities, including cleaning the locker room, the drills on the ice, and the team bonding week over Thanksgiving. Every detail was planned by Coach and the sum of it all culminated in a disciplined and responsible approach to success.

That was an interesting lesson for a high school student to learn from a Coach, and I wondered how Cooper would use it later in life. I had no doubt that he would. It was time to bring the interview to a close, and I asked if Cooper had anything else to add.

"Thanks for making our lives easier," said Cooper.

I realized that helping him be a more effective captain was more important to him than winning the state championship. In fact, he hadn't even mentioned it. This supports the scientific research that reveals that we remember less about what we do than how we feel as we do it.

"By the way," added Cooper, "My dad has been watching Cranbrook hockey for eight years. He said that after we did the StrengthsFinder exercise, it was the best team he's seen in that entire time. It might have been even better than in '07, when we had Andrew Miller. Maybe it was the 13 seniors."

"My dad has been watching Cranbrook hockey for eight years. He said that after we did the StrengthsFinder exercise, it was the best team he's seen in that entire time."

Maybe. Or maybe it was the energy generated by a talented team that understood and honored the strengths of the individual and placed them in a position where they were valued and utilized.

Working with the Cranbrook hockey team had given me deeper appreciation for the approach I had developed. I was beginning to see new potential around my own value proposition. It felt really big to me, and I was struggling with specific words to bring it to life. I was confident that with enough reflection, the precise words would reveal themselves. It turns out, I was right.

PART 4: WHAT THE WORLD SAW

Chapter 17: No Teammate Left Behind

"The strength of the team is each individual member. The strength of each member is the team."

Phil Jackson

* * *

With the interviews behind me, I was seeing the value of the Clifton StrengthsFinder through the eyes of Coach and the players. It was enlightening. Focusing on the strengths of the team brought relief and it also oiled the talent machine so that they became a finely tuned engine delivering maximum power. It built team understanding and awareness. Everyone had a role, and all roles were equally valuable. I was reflecting upon Coach's determination to help each young man contribute in their own way, when a snappy catchphrase entered my head: **No talent left behind.**

Every single strength, in every single player, was valuable and put to use. The talent was not just assigned by Coach Weidenbach but harnessed through a process of individual ownership and a public commitment to the team. On the ice, off the ice – it did not matter. No talent was left behind. I spoke to Coach about the idea and he provided another level of understanding. **When no talent is left behind, then no teammate is left behind.**

All the ability of every single Cranbrook hockey player was considered useful in the mission to win the Michigan state championship. It did not matter how old the teammate was, how many minutes they played, or what their specific hockey ability was. Coach wanted to leverage every player in the room by fully understanding, valuing, and utilizing their strengths. This process offered an enormous value proposition. When no talents or teammates are left behind, everyone is valued, all voices are heard, and higher performance is achieved. This results in a distinct competitive advantage for those willing to make the investment.

Imagine a world where every available human talent is brought to bear to solve the problems of the day. Imagine a world where people are valued for being valuable and are put in well-defined roles where they can deliver superior performance by leveraging their strengths. Imagine a world where teams define success from a holistic point of view, including business and human objectives, and then align their powerful strengths, skills, and experiences behind it. The path leads us to a world of self-actualization and maximum contributions to the universe. This is the No Teammate Left Behind approach to success.

I decided right then and there that No Teammate Left Behind would become my signature offering to my clients. It so clearly defined how we would achieve success through our work together.

The No Teammate Left Behind value proposition is not a pipe dream. It is available today. Coach Weidenbach and the Cranbrook hockey team had proved it, and I had experienced it in the corporate world as well. Of course, this value proposition is possible only when we know what people's strengths and talents are. That is the power and beauty and significance of the Clifton StrengthsFinder tool.

If It Was Easy, Everyone Would Do it

One cannot make such grand pronouncements without acknowledging that the process of harnessing every ounce of talent on the team is no walk in the park. My experience shows that many coaches, managers, and leaders are unwilling to engage in the challenging work required to make the journey. The team also requires a maestro like Coach Weidenbach. Leadership is required. A No Teammate Left Behind program is difficult and demanding, but the payoff is magnificent. I am not referring to championships. I am referring to building a team that has heart and character and respect and discipline and brotherhood and chemistry. We want more of those in the world, don't we? In business? In schools? In non-profits? The benefits accomplished by Coach and his team are not limited to the sports arena. It is a strategic success plan for any team.

To further understand how Coach culled all the talent from the team, I summarized at a high level how he helped the players leverage their strengths and align to the success statement.

Cranbrook's Success Statement: The 2014/2015 Cranbrook Hockey Team is determined to win the state championship by recommitting to unselfish play, discipline, focus, trust, respect, team chemistry, brotherhood, and by caring for one another, on and off the ice. We refuse to let anyone fail.

Player	Formal Role	Human Role	Strengths to Use	Impact on Success Metric
Mason Schultz	Forward	Energize the team	Woo, Communication, Restorative, Includer, Strategic	Keep them fired up and encouraged
Nolan Rogow	Goalie	Human glue, Harmonizer	Harmony, Relator, Communication, Futuristic, Competition	Smooth ruffled feathers
Jack Blumberg	Defense	Observer, Leader, Inspirer	Learner, Command, Activator, Competition, Achiever	Keep team on track and healthy
Jake Nestell	Forward	Observer, Analyzer	Restorative, Adaptability, Strategic, Futuristic, Analytical	Identify and share chinks in opposing team's armor
Blake Rogow	Forward	Team competitor, penalty killer	Restorative, Deliberative, Achiever, Analytical, Competition	Lead team competitiveness and prevent goals
Austin Alger	Forward, Co-captain	Construct team success	Consistency, Arranger, Harmony, Competition, Significance	Refuse to let team fail by sticking to the system
Cooper Stahl	Defense, Co-captain	Insert calm & confidence	Futuristic, Developer, Relator, Adaptability, Significance	Glue team together to stay engaged in high pressure situations

If you took the StrengthsFinder, try building your own chart that summarizes your roles, strengths, and impact on your success metrics.

In the meantime, I had plenty of content to chew on. Coach and I had partnered to achieve success. He had maximized a formal system that resulted in great hockey skill and strategy development. I had maximized a human system that resulted in identifying and leveraging the team's strengths and forging an emotional connection to the definition of success. Together, our systems formed a powerful combination. Our method could be summarized in a mathematical sense as follows:

Well-Developed Formal System + Well-Nourished Human System + No Teammate Left Behind + Alignment to Success Metrics = Higher Performance

In the case of the Cranbrook hockey team, we could break it down a bit further. If you are following along with your own sports or business team, the breakdown would vary based on the purpose of your organization.

Well-Developed Formal Hockey System (external, physical, drills, plays)
+
Well-Nourished Human System (internal traits that have external manifestation, strengths-based)
+
No Teammate Left Behind Approach (fully leverage every person/strength)
+
Alignment to Success Metrics (formal and human)
=
Higher Performance

In the business world, the formal system would vary. Every company lives and dies by management and business controls. These are akin to the hockey team's formal system in the formula above. A sales team would require the talent, training and tracking mechanisms to be successful. The formal system for sales is quite different from one required to support patients, nurses, and doctors in a hospital. A consulting organization focused on accounting and audits would require yet another formal system. Lots of energy and precious

However, many companies assume the formal system is enough to drive success, and they underestimate or ignore the human system. This is a fatal strategic blunder. We need both.

resources are invested in formal systems, which is as it should be. However, many companies assume the formal system is enough to drive success, and they underestimate or ignore the human system. This is a fatal strategic blunder. *We need both.*

Here is an example of what happens when the human system is ignored.

Imagine two farms of similar size. Both farmers have rich soil, wonderfully sharp plows, and they plant the same seed. Successful crops require a field well-prepared for planting. Each farmer has a pair of oxen to help plow the field. One farmer views the oxen as a valuable asset, and feeds, shelters, and cares for them so that they grow and remain strong. Why? This farmer realizes that without strong oxen, the value of the plow is diminished. A strong pair of oxen will plow deep, straight furrows and complete their work more swiftly. The seed is planted at the right depth, resulting in a better crop yield. The farmer fully utilizes his resources, which drives greater productivity and profit.

The other farmer views his team of oxen as an extension of the plow. They are a tool to be used. He saves money by feeding the oxen just enough food and water to exist. They plod along in survival mode, exhausted and thin. The furrows they plow are not very deep or straight. The seed is planted at a shallow depth, making it difficult for the plants to develop strong roots. The crop returns lackluster results. The farmer squeaks by on a sub-optimized farm.

Which farmer will be in business 20 years from now? Which farmer would you invest in? Which farmer would you prefer to buy from? Which farmer is more likely to have higher quality, a safer workplace, and engaged workers who care about the product? Which farmer would you like to work for? Which farmer gains the competitive advantage over the long haul?

When there is a corporate field to plow, teams of well-nourished oxen will always outperform teams of starving oxen, regardless of the formal system in place to drive them forward.

When there is a corporate field to plow, teams of well-nourished oxen will always outperform teams of starving oxen, regardless of the formal system in place to drive them forward. Imagine how a well-nourished global workforce would perform! Imagine how your well-nourished teams would perform.

It was time to test my concept on my brother. I called Marty and shared the idea of my No Teammate Left Behind approach. He confirmed the value of the notion, and we proceeded to dissect it even further, acknowledging the importance of other critical success factors that manifested themselves in the Cranbrook story.

We discussed the implications of combining an amazing leader, a talented team with a strong desire to succeed, and the power of a strengths-based system. It gave the Cranbrook hockey team a distinct advantage over the competition. We also agreed that the same ingredients would offer a performance advantage to teams in the corporate world. In short, we were on the right path by helping strong leaders harness the strengths of individuals and teams, and align it with succeAfter we concluded our conversation, my mind was still whirling and processing the concept. I was meeting with a new client and figured that expressing the value proposition of a No Teammate Left Behind program would help them envision their team's better future. I began to jot down a few questions.

1. **Do you want to create a competitive edge with your team?**
2. **Do you want to invest in and nourish the human system and merge it with the formal system?**
3. **Do you want to leave no talent or teammate behind to accomplish the important work of your organization?**

Not 30 seconds later, my phone rang. It was Marty. "I'm a freaking genius, and I can prove it!"

"Well it's about time," I replied.

"You gave them a power play! When the team knew their strengths, it gave them a competitive advantage, just like a power play does in hockey. They basically had an extra man on the ice!"

"That's it!" I said, practically leaping out of my chair. "Implementing the StrengthsFinder is a power play! Teams who know and leverage their strengths have the competitive edge over teams that don't."

"Exactly!" he said. "And on a power play, the team is energized and focused because they are in a position to dominate with the extra man advantage. The other team is demoralized because they know they are at a disadvantage. They can see it. They can feel the energy gap. They can't even think about winning; *they have to focus on preventing a loss.*" My brother paused for a few moments, and then added, "It is almost unfair, and it's a game changer."

It was a game changer. We had executed a strengths-based power play. Our power play was the culmination of all the momentum associated with identifying success, investing in the trust bank, leaving no talent or teammate behind, valuing people for being valuable, and positioning them in a role to succeed. It generated a tidal wave of energy that provided a competitive advantage. When wielded with intent, the Clifton StrengthsFinder is not just a tool. It is the extra player whose sole purpose is to ignite all the talent on the team. The process of fully exploiting every talent and harnessing the full potential of every teammate is the power play. It offers a distinct competitive edge that separates the great teams from the good teams. Adding to the attraction of the No Teammate Left Behind power play is the fact that the journey is rewarding and joyful. It is the experience of a lifetime.

The Clifton StrengthsFinder is not just a tool. The Clifton StrengthsFinder is the extra player whose sole purpose is to ignite all the talent on the team.

This power play is available to any team, in any industry, in any region. It is simple, but not easy. And it is only a game changer if the team is willing to do the hard work along the way. Coach Weidenbach and the Cranbrook hockey team had taught us that.

I told myself to calm down and think it through. I began by reviewing the definition of a power play. From the Oxford Dictionary online, the power play was described as offensive tactics in a team sport involving the concentration of players at a particular point.

I modified the definition.

Our power play is the system of measuring, concentrating, and aligning the team's talent with the measurement of success, resulting in a competitive edge.

Our formula expands, describing how the competitive edge is achieved.

Power Play:

Well-Developed Formal System + Well-Nourished Human System + No Teammate Left Behind Program + Alignment With Success = Competitive Edge

It is possible that the competitive tone of my formula may rub some corporate folks the wrong way. However, let us remember that the goal of a team or a company is sustained success over time. Think about the farmer who invested in his oxen so that they remained strong and productive. Or think about the fact that only 12% of the Fortune 500 companies around in 1955 were still here in 2014. Back then, the average lifespan of a Fortune 500 company was expected to be about 70 years. Now, it is less than 15 years. When a company goes out of business, everyone loses. When a company grows with a holistic approach to success, everyone wins. A strategic competitive edge is more important than ever. We need not apologize for fully valuing the talent on the team to deliver sustainable performance. No Teammate Left Behind is a power play available to every single person and team on this earth.

Or think about the fact that only 12% of the Fortune 500 companies around in 1955 were still here in 2014.

Also, let us not forget that winning has many faces. Winning can be the result of investing in the human glue of the team. It can be the outcome of refusing to let anyone fail. It can be the result of leaving no talent or teammate behind. These strategies drive extraordinary team energy which is always a sight to behold. It is contagious, reciprocal and inspirational. When you give me energy, I am infected by your energy. I raise my energy to reciprocate, which further elevates your energy, and I feel inspired by the process. I share my increased energy with someone else on the team, and the same thing happens. This ladder effect is how team energy is created. The power play amplifies and directs that energy. It is unfortunate that I do not have a StrengthsFinder energy meter to prove that it is true.

Or do I? Do I have a way to prove the competitive advantage gained by a No Teammate Left Behind power play? I believe they call that data.

Chapter 18: What the Data Showed

"In God we trust, all others bring data."

William Edwards Deming

* * *

Was there more to our power play motif than wins/losses and trophies? We certainly had qualitative data. The players said they had treated one another differently after we worked together. Coach leveraged the results to shape the holistic role of each player. The energy boost and improved teamwork was discernible, even to people in the stands. The process had a clear and lasting impact on the boys – the exit interviews proved that. Those outcomes were a direct result of our investment in the human system and that generated a magnificent power play. The Cranbrook hockey team went 10-1 after we crafted our success statement and focused on the individual and collective strengths of the team. But beyond the winning record and state championship trophy, was there any other useful information buried in the numbers?

I am not a statistician. Data does not taste like Godiva chocolate to me. However, I was curious, and in my brain, curiosity is closely followed by energy, because Learner is my third strength. I did not want to get lost in the weeds. Yet, at the same time, I did not want to miss an opportunity to measure how the investment in the human system impacted the formal system. I concluded that there were some basic hockey metrics I could explore on the individual and team level.

1. Were there individual performance improvements?
2. Was there an uptick in the number of shots on goal per game after our workshops? Did the team score more goals? Those would be signs of a more effective offense.

3. Was there corresponding data that reflected an improvement in defense? Fewer shots on goal for the opposition? A reduction in the average number of goals scored against Cranbrook?

In short, was there a *strengths inflection point*, a moment in time where the impact of nourishing the boys with high octane rocket fuel was realized and reflected in the data? Was the resulting power play visible and measureable?

I turned to the source of all things: the internet. I'm glad I did.

The Numbers

I started by visiting the webpage that held the league records and noticed a few interesting statistics.

- One Cranbrook player had 15 minutes of penalties in one game. Wouldn't it be interesting to sit down with that player and explore what was going on? It is possible that he was unlucky or perhaps he was lost in any number of emotional tidal waves that happen in sports. On the other hand, it might also be an occasion for coaching and discussing his strengths. Was his Competition strength running amok? Was there some other burner set too high? If so, which one? Why? How could we dial it down? We own our strengths; they don't own us. Regulating our strengths is one of the biggest challenges we face, but it is an essential part of becoming a team asset, not a liability.

We own our strengths, they don't own us. Regulating our strengths is one of the biggest challenges we face, but it is an essential part of becoming a team asset, not a liability.

- Austin Alger, the Cranbrook co-captain who was voted Mr. Hockey, held the league record for the most assists in one game. What strengths may have contributed to that? Yes, he had Competition, but he also had Arranger and Significance. He told me in his interview that he liked constructing team success. Feeding the puck to another and watching that player score a goal would be a huge strengths payoff for him. The timing of his accomplishment was interesting. It happened after we invested in the strengths of the team.

- Austin Alger also had one of the longest point streaks in the league. He scored 29 points (goals and assists) over 10 consecutive games. Austin's point streak began after our workshops and ended with the state championship. Nolan Rogow had observed that as Austin went, the team went. A strong performance from Austin would energize the team.
- Mason Schultz had an eight-game point streak that started after our workshop. When I interviewed Mason, he talked about how he leveraged his strengths to inject more energy into everything he did. His energy boost would have occurred right about the time his point streak began. Were the two related? Possibly. Again, it is an opportunity for a strengths-based success conversation so that the player understands the connection between leveraging his strengths and achieving performance in his role.
- There were some team records of interest as well. Cranbrook had the second longest win streak – 10 games. Those wins came after we held our workshops on their run to the state championship.
- Cranbrook held the league record for the most goals scored in a game (11) and the largest margin of win (11). Again, it happened after our workshops.

Was our focus on success, strengths, and the human system the only contributing factor to these amazing individual and team accomplishments? Of course not. Did it help? Well, the timing is suspiciously lovely.

I moved away from the league records page and began to focus on individual games. I started by building a table with statistics from all the games.

The Cranbrook Hockey Team's 2014/2015 Data:

	Date	Opponent	Shots on Goal	Score	Win / Loss /Tie
1	11/21	Grosse Pointe North	39-24	**5-3**	**W**
2	11/22	Port Huron Northern	38-14	**8-1**	**W**
3	11/26	Trenton	26-21	**5-2**	**W**
4	11/28	Livonia Stevenson	50-23	**2-1**	**W (OT)**
5	11/29	Rochester United	23-41	**4-6**	**L**
6	12/5	Calumet	43-9	**5-1**	**W**
7	12/6	Calumet	58-15	**7-2**	**W**
8	12/12	Grand Rapids CC	45-14	**4-0**	**W**
9	12/13	Flint Powers	47-12	**5-2**	**W**
10	12/17	St. Marys Prep	53-40	**4-2**	**W**
11	12/20	Brother Rice	31-24	**4-2**	**W**
12	1/10	Catholic Central	32-20	**1-1**	**T**
13	1/16	De La Salle	56-18	**4-3**	**W (OT)**
14	1/17	St. Marys Prep	31-27	**4-5**	**L (OT)**
15	1/23	U of D Jesuit	42-21	**2-2**	**T**
16	1/24	Plymouth	36-23	**1-1**	**T**
17	1/30	Catholic Central	32-36	**5-4**	**W**
18	1/31	Grosse Pointe North	31-18	**4-0**	**W**
19	2/6	Port Huron Northern	29-15	**3-1**	**W**
20	2/7	U of D Jesuit	29-20	**2-0**	**W**
Completed Success and StrengthsFinder Workshops on 2/8					
21	2/13	Notre Dame Academy (WI)	25-34	**1-2**	**L**
22	2/14	Rochester United	31-18	**6-2**	**W**
23	2/20	Brother Rice	40-29	**4-1**	**W**
24	2/21	De La Salle Collegiate	37-22	**6-2**	**W**
25	2/27	Trenton	37-24	**6-4**	**W**
26	3/2	Royal Oak Shrine	46-7	**11-0**	**W**
27	3/4	Notre Dame Prep	48-3	**8-0**	**W**
28	3/7	Detroit Country Day	37-15	**4-1**	**W**
20	3/11	Wyandotte High	54-24	**9-4**	**W**
30	3/13	Riverview High	53-2	**8-0**	**W**
31	3/14	Houghton High	50-13	**4-0**	**W**

By examining the Win/Loss/Tie column, I could see the arc of the team's journey. Coach had said they performed well before Christmas, and then things began to go downhill. They were not playing up to their potential in January, and they were not playing as a unit. The ties were symptoms of trouble. The team was talented, but struggling. I calculated the team's win/loss rate.

CRANBROOK	Pre-Workshop	Post-Workshop
Win/Loss Record	15-2-3 (.750)	10-1 (.909)

The team's win rate before we worked together was 75%. Nothing shabby about that. If Cranbrook had won the three games that ended in a tie, it would have been 90% which was nearly identical to the post-workshop win rate of 91%. Remember, Coach is building great men through hockey. He wasn't particularly upset about the team's win/loss record. He was unhappy with their inability to play like a team.

This is the problem with statistics in sports. It is an output metric, a lagging indicator like the price of a stock on Wall Street. It is the result of the talent, skills, experience, and the intangibles that each player brings to the game. Those parameters are an input to the system. Statistics cannot measure the impact of an athlete's intangible characteristics. They can only be discerned by repeated exposure and contact with that player. Yet greatness often lies in that mysterious place inside a team's heart and soul, where the intangibles blend and brew in a magnificent cauldron. The No Teammate Left Behind program is an investment in human alchemy because it positively impacts traditional success metrics. We pour energy into the front end of the success system to drive better outcomes on the back end. More on that in a moment.

I studied the table but felt edgy and uncomfortable. The data looked like visual chaos to me. I couldn't see patterns – it was too much information. Knowing that analyzing numbers is not my strong suit (my Analytical comes in at 24 out of 34 strengths), I decided to throw it all in a spreadsheet and plot it. My heart pounded as I examined the graphs associated with goals scored and shots on goal. There were trend lines! There was a strengths inflection point. Identifying the Cranbrook hockey team's strengths and adopting a No Teammate Left Behind approach had fostered team chemistry that had compounded over time. The guys had been empowered by Coach Weidenbach to bring their unique strengths to their specific role on the team. The team responded well because it was like asking a fish to swim and a jaguar to run. The high powered race cars were aligned and pulling in unison towards the team's definition of success. The culmination of all these factors was like having an extra player on the ice. It had provided a competitive advantage. Check out the chart below.

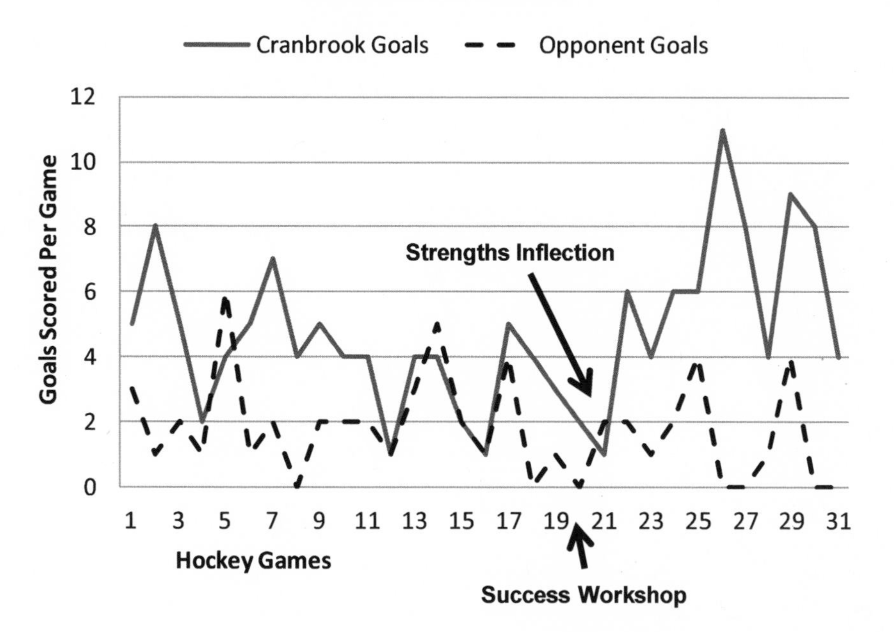

This chart represents the Cranbrook and opponent goals scored per game over the entire season of 31 games. I made note of a few interesting facts. I realized for the first time that the Cranbrook players had never been shut out. They scored at least one goal every game. Over a 31-game season, that's a powerful nod to the talent on the team. Cranbrook shutout four teams in the 11 games after our workshop, compared to three shutouts in the previous 20 games. The Cranbrook team lost the first game after our workshop (game #21 along the bottom axis) but Coach said it was the best they had ever played as a team. The strengths inflection point occurred at game #22. Over the last 11 games, Cranbrook scored 67 goals. The competition scored 16 goals. That is an enormous gap.

I eagerly plotted a similar graph of the shots on goal data. Had they peppered the opposing goalie more frequently after adopting a No Teammate Left Behind approach to success? Boy, did they ever!

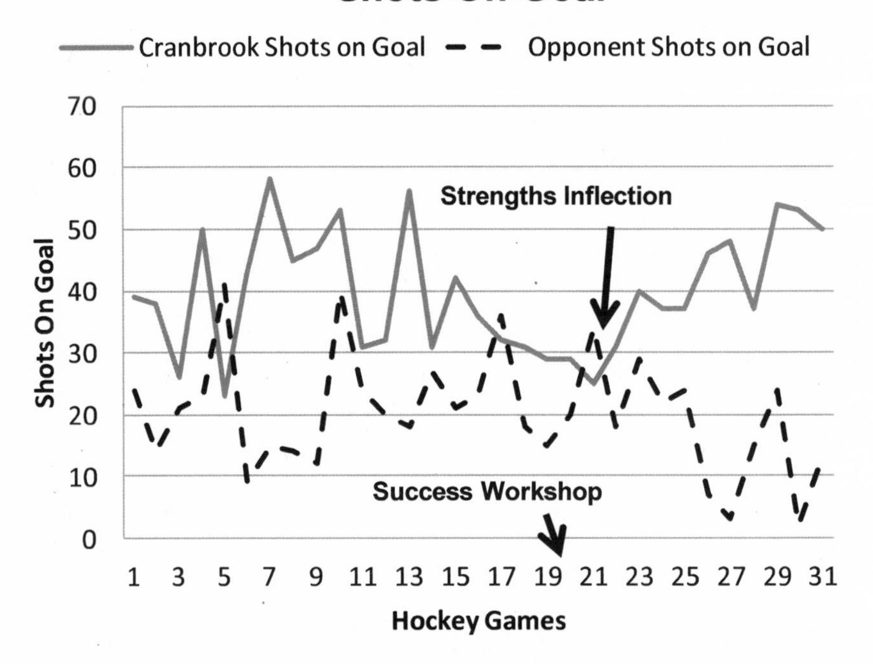

This chart represents the Cranbrook and opponent shots on goal over the entire season of 31 games. Notice that there were only three games all season where the opposition outshot Cranbrook. Two of those games were losses. Post-workshop, Cranbrook not only attacked the opposing goalies with more shots, they also prevented more shots. There were three games where the opposition had fewer than 10 shots on net. Winning without shooting the puck is downright impossible. Combined with the additional stress from the increased offensive pressure from Cranbrook, it would make for a miserable experience for the other team. After we evaluated their strengths, refined their roles, and focused on team success, there was a growing and insurmountable chasm between the shots on goal achieved by Cranbrook versus the opposition. Look at the trend lines after Game #22 – that team was on fire! The post-workshop data reflected the perpetual, "extra man" advantage described in the previous chapter. Cranbrook was out-shooting and out-defending the opposition.

I now had two sets of data supporting the improvement in the team, but my data adventure was not yet finished. I discovered that there were more jewels hidden in the averages.

Post-workshop improvements include:

- Cranbrook outshot the competition by an average of 24 shots per game, reflecting an eight percent increase.
- A 20% decrease in the average shots on net for the opponents.

What did the average goals per game statistics reveal?

Cranbrook's Average Goals Per Game

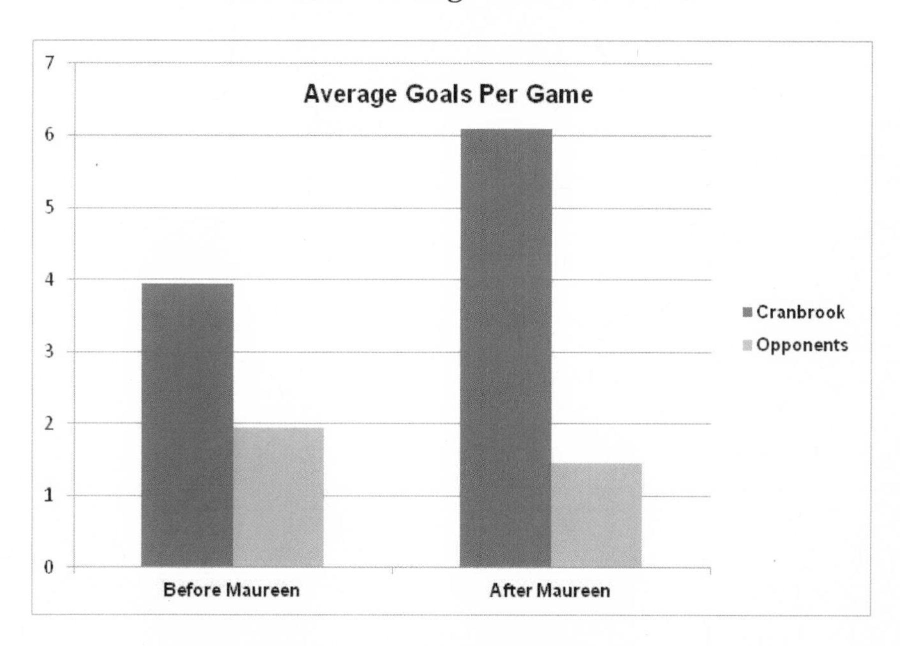

This was like winning the Kentucky Derby by 10 lengths versus winning in a photo finish. *The Cranbrook Hockey team was not squeaking by. They were dominating.* The No Teammate Left Behind competitive advantage was present on both sides of the blue line.

I made note of a few caveats. The post-workshop game count was lower than the pre-workshop. Any number of factors can impact a win or a loss. The teams they played were not the same. It was later in the season so the boys were more experienced. Success is not formulaic in nature. There were also other factors.

Maybe the individual players took higher quality shots. Perhaps it was a result of the improved team chemistry, and every player experiencing "flow" at the same time. Maybe the goalies and teams they faced after we worked together were not as strong. There were many variables, but the improvement was undeniable.

The real purpose of my data analysis was to identify a marker associated with our No Teammate Left Behind journey. I wanted to evaluate the return on investment that Coach Weidenbach had made in the human system. Did the data reflect the outcome of increased self-awareness and team awareness, and a strong connection to their definition of success? When they refused to let anyone fail, did that increase the success of individuals and the team? Was it the result of oiling the talent engine? Was it a direct outcome of increasing the human glue or harnessing all the influencing strengths? I believe the answer to each question is "Yes." These investments provided a clear and visible competitive edge that is "the rest of the story" behind the statistics. That, combined with the fact that these were hockey players who had extraordinary physical talent, is what made them seemingly unbeatable by the end of the season.

A Strengths Revolution in Sports

As I considered the intersection of data, talent, and success, my Ideation and Strategic strengths kicked in. Suddenly, it hit me. Coach and I had pulled off a *Moneyball*-like experiment. We had taken my corporate focused strengths-based success system and injected it into a sports team. We had merged the formal system with the human system, investing in both to achieve greater success. My before and after data analysis highlighted the improvements in performance gained by investing in the internal characteristics of the talented hockey players. My interviews with the players underscored the value of our No Teammate Left Behind approach. We had merged tools and ideas from Wall Street and brought them to Hockey Street. That parallels what happened in *Moneyball.*

If you are not familiar with *Moneyball*, let me briefly explain. *Moneyball* is a book written by Michael Lewis that documents the true story of how smart guys from Harvard and elsewhere, with an interest in baseball, revolutionized the data used to predict the future performance of baseball players. It is the journey of the Oakland A's baseball team general manager, Billy Beane, and his unconventional approach to selecting baseball players based upon statistics that were ignored or undiscovered by traditional gurus of the sport. Think *Revenge of the Nerds* meets *The Bad News Bears*.

The cornerstone of the *Moneyball* approach was to identify players that were pegged as losers when measured by traditional metrics, but scored well in statistics that Billy Beane knew were better predictors of future success. He was the first real believer in this merger of brains and brawn and was in a position of power to leverage the data available. It allowed him to build winning teams at a lower cost because other teams did not want the same ballplayers that Billy wanted. Billy Beane valued and deployed players differently than other general managers. It was a winning strategy, and it was cost effective. *Moneyball* was a money saver for Billy Beane.

I am not interested in the money side of this equation. I am interested in knowing and leveraging the secret weapons inside a championship player (or employee). Not just the physical talent but the internal strengths that fuel his or her greatness. These are the intangibles that each of us bring to the universe. Through the StrengthsFinder, we have access to human data that can help us understand the hearts and minds of talented athletes so that we can help them achieve breakthrough performance in their sport. It is useful information for coaches.

Selecting talent in sports (and in business) is a form of gambling, of betting on a future that may or may not come to fruition. Considering the amount of cash and pressure associated with the sports industry today, including at the high school and college levels, wouldn't we want to know everything we can about that player so we can help them perform at their best? What if coaches were to nourish a player's strengths like they do their swing or slap shot? Wouldn't it make sense to know the source of a player's internal rocket fuel? Wouldn't we leap at the opportunity to understand their lens to the world? Wouldn't the head coach of any Big Ten sport want to know how to fully capitalize upon every ounce of talent they have on the team? The answer is an absolute,

"Yes!" This should not be new news to you. Coach Weidenbach said exactly the same thing about his team way back in Chapter 3.

Conversely, from the player's point of view, wouldn't he or she like to describe with confidence and clarity what makes them valuable, beyond their physical capabilities? Wouldn't it be great if they could offer examples of how they had helped the team win with their heart, spirit and soul, in addition to their athletic prowess? Wouldn't it be amazing if athletes could describe how they inspire their teammates or how they lead in the locker room? What they love most about the sport and how they bring their complete selves to the game? If athletes possessed a deep understanding of their strengths, they might choose the school or coach that would most value them for being valuable. Ditto for job interviews in the corporate world, by the way.

I decided to reread *Moneyball* and explore how the No Teammate Left Behind approach might have helped the smart guys and Billy Beane make even more effective choices. Could they have eliminated some of the guesswork in understanding and selecting baseball players? I swiftly realized that there remained an information gap that could have been minimized by the journey that Coach and I had made with the Cranbrook hockey team. Armed with better statistics for measuring and predicting performance was not enough. Our No Teammate Left Behind program would have been extremely useful. Billy Beane and his staff were still searching to identify those intrinsic, internal, intangible characteristics that do not show up in a stat sheet, yet can make or break a player, a game, or even a team.

These intangible characteristics have descriptors, including words like heart, grit, respect for the game, scrappy, impatient, patient, hungry, smart, mentally tough, curious, presence, resilient, confident, gutsy, coachable, clutch, thoughtful, unflappable, feisty, gamer, solid, resourceful, persistent, and single-minded. You will not find formulas for these critical success factors in a spreadsheet. You will find clues to them, and others, in the Clifton StrengthsFinder assessment.

In *Moneyball*, I discovered multiple examples of how these internal components of a person's holistic being were desirable or impacted the success of the team. Here are a few examples.

We can measure internal patterns of excellence that manifest themselves in an external manner.

1. When evaluating a powerful hitter, the baseball scouts spoke about a particular player as having "presence". This is a word often used to describe those people with influencing talents in their StrengthsFinder profile. When they walk into the conference room or the locker room, people notice them. It might be Command or Self-Assurance or Significance. It might also be an executing strength like Focus or Restorative. We would have to know their strengths and explore them with each player to understand with certainty. The point is this: we can measure internal patterns of excellence that manifest themselves in an external manner. By the way, having that "presence" did place the player in the "yes" column. He was selected.
2. One scout, in dismissing a player, said he simply didn't look like a baseball player. Looks, schmooks! Billy Beane was great at smashing down that theory with metrics that measured future success for baseball players, like getting on base. However, he remained in the dark about how the player thinks to solve problems, executes tasks, builds relationships, or influences others on the team. We can't tell anything about those capabilities by looking at the player. My No Teammate Left Behind approach helps us measure and fully exploit that information.
3. One of the most moving stories in the book is about a player who suffered a career-ending elbow surgery. He could no longer throw the ball, but he could still hit with the best of them. Billy Beane grabbed a hold of this guy and moved him to first base, a role which traditionally requires less throwing. With encouragement from the infield coach (and we all need encouragement when we are trying something new), the player eventually became comfortable in his new position. There was another unexpected benefit. It also allowed him to bring his whole self to

the game. For him, baseball was a social experience. From a StrengthsFinder standpoint, he might have Woo, the gift of never meeting a stranger, or Communication, the gift of verbal engagement. In his new position at first base, he chatted it up with the opposition, and in the process, had more fun. Having more fun made him more confident on the field and in the batter's box. His numbers went up. Billy Beane realized that when other teams had tried to limit this player's social talent, it had actually undermined his performance. Bringing his holistic strengths to the game was critical to the first baseman's ability to deliver his maximum contribution to the team. He needed that strong connection between his soul and his role. It also paid off in other ways. This player was able to share information he received from opposing players when they were on first base. He used it to encourage and provide feedback to a struggling pitcher. When the pitcher received the information, his confidence bounced back, and he mowed down nine out of 10 batters in the playoffs. Imagine if Billy Beane and his staff had known the strengths of the whole team and had leveraged all that talent on and off the field.

Bringing his holistic strengths to the game was critical to the first baseman's ability to deliver his maximum contribution to the team. He needed that strong connection between his soul and his role.

There are other examples, but these are enough to support my point. Statistics do not measure the secret powers within the heart, soul, or mind of a player. Deploying the No Teammate Left behind program can unlock and harness the internal characteristics that contribute to an athlete's external success.

We can help coaches and players and teams become higher performing in the same way that leveraging innovative statistics helped Billy Beane build a successful baseball team. The proof is found not so much in the compelling data as it is in the stories of those fabulous young men documented in earlier chapters. When they were expected to bring all their talent to the team, they soared. Coach Weidenbach, an extraordinary and experienced sports leader, recognized it, too. As a reminder, this approach is not new. It's new to sports.

At its core, the No Teammate Left Behind program is the sum of my ten years of experience in building winning teams. I have my work with dozens and dozens of organizations to lean on. I have discovered untapped talent sitting idle and undervalued in cubicles all around the world. I have found buried human treasure in Singapore. In Brazil. In the Netherlands. In Spain. In New York. In CEOs and interns. In boardrooms and locker rooms. In tech teams and sales teams. I have helped individuals and teams fully exploit their talent so that they achieve success and fulfillment. My work with Coach Weidenbach and the players has deepened my belief and broadened my sphere. There is only one stipulation: The group must be hungry for greatness and be open to exploring their internal world to achieve external results. Is the team's desire for success running deeply through their veins?

I have always wanted to divide the world into two teams: those who deeply desire to achieve their full potential and those who do not. I want to stand at the front of the masses and ask, "Who wants to work hard to understand and leverage their God-given greatness to achieve their full potential?" Those who raise their hand can move to the left and be on my team. Those who do not can move to the right and be on someone else's team.

I will pour my heart and soul into those on my team, helping them understand their strengths, define success, and bring their holistic excellence to bear. I will get down and dirty and work in the trenches with them. That is what I do best. It is my value proposition to the world.

After one year, we could compare my team's level of success, well-being, and happiness with those who did not wish to invest in themselves. My team will thrive through increased self-awareness, team awareness, and a real understanding of their value proposition. The other folks will survive and stumble along, hoping that somewhere, sometime, someone will help them figure out how to be at their best. I know this to be true because I am still receiving grateful emails from people inside The Company whom I coached years ago. They are thriving in difficult times, while others are barely surviving.

So, to those of you in the industry of sports, I ask: Who wants to work hard to understand and leverage their God-given greatness to achieve their full potential? Who wants to deeply explore their intangible awesomeness and make tangible use of it? Who wants to know the holistic makeup of their team – how they think, execute, relate, and influence – so that they can align it with a common definition of success? Who wants help mining untapped talent? Who wants to productively lead the high-powered engines in the locker room? You do? I am all in.

Let's find those Thinking Men, those Harmonizers and Energizers, those Constructors and Calminators, and the others on your team who are currently undervalued and underutilized. Let's exploit the internal talent on your teams to optimize performance. Let's launch a strengths-based revolution in the world of sports. If you start today, in five years you will be light years ahead of your competition! Your teams will compete with greater energy, chemistry and success. There will be no talent or teammate left behind. You will know the satisfaction and momentum of maximizing the internal and external strengths of your team. You will be in on the ground floor of this revolution, and will be a better coach, leader, or athlete as a result. It is a compelling vision.

If you are not all in, I am sorry because you will miss the opportunity to discover, value, and harness the talent on your team. That is unfortunate for the players or people you lead.

I suspect this story will reach a small, but select, group of coaches, athletes and leaders who seek to build their best teams and achieve their highest performance. I want to work with you. If we bring my No Teammate Left Behind program to your people, I know we can make a difference for them. We have already accomplished that for a group of talented young men with a deep desire to achieve their full potential. We have compelling qualitative and quantitative data to support it.

Enough said on that topic. Let us return to the journey made by the Cranbrook hockey team.

When no talent or teammate is left behind, untapped power is discovered and leveraged. We could measure it.

For our heroes, the Cranbrook varsity hockey players, the statistics shared in this chapter reflect the impact of valuing and leveraging all strengths from all members of the team. It is a nourishing experience. What happens when we nourish our kids, our plants, or our employees? Growth happens. Performance improves. Morale rises. Collaboration and engagement increase. These benefits are what the boys spoke about in their interviews, and they would have felt them with or without a state championship trophy. When no talent or teammate is left behind, untapped powers are discovered and leveraged. We could measure it.

My mind leapt to any number of maxims associated with sudden and spectacular changes in behavior. When we tapped the innate strengths of the players, what happened? Had we released the hounds? Awakened the sleeping giant? Poked the bear?

A Coach's View

In an attempt to mitigate my flair for the dramatic, I decided to engage Coach Weidenbach. He was the voice of reason. He understood the team, the statistics, and the experience better than I did. I emailed my data, charts, and list of caveats for him to review.

He replied:

One thing to note – our opponents in the last half of the season were not quite as strong as the first half of the season. We played more MIHL opponents (a tougher league) before Feb 1.

However, I do believe we played way better the second half and in the playoffs. The chemistry was also way better. There is NO doubt in my mind that the StrengthsFinder program was the main factor.

I thanked him for his input, and said I would add that point about the weaker opposition to my caveats. I asked if the data surprised him. He quickly replied that he found the data interesting but not surprising. However, Coach was surprised by the competitive advantage gained by inserting the StrengthsFinder assessment tool.

I am surprised on how our players reacted to StrengthsFinder and the long-lasting positive effects. StrengthsFinder helped us turn the corner for sure.

Once we got rolling after Feb 1st, there was no stopping us. It was an unbelievable feeling to experience the energy and momentum.

The team had migrated from a discouraging place of being talented and struggling to an elevated state of being talented and unstoppable. The energy and momentum was prominent to a point that it even excited Coach – and he has been around hockey for decades. It was the feeling of being unstoppable that overwhelmed the opposition. This joyful sense of performing without drag is the desired outcome of my No

Teammate Left Behind program. It is what happens when we take a highly talented team and nourish their internal greatness. They flourish in ways previously unimagined. They breathe rarefied air comprised of camaraderie, trust, effort, and a deep belief in one another. **When this occurs, the team arrives at Destination Unstoppable**. The Cranbrook hockey team reached that place, and remained there for the rest of the season.

It was the sense of being unstoppable that overwhelmed the opposition.

I wondered if the other Cranbrook coaches or player parents might have their own perspective on how the team reached Destination Unstoppable. I reached out to a few people, and received powerful and touching observations.

Assistant Coach Patrick Ronayne noticed that after our workshops, the team was more focused on a common vision of success. "In the beginning of the season they seemed like a herd of young colts running around, sometimes in circles with no direction or focus," said Coach Ronayne. "Later they were like a herd of stallions, running in a pack toward the same goals, not asking questions, just doing and achieving."

There is something primal and inescapable about a pack mentality. It strikes fear in the minds of their prey.

Pause for a moment and imagine how the opposition might have felt when that determined pack of stallions thundered upon them with unrelenting fury. Hearts pounded. Defense crumbled. Mistakes were made and paid for. Panic set in. Courage and morale sank. It was over. That's what Destination Unstoppable looks like and feels like. It is a perfect visual for how the Cranbrook hockey team played the game.

Assistant Coach Scott Lock was aware of a drop in selfish behavior. "Some players thought they were entitled to more ice time, etc. After (the workshops) I believe everyone's roles became clearer and each player did their particular part in the success of the team."

Coach Lock also spoke about the difference between being a great player and being a great teammate. "We knew we were a skilled team but during parts of the season we did not play for each other." Once everyone knew their strengths and understood what success looked like, players and coaches were more supportive of one another and helped each player succeed in their role. "We knew if we played the right way, no other team would beat us this year unless we let things happen. The players decided to make things happen and it was a blast. The journey was the best part of it all."

Goaltender Coach Ron Slavick shared insight into how the workshops impacted goalie Nolan Rogow. "I saw Nolan looked at a little differently in the locker room. He was still the same personable, funny guy that everyone loved, but now he was there being a teammate and not just a buddy." Nolan would use a joke to bring someone up or bring someone down so that they didn't get too high on themselves. "If I heard the term 'glue guy' once, I heard it a million times regarding Nolan. He truly did become a glue guy for this team."

Coach Slavick also noted an improvement in the team's chemistry. "The team needed that extra push to take us from a great team to a championship family," said Coach Slavick. "In my opinion, you don't win a championship without that. In every family, the members know the strengths and weaknesses of each other. I believe this is what happened after doing the workshops with you. It allowed us to work harmoniously to achieve our goals."

One parent observed a transformation in the team's demeanor after we focused on strengths and success. "There was a calm factor when (the boys) came out of the locker room. They already believed they would win. They all had a role on the team, felt secure in that role and secure in what the outcome would be. It was extraordinary to watch. These distracted, unfocused teenagers became confident young men, playing a team sport by delivering important contributions through their personal strengths."

Coach Lock confirmed that observation, and added, "During our journey to the state championship, I noticed that our players never got rattled. We were so confident in each other that the hockey part just took care of itself."

Did anyone notice a change in their son's play? They did. "Before his role was defined, he was always trying to 'figure it out', trying to do it all and wasn't overly effective," said one father. "(After the workshops) our son had harnessed his energy and focus. He was happy to have a clear role. He was happy to be confident in his role. His play for the remainder of the season reflected confidence, energy and higher performance." One mother said that many parents marveled at the improvement in their own boy's performance on the ice and confirmed the connection to the rapidly increasing momentum of the team.

Parents also saw benefits that will last beyond high school and hockey. "'This 'cheat sheet for life' made him feel relaxed in knowing why and how he could use his unique strengths for the first time. He was more self-assured, more relaxed knowing his natural abilities and he was more effective in all that he attempted to accomplish. Understanding his strengths gave him the extra confidence to transition smoothly into a wonderful college experience."

Another parent said that we created cohesion out of chaos. One father spoke about the difference in the team after we worked together, describing it like flipping a light switch. The increase in performance was instantaneous and remarkable.

These observations support the advantage of implementing the No Teammate Left Behind program. It is a success strategy. Players and employees feel empowered, confident, and valued for being who they are. They are relieved of the burden and futility of being someone they are not. Being who they are is the surest path to a happy, engaging, and meaningful life. Success is a byproduct.

Our investments in the human system drove improvements in the formal system, and we had the data to prove it. No talent was left behind because we had harnessed it all. No player was left behind in the quest to win the state championship. The team achieved the sense of momentum gained by identifying individual strengths, aligning them with success in the role, and aligning that with success for the team. The result was a power play that delivered a measurable competitive advantage. This Cranbrook hockey team was not to be denied. Destination Unstoppable was on their horizon, and they reached it.

My methodology, which had so often been tested in a business environment, had played an instrumental role in the hockey team's achievements. I again felt valued for being valuable and appreciated the good fortune associated with the opportunity to work with the Cranbrook coaches and players.

To test the readability of my analysis, I emailed it to my brother, Marty. He manages an automotive test lab and reviews data for a living. Later that evening, he called.

"The data," he began, "is unbelievable. It took me a while to figure it out, but the shots on goal stats are amazing. The trend lines, the gap between Cranbrook and the other teams – it is truly impressive."

"I know! It is exciting. Do you see the inflection point?"

"There is a clear difference in the before and after data."

I began to share what I thought had happened and how investments in the human system had driven results in the formal system, when he interrupted me, offering a test engineer's point of view.

"You helped remove interference from the system."

I liked his choice of words. The idea of removing interference had both a physical connotation and a mental one – think of removing the background hiss on a conference call or tweaking a dial to eliminate static on the radio. Conversation and information is much easier to process without the distraction from that hideous noise. Frustration would decrease, resulting in improved understanding and team chemistry. In the physical world, when there is no interference, power is uninhibited and momentum increases! That sense of being unstoppable rises from the team and perpetuates like a magnetic flywheel.

I supported his point with feedback from the players. "The players often used the word 'relief' when they spoke about the impact our work had on them personally. I think that's a result of removing the interference," I replied. "There was less conflict. They had clear expectations for their role - on and off the ice. They understood their strengths and the strengths of other players. They had defined success and that served as a compass for the team. I believe all those things removed interference. It was like defying gravity."

"I can see that," replied Marty. "What is amazing though is how it is reflected in the data."

It was amazing. I had a wide grin on my face as I shared some of Coach Weidenbach's thoughts with Marty. Post-workshop momentum was evident in the charts and tables. The players had felt it, the coaches and families had seen it, and I had the statistics to prove it. There was an inflection point that demonstrated the power achieved by harnessing the untapped talent on the Cranbrook hockey team. "We felt unstoppable!" was the cry of the warriors who made the long, hard journey to achieve their destiny. It was glorious.

Chapter 19: What Success Looks Like

"Success is peace of mind, which is a direct result of self-satisfaction in knowing you made the effort to become the best of which you are capable."

John Wooden

* * *

My interviews were done and my adventure in data mining was behind me. So I began to wrap up my writing.

I did not ask Coach Weidenbach if he would like to see the boys' interviews. I just assumed he would and I printed a draft copy for him.

On my drive up to Cranbrook, I thought about the sports maxim: "Leave it all out on the field." It is a phrase that implies 100% effort and commitment to success during a game. I get it, but I thought the phrase was missing something.

**A team's best effort can be achieved only when everyone's best is leveraged.
If a leader overlooks or undervalues an immensely talented person on the team, then it is not possible for that team to reach its full potential.**

With Coach's guidance, not only did the players *leave* it all out there, they *brought* it all out there. That is a more powerful value proposition. The Cranbrook hockey team left no talent or teammate behind on their winning journey. Therefore, they had more horsepower to bring to a full effort commitment. Leaving it all on the ice is a great accomplishment only after a team has identified and harnessed all the holistic strengths to bring to the game. A team's best effort can be achieved only when everyone's best is leveraged. If a leader overlooks or undervalues an immensely talented person on the team, then it is not possible for that team to reach its full potential. Why? You have one less person pulling on the rope. The team is sub-optimized, making them less effective. This result is the opposite of a power play. Leaving it all out there is not a winning strategy unless the leader brings the full horsepower of the team to the effort.

My experience in developing successful leaders and teams, validated by our journey with the Cranbrook hockey team, reveals additional critical success factors, including:

1. **Strong Leader Focused on the Human System:** Achieving maximum performance requires a coach (or leader or manager) that is committed to go far beyond the formal system and invest deeply in the human system. The No Teammate Left Behind program is not a one and done. It is a process which demands focus just like improving the physical talent on the team. The resulting increase in team chemistry is worth its weight in gold.
2. **Strengths Expert**: It requires an expert in the Clifton StrengthsFinder to foment the conversations around the human system and help each player understand how to fully utilize their strengths and the strengths of the other people on the team. This person must have deep experience with teams and must be confident enough to respond well to challenges from high-powered athletes, leaders, and executives. There is no melting on the road to greatness and this rule applies equally to everyone involved with the team's success.
3. **Team First Mentality:** It requires a unit willing to collaborate on the definition of success, and focus on "we" more than "me." Being a great teammate *and* a great player is the goal.
4. **Commitment to Success:** The team must be hungry. Players or employees must have a deep desire to complete the sustained internal work required to achieve external success. This is always a challenge because many teams and companies have an execution-focused culture which absorbs precious time and energy. We need time and energy to complete the internal work. We also need encouragement and support from leaders.
5. **Follow the Destination Unstoppable Roadmap.** I provide a detailed Destination Unstoppable roadmap in Appendix A. It is comprehensive in nature, so don't be intimidated or overwhelmed. It

is unlikely you would adopt each step. Like all plans, it is meant to be modified by you. I do the same with each team I work with.

Teams that demonstrate the presence of all five critical success factors are rare, which is what makes long-term success so difficult to achieve in sports and business. It is also why so few teams reach their full potential. I hope you are on one of those rare teams, or want to engage in building one.

I dropped off final versions of the player interviews for Coach Weidenbach to review. He was at lunch, so I left them for him. Later, he sent me an email.

Thanks for dropping off the player interviews. I just read every one of them. WOW! I have never been happier. To know that the hockey program has done so much for them makes me smile. It is definitely more about the journey than the destination.

When I read Coach's email, I realized that the collective understanding of everyone involved had increased dramatically. I was not sure how much Coach knew about how the boys felt, or if he was previously aware of the details captured in my interviews. His email indicated that there may have been a few surprises. I suspected that Coach may have received what we were all seeking – to be understood and valued for our value proposition. From his players' own remarks, he received a tremendous gift. Their experiences validated Coach's approach, belief system, and determination to use hockey as the vehicle to transform young men into great men.

I pulled up Coach's email where he had defined what success looked like for him. His personal goals included:

1. To build a team with great chemistry.
2. To have players respect each other at all times.
3. To have players who care about each other and the success of the team more than just caring about themselves.
4. To win a state championship (optional)

He explained that he had good kids, but no Patton or Braveheart, and he placed importance on the players taking ownership for their success. He reminded me that successful teams are not created when the coaches care more about the outcome and goals than the players do.

Read his email, and then consider the transformation of the team. The Cranbrook hockey team had developed great chemistry. Respect had replaced disdain. Players were invested in each other and the success of the team. They adopted an "I refuse to let you fail" mentality. And as a result, they dominated the playoffs and won the Michigan Division III State Championship. By his own measurements, Coach had achieved his goals. That was what success looked like for him.

What I love most about Cranbrook's journey is that the team did not need a William Wallace or General Patton in the locker room. Instead, they required a fully leveraged Austin Alger, Cooper Stahl, Nolan Rogow, Blake Rogow, Mason Schultz, Jack Blumberg, Jake Nestell, and many others. Our No Teammate Left Behind strategy accomplished the goals by fully capitalizing upon the strengths the boys did have rather than lamenting over what they did not have. They were not broken. I did not fix them. I helped them become more of who they already were, focusing on the abundance within. That's what success looks like for me.

They were not broken. I did not fix them. I helped them become more of who they already were, focusing on the abundance within. That's what success looks like.

I thought about the dozens and dozens of teams I had seen in The Company that would never know the experience shared by the Cranbrook hockey team. These young men had learned more about their individual and collective talents than some people learn in a lifetime. They had internalized that information for their own benefit and had used it to deliver peer-to-peer coaching. More importantly, they understood the value of that knowledge and could apply it throughout the rest of their lives. We were building strengths-based leaders. The future of Michigan – heck, the future of this nation – rested upon people like them, those who would value and leverage the holistic abilities of their colleagues. Won't it be fun to watch where they go from here?

I know what success looks like, because I have seen it from the inside out. I have worked with a maestro who said, "I tell them all the time that we have to make music, not noise. The maestro makes the music happen. If they don't make music, it's the maestro's fault." I watched the boys play with determination, focus, and energy. They became a high-performing unit. The interviews are compelling, and all share a common thread: the journey to become a great team was their Destination Unstoppable. The trophy was simply a footnote.

The Ending to Our Story

We started our adventure with the goal of refuting a common premise: "Fix your weaknesses and you'll be a rock star!" No. Hone your strengths, and you'll be a rock star. Manage your strengths and weaknesses with aplomb, and watch your performance soar. It is a key component of an effective success strategy.

Our experience focused on the transformation from talented and frustrated, to talented and unstoppable. To have friction and unproductive conflict removed from the system by helping people do what they do best. To experience the joy of learning about one's greatness, and have that greatness be developed, leveraged, and celebrated. To have all that talent honed and focused on a team success statement. To have one's strengths honored for contributions made on and off the ice. To be deeply understood, and valued, for how one thinks, relates, influences, and executes tasks. To play for a coach committed to building great men by molding each player in a way that reflects their individuality. That is what success looks like.

The Cranbrook hockey team, like many teams, had people that were operating as individuals, sniping at one another, playing with a chip on their shoulder, and viewing teammates as opponents. They did not have challenges associated with shooting or skating or stick-handling. Coach had that well under control, and that was not what was wrong with the team. They had human problems, and those human problems became hockey problems. These problems became losses, ties, and a long, collective tumble into the deep well of frustration.

The Cranbrook hockey team won by identifying the strengths of the individuals, and then empowering each young man with the expectation that they contribute their strengths, regardless of age, grade, position, power, seniority, or social status on the team.

My contribution was convincing them to focus on the human problem and to do that from a position of nourishment and abundance. The Cranbrook hockey team won by identifying the strengths of the individuals, and then empowering each young man with the expectation that they contribute their talents, regardless of age, grade, position, power, seniority, or social status on the team. Coach wrung every last bit of awesomeness out of those young men, and they loved it. It was a huge relief for them to let go of whom they thought they should be, and just be who they were. Who they were was perfect for their role. That is what success looks like.

I learned that I am perfect, too. I am perfectly suited to help a talented young team with a strong desire to succeed, and their leader, who understood that fully exploiting the strengths of his team was a worthy, noble endeavor. I was valued for being valuable, and my corporate scars no longer pained me. I was at peace because I had helped the Cranbrook team achieve Destination Unstoppable and was appreciated for it. I was proud of the coaches and players – and proud of my own contribution to their success. And frankly, I had a blast. That is what success looks like for me.

Coach Weidenbach is perfect – perfectly wired to help boys grow into men, one player at a time. Coach exemplifies the strengths-based notion of achieving near perfect performance in his role. He understands that our No Teammate Left Behind program is a success strategy that helps him fully develop the internal and external talents of the players. He believes that it helps them build a better future. Hockey is his teaching tool of choice, fueled by his secret sauce of strong, caring, and individualized leadership. That is what success looks like for him.

The Cranbrook hockey team, Coach Weidenbach, and I demonstrated the art of the possible. We verified the power of mining the untapped talent of an extraordinary group of young men. We identified and celebrated their strengths using the Clifton StrengthsFinder. We aligned their innate horsepower behind the success statement. We upped their commitment to one another. Those actions altered the team chemistry and helped the team coalesce. Once we made those important steps, the hockey problems began to take care of themselves. The human engine was well-fueled and well-oiled. The interference was removed on the ice and in the locker room; momentum and energy grew in its place. It was palpable. Together, we formed our own strengths-based power play and the team became unstoppable.

Transforming the Cranbrook hockey team is our Destination Unstoppable story. It is a magnificent tribute to the players that became a high performing unit at exactly the right time. The experience helped them become greater young men with a bigger and more fulfilling future ahead of them. The state championship trophy will sit in some cabinet collecting dust. In contrast, their personal journeys will be etched forever in the hearts of and minds of a remarkable team, and will impact the world with compounded interest. That's what success looks like.

Destination Unstoppable is available to any team that has the will to harness the strengths of the group and align that energy behind a collective definition of success. It is rooted in winning with brotherhood, respect, caring, full-effort and refusing to let anyone fail. Our power play can be your power play, because this is more than a hockey story. It is a team story. The world runs on teams. Volunteer teams. Sports teams. Family teams. Educational teams. Leadership teams. Medical teams. Technology teams. Sales teams. Military teams. Customer Support teams. How many teams are you part of? Have they reached their full potential? What does Destination Unstoppable look like for your team?

Our power play can be your power play, because this is more than a hockey story. It is a team story. The world runs on teams.

We, the Cranbrook hockey team, Coach Weidenbach, and I, have shared our story to inspire you to follow in our footsteps. We want you to feel unstoppable. We hope you will leverage the game changer – the Clifton StrengthsFinder – to focus on what is right about your people, not on what is wrong with them. We hope you will explore what success looks like for you and for your teams. We hope you will make the journey of No Teammate Left Behind to fully maximize your team's performance and achieve your competitive edge. We hope you will build your own power play and leverage it to leave a positive impact on the universe. We hope you will move mountains in ways yet unknown, and race towards the finish line of your team's Destination Unstoppable.

We will be waiting for you.

Appendix A: Destination Unstoppable Roadmap

Destination Unstoppable can only be reached when no teammate is left behind. Destination Unstoppable is momentum. It is the outcome of identifying untapped talent, aligning strengths with our role, and aligning our roles with a common view of success. It is the process of achieving a team's full potential. It is an arduous undertaking so I am offering a high level roadmap for you and your teams to work with. This roadmap is a best practice plan created through my lens and my extensive experience with building winning teams. However, you are the commander of your own ship. I encourage you to implement this plan and then customize it to drive great results with your teams. I only ask one thing in return: **Do not let this become a "one and done" initiative.** That is a disservice to your players and employees. Will you commit to a six-month focus on your team's internal talents and develop them with the same intensity with which you develop their physical talents? What about one-year? This is how we achieve breakout performance with individuals and teams.

This roadmap is like a memory foam pillow. We slowly absorb the strengths of people and teammates to build the confidence and awareness associated with that knowledge. It takes time to integrate information and behavior. Practice makes permanent. There are no short cuts. Athletes know that better than anyone. The Destination Unstoppable journey is no different. Execute the plan in stages rather than all at once.

Coach Weidenbach and I are also available to provide support should you wish to engage us. Feel invited to reach out to us at www.maureenmonte.com.

Ready to start?

High Level Roadmap

- ☐ **Assess The Team's Willingness to Complete the Journey**
- ☐ **Find a Gallup Certified Clifton StrengthsFinder Expert**
- ☐ **Define Success and Build a Success Statement**
- ☐ **Leverage the Game Changer: The Clifton StrengthsFinder**
- ☐ **Evaluate the Data**
- ☐ **Revisit the Success Statement**

- ☐ **Identify Three Roadblocks to Success**
- ☐ **Leave No Talent or Teammate Behind!**
- ☐ **Maestro, Lead by Example**
- ☐ **Athletes, Study Yourself Like You Study Your Craft**
- ☐ **Avoid Pitfalls**
- ☐ **Celebrate Wins**
- ☐ **Reach Out To Us For Help**

Detailed Roadmap

1. **Assess The Team's Willingness to Complete the Journey**

   a. Is there a Maestro willing to lead the effort? Is it you? If not, who?

   b. Do you have the budget for delivering the Clifton StrengthsFinder to your team, including all coaches and support staff?

   c. Do you have the budget for hiring a StrengthsFinder expert to guide you along the path?

   d. Will you commit to weekly investments in the human system via informal conversation and formal exercises?

   e. Will you provide yourself and the team time to explore their greatness? How much time? Will you commit to one year?

   f. Is the team's desire for success running deeply through their veins? Is everyone on board? If everyone is not on board, how will you fix that?

   g. Do you know what success looks like for you? Why do you coach or lead? Can you articulate it with specifics?

   h. Have you reviewed and tweaked our power play formula to include your formal system of player or employee development?

   Power Play: Well-Developed Formal System + Well-Nourished Human System + No Teammate Left Behind Program + Alignment With Success = Competitive Edge

   Note: Do not move forward until you have a positive response to each question above.

2. **Find a Gallup Certified Clifton StrengthsFinder Expert**
    a. If you care to work with Coach Weidenbach and me, contact us via my website at maureenmonte.com. Also, there is a directory of Gallup Certified coaches at the StrengthsFinder website.
    b. If you interview Gallup Certified Coaches, make sure they have proven success in working with teams. Make sure they have the confidence to work with high-energy athletes and laser-focused leaders or executives. There may be egos, energy, and struggles for control as part of the engagement. It is not for the fainthearted. Experience matters.
    c. Make sure they can be a great strategic partner to you and your organization over the long haul.
3. **Define Success and Build a Success Statement**
    a. Revisit Chapter 4. See what we did with a team trust bank and by refusing to let anyone fail. These commitments are critical because they require action, and we all know that action speaks louder than words. Action injects energy. Practice makes permanent.
    b. For you: "What does success look like in my role?"
    c. For your team: "What does success look like for our team? Where is our Destination Unstoppable and what does it feel like for us?"
    d. Shape the team success statement with input from all.
    e. Be holistic. Consider all forms of success, and do not leave out any stakeholders.
    f. Review your success statement over time. It is a living document, not the Ten Commandments. Also, it may, and likely will, vary year to year. Let each team craft their own, with guidance and leadership from you. Ownership is key.
4. **Leverage the Game Changer: The Clifton StrengthsFinder**
    a. For you.
    b. For your leaders/managers (do them first). Debrief on what you learn about one another, and how you have seen your strengths manifest themselves in your work with the team and in your own personal success. Focus on and explore your Insight Reports. Complete the Success Profile in Appendix B.
    c. For your employees or teams.

d. My Team Analysis tool will be available at my website to help you with the next step of evaluating the data.

5. **Evaluate the Data**

a. What strengths categories are most common, least common?

b. What strengths are most common?

c. What strengths are least common?

d. How does your team's strengths data provide unique insight into the challenges faced by the team? What jumps out at you? Is your team low in thinking strengths? Are they low in human glue? I recently had a women's lacrosse team that was young and lower in human glue move through an exercise to help them invest in their connections with one another. I asked them to think of a time when a teammate had put the team first. Once they selected a player, I had them tell that person what they had done that demonstrated the team-first mentality, note the impact on the team, and then thank them for it. This exercise and others like it can be repeated weekly to develop and reinforce are-as of the team chemistry that need improvement. All teams struggle! Let's help them with strengths data, focus, and encouragement.

e. Now that you know your team's strengths, what can you do differently to engage with the individual players and the team?

f. What is your team's competitive edge, and how can you best nourish and leverage it?

6. **Revisit the Success Statement**

a. Is it different now that the team knows their strengths? Ask them.

b. For you: Are there any modifications to your response to "What does success look like in my role?"

c. Reshape with insight and energy gained from the Clifton StrengthsFinder if it makes sense to do so. Allow the team to own this process and the outcome.

7. **Identify Three Roadblocks to Success**

a. For you: "What three things are preventing me from achieving success in my role?"

b. For your team: "What three roadblocks are preventing us from achiev-ing our success statement?"

c. Identify strengths/people/actions to tackle roadblocks.

d. What does progress look like?

e. How do we measure progress?

f. Seek and share examples of teammates who make a dent in the roadblocks. These are investments in the team trust bank. Consider creating a physical team trust bank (a jar would do) and have people insert notes of gratitude in the bank. Make this a weekly event and an ongoing conversation.

8. **Leave No Talent or Teammate Behind!**

a. Refine role definition to leverage strengths and align to success.

b. For each person on the team:

- What is the formal role?
- What is the human role?
- What strengths will be leveraged – leave no teammate behind!
- How does each player connect to the definition of success?
- How can they help solve the challenges and roadblocks above?
- This conversation may start in private. Maintain it in public so that everyone understands roles and expectations. This helps teammates hold one another accountable, and refuse to let anyone fail.

c. Revisit frequently. This is a process, not a pill.

d. Keep strengths conversations alive by asking for strengths stories during meetings. What did they do yesterday? What was the best part, the hardest part? Connect that information to their strengths.

e. Catch teammates using their strengths and acknowledge it.

f. Have the team strengths chart visible everywhere, including at the desks, lockers, or workstations of every team member.

g. Have each player complete their Success Profile in Appendix B.

9. **Maestro, Lead by Example**

a. The more you refer to the team's strengths and the success statement, the more likely your players or teammates will do so as well. Remember, **practice makes permanent.**

b. Review each person's StrengthsFinder Insight report with them individually, exploring what they highlighted and why. Ditto with the Action Planning Guide report.

c. Share your Insight Guide, exploring what you highlighted and why.

d. Ask them what they like best about the sport or role. What strength(s) are they using when they feel at their best?

e. Ask what gives them the most trouble, or what they find most challenging. Is it a skills or experience problem? Do they need training and practice? Explore ideas for using their strengths to help.

f. Ask "What's your favorite strength today?" followed by, "Why?"

g. Explore the strengths in more detail using resources at Gallup's website, www.gallupstrengthscenter.com and by visiting their YouTube channel. There are StrengthsFinder videos of real value there, ranging in length from five minutes to 45 minutes.

h. Have your players review the videos of their top 5 strengths. Ask, "What strengths video have you watched? What did you learn?"

i. Invest in the team trust bank by making positive deposits. It is possible to be both honest and encouraging when guiding teams.

10. Athlete, Study Yourself Like You Study Your Craft

a. Dig deep into what you learn about your StrengthsFinder results. When have you used those strengths for personal achievement or to impact the team?

b. Ask others who know you well to read your Insight Guide and highlight those phrases that reflect when they have seen you be at your best or add value to the team.

c. Select items from your Insight and Action Planning report that can help you develop your strengths. Focus on the context of your formal role and human role – which statements support those roles specifically? If I were a researcher trying to cure cancer, I could read my Insight report and highlight those statements that help me on my quest. If I am also a parent, I might highlight different statements that support my goal to engage deeply with my children.

d. Form a paragraph from the statements you highlighted in your Insight report. What does it say about you as a person and how you bring excellence to your role?

e. Once you have a basic understanding of your strengths and what they mean to you, focus on one strength a week. Note when you see your strength in action and what the impact was for you and for your team.

f. Explore the strengths in more detail using resources at Gallup's website, www.gallupstrengthscenter.com and by visiting their YouTube channel. There are StrengthsFinder videos of real value there, ranging in length from five minutes to 45 minutes.

g. Invest in the team trust bank by making positive deposits through encouragement and conversation with your teammates and coaches.

11. Avoid Pitfalls

a. Athletes are by nature competitive. So are sales people. So are many executives. Beware the strengths envy trap, where people on the team compare their results to others, seeking an advantage or conversely, feeling "less than" someone else. I avoid this problem by meeting with them individually before we gather as a team. A dive into their natural gifts often results in them owning their strengths and diminishes the need to compare their results to others. Consider having your certified StrengthsFinder coach meet with teammates individually first, especially if the team has a history of conflict or poor team chemistry.

b. Some people will be less eager to share their results or comment on their results in a public forum. Don't force it. It's likely a strengths statement resulting from talents like Intellection, Deliberative, and others. Or maybe they are feeling left out or are struggling with something else. Honor those strengths and feelings just as we honor those that are more lively and energizing in nature. Invite them, don't make them. The journey is compelling and people will get on the train when they see progress with teammates and leadership.

c. Avoid assumptions. Just because something is totally clear to you does not mean it is totally clear to others. This common problem is worsened by the fact that we all see the world through the lens of our strengths. Ask questions about a how a person views a given situation. This experience is like asking about the temperature outside. I hate the cold, you love it. I believe it is not hot enough, and you believe it is too hot. It is 62 degrees out – how we perceive that temperature depends on our point of view. The same is true of our strengths. You move too fast in my eyes. I move too slowly in your eyes. What is most effective for the moment at hand, fast or slow? Thinking about the future or thinking about the past? It is all valuable, and making good use of it should be the goal of a great leader or coach.

d. Be curious, not furious. Ask open ended questions even if you don't agree with what someone has said. We all have a different lens to the world, remember? Some of my favorite responses are: Tell me more. Why is that important to you? Can you give me an example?

e. Don't be like Dwight Schrute from *The Office* who is so serious that no one takes him seriously. Being too serious shuts people down and instills fear. Have fun with it. The No Teammate Left Behind journey lightens the mood, which contributes to the improved chemistry. We unlock the joy of helping people do what they do best, on and off the ice. It is how we achieve that Destination Unstoppable momentum.

12. Celebrate Wins

a. I'm not talking about wins in the win column. I'm talking about wins in strengths understanding, team chemistry, investments in the trust bank, and putting the team first. Keep the momentum alive by celebrating when progress is visible or measurable, both in results and in effort and understanding for individuals and the team.

b. Don't forget to share your stories with us! Visit www.maureenmonte.com and tell us about your favorite Destination Unstoppable example.

13. Reach out to us for help

a. Embrace the Destination Unstoppable and No Teammate Left Behind experience. It is similar to learning a new language or sport. It takes repeated exposure and practice to develop a capability in it.

b. Be patient with yourself and with your players or employees. This is a great time to have that beginner's mindset, and know that each day, person, and journey is different. It's also never-ending.

c. If you get stuck, and we all do, reach out to Coach Weidenbach and me at www.maureenmonte.com.

All strengths are useful when they are valued and leveraged to support the team's mission. Please tattoo this on your forehead.

I hope this roadmap, combined with the Success Profile in Appendix B, helps individuals and teams form and document the connection between strengths, team success and the goal of reaching Destination Unstoppable!

Appendix B: Success Profile Template

Name:

Top 5 Strengths:

1. ______________________

2. ______________________

3. ______________________

4. ______________________

5. ______________________

If you knew my strengths, you would know that I:

Our team success statement is:

The strengths I use most often to support the team success statement:

Formal Role

My formal role on the team is:

Success in my formal role is when I:

The strengths I use most often to support success in my formal role are:

My favorite Insight Guide statements that support my formal role are:

Human Role

My human role on the team is:

Success in my human role is when I:

The strengths I use most often to support success in my human role are:

My favorite Insight Guide statements that support my human role are:

I am a great player when I:

I am a great teammate when I:

My Performance Toolkit

(see Coach W's example in Chapter 10)

	Influencing (Horsepower & Energy)	Executing (Task Orientation)	Relationship-Building (Human Glue)	Thinking (Navigating & Solving)
Top 5 Strengths				
Resulting Outcome of Top 5 Strengths				

Valued & Misunderstood

I feel most misunderstood on this team when:

I feel most valued by this team when:

I feel most misunderstood in school/work/home when:

I feel most valued in school/work/home when:

Appendix C: Cranbrook Hockey Team vs. Everyone

How different is the team strengths profile of the Cranbrook hockey team? Very different! Check out the chart below which compares the hockey team's most common strengths with a few other teams I have worked with. Those teams cross multiple industries and roles, including a medical executive team, a high tech startup, and the leadership team associated with a large sales organization in Europe. I also added the global norm provided by Gallup. This provided a comparison between each team and the top five StrengthsFinder results in the global population.

I added Learner to the chart because I had never seen a team of 25 people with only one person having the Learner strength in their top five strengths.

Cranbrook Hockey Team vs. Everyone – Top Five Strengths Frequency*

Most Common Strengths on Cranbrook Team	Cranbrook Hockey Team (28 people)	Medical Leadership Team (10 people)	High Tech Startup (25 people)	European Sales Leadership Team (60 people)	Global* Population (11 million)
Competition	72%	0%	25%	18%	11%
Restorative	48%	0%	14%	7%	17%
Futuristic	44%	30%	4%	15%	12%
Achiever	40%	60%	57%	45%	32%
Relator	28%	40%	25%	50%	28%
Significance	28%	10%	7%	3%	6%
Strategic	24%	40%	36%	32%	23%
Command	20%	0%	14%	2%	5%
Responsibility	20%	40%	32%	27%	29%
Learner	4%	70%	43%	12%	28%

* The global population information was provided by Gallup and is based upon the top five StrengthsFinder results from 11 million people.

The largest gap was in the strength of competition where the hockey team was dominant. The startup employees with Competition in their top five strengths included the vice president of sales and three of his team; the director of marketing; the marketing intern; and the chief technology officer.

Restorative is the consummate problem solver strength. People high in Restorative notice and anticipate roadblocks and then work to prevent them. It is not the same as thinking to solve a problem; it is *acting* to solve a problem. It is perseverance with a bulldozer – that roadblock will be removed. People with Restorative are more impervious to pain. They continue to fight despite the physical, emotional, or mental pain. They don't give up. The Cranbrook players had considerably more Restorative than any other team.

Most interesting to me, beyond the Competition strength, was Futuristic. On the hockey team, eleven players possessed it, and yet only one tech team member had Futuristic in their top five strengths. I expected higher amounts of Futuristic on the startup team simply because they are a startup. However, that is an example of me projecting my thoughts on what success looks like on a tech team focused on the future. One can focus on the future without having Futuristic. Plus, Futuristic is a low-frequency strength in the global population, appearing less than 10% of the time in a top five strengths profile. Notice how many of the medical team had Futuristic. We do want our doctors seeing a better future for us, don't we?

Perhaps the presence of the Futuristic strength on the hockey team reflects the need for athletes to look forward, not backward. Dwelling on mistakes can drain athletes of energy and cause them to lose focus in the moment. High Futuristic could empower them to set the last play behind them and be energized and focused on the next play.

One example of a "next play" mentality and proof of its success is an approach developed by the most winning coach in college basketball history, Coach Mike Krzyzewski of the Duke Blue Devils. Coach K (his name is reduced to K for obvious reasons) has his players shout, "Next Play!" on every trip up and down the basketball court, whether they score or not. He was interviewed about this concept and said, "You cannot do anything for the last play. Someone who is always looking in his (or her) rearview mirror will never make the most of the current moment. The next play is the next moment. Why wouldn't you want to be at your best for the next moment?" The complete interview is available online at thefilmroomproject.org.

Focusing on the next play does not mean that you do not learn from history or from your mistakes. It means that you do not live there when your full performance is needed now. Imagine a CEO giving a public update to shareholders. In the middle of an important point, this person stumbles over their words, and things get a bit muddled. It happens. How the leader responds to the next sentence determines the measure of the man or the woman. Can they move past the mistake?

If you watched the movie, *The King's Speech*, you will know how challenging it can be. In T*he King's Speech*, the British people wanted the King to overcome his stuttering. They wanted him to succeed. He just had to give them the reason and opportunity to root for him. Smile, pause, collect yourself, and move on. Restate it, or give your all to the next remark and the rest of your speech. Next sentence. Next word. Next moment. Next play.

Imagine if we asked our business teams to say, "Next play!" after each setback or successful milestone of a project.

The athletes had considerably more Significance in their top five strengths than the technology team. Significance is the need to make an impact and be rewarded for success. They like their efforts to be recognized because it makes them feel like their work is important and valuable. Striving to win a state championship would feel significant.

Now, I need to make a couple of key points here so that this data is not misinterpreted and so that we do not jump to inaccurate conclusions.

1. **Small Data Samples:** These are relatively small data samples, so we cannot consider them statistically valid. They are, however, interesting, and reflect the unusual characteristics of the Cranbrook hockey team.
2. **We Are More Than Our Top Five Strengths:** We all have talent beyond that provided in our top five StrengthsFinder profile. Our true performance toolkit is comprised of our top 10 to 15 strengths. We only have the top five StrengthsFinder results for the players on the hockey team, so that is our point of comparison with the other work groups.
3. **Medical Leadership Team:** If we examine the doctors who appear to have far fewer influencing strengths in their top five, let's consider their occupation. They are scientists first, leaders second. If we were to look at their entire StrengthsFinder profile (from 6-34 strengths), we would see the emergence of influencing strengths. I know this is true because I have their entire 34 StrengthsFinder profile. However, scientists are thinkers. They do research and noodle on results and create studies. These activities require considerable thinking horsepower. This group tends to think first and influence later, often wielding the outcome of their thinking. We want our doctors to learn as much as possible about their field of expertise. They have Learner like the hockey team has Competition.
4. **High Tech Startup Team:** They are a relatively competitive group. In addition, they are highly driven and productive (Achiever) and many of them work weekends. Stamina is a big part of success in entrepreneurship and hockey. The technology company was higher in thinking strengths as a category, which was not surprising considering that many had an engineering or information technology background. The hockey team was energized by the future (Futuristic) and by removing roadblocks (Restora-

tive). I was surprised that the startup company had lower Futuristic and less Restorative, but that is why we take the assessment. Our assumptions are often proven incorrect. Knowing the internal makeup of the team helps us lead them more effectively and helps us celebrate and maximize their contributions.

5. **Sales Leadership Team:** The sales folks are higher in Competition when compared to engineers or doctors. This is logical because sales people are in the business of influencing a customer to buy something. They often have quotas and compete with other sales people and teams to generate the most revenue. A sale is a win, and it means the competition lost. This group had the highest amount of the Relator strength, and forming deep relationships with clients over time would likely help them sell more goods. We purchase from people we like.

The bottom line is that the Cranbrook hockey team had higher amounts of some uncommon strengths (Competition, Command, Significance, Restorative and Futuristic) when compared to all the teams and to the global population. This contributed to the extraordinary amount of energy and horsepower they generated and the determination with which they pursued their goals. They were very different from my other clients, and as such, had different needs.

If you have made this journey with your team, compare your results to those listed in the chart!

About The Author

Maureen Electa Monte builds winning teams. She has been focused on the success of individuals and organizations from the moment she graduated from the University of Rhode Island with an MS in Mechanical Engineering. Her life is the culmination of global projects that have provided her with a rich variety of experiences. Each adventure contained unexpected treasures that shaped her understanding and perspective of the world around her.

While working for a software company in Paris, she discovered that she had an eye for photography. She returned to the United States and became an award winning photographer with clients that included American Greetings, Farmer Jack, La-Z-Boy, Detroit Tigers, Detroit Red Wings, American Cancer Society, Jack's Place for Autism, and others.

When she graduated from Duquesne University in 2006 with a MS in Leadership, she was already coaching people with the Clifton StrengthsFinder. She now serves clients with her No Teammate Left Behind program so that teams achieve their fullest potential and discover Destination Unstoppable.

She is guided by her Vision, Mission, and Purpose statements:

MY VISION is a world where everyone courageously searches their heart, pursues their dreams with excellence, honor, and self-respect, inspiring others along the way.

MY MISSION is to reveal and honor the strengths of everyone I meet.

MY PURPOSE is to help people and teams accomplish what they were put on this earth to achieve.

Maureen Electa Monte currently resides in Michigan.